ALTERNATIVE TEACHER CERTIFICATION

A State-b...   ...s 2008

C. EMILY F

TABLE OF CONTENTS

INTRODUCTION

Alternative routes to teacher certification continue to grow and change rapidly. They also continue to have a major impact on who is entering teaching, where they teach and how they enter the profession.

In 2008, all 50 states and the District of Columbia report they have at least some type of alternate route to teacher certification. All toll, 128 alternate routes to teacher certification now exist in these 50 states and the District of Columbia. In addition, these states report that nearly 500 alternate routes programs are implementing the alternative routes to teacher certification they have established.

Based on data submitted by the states, NCEI estimates that approximately 57,000 individuals were issued teaching certificates through alternative routes in 2006-07 slightly fewer than the 59,000 estimated in 2005-06, but up from approximately 50,000 in 2004-05 and 39,000 in 2003-04. As shown in the figure below, the numbers of teachers obtaining certification through alternative routes have increased substantially since the late 1990s. Nationally, approximately one-third of new teachers being hired are coming through alternative routes to teacher certification.

Number of Individuals Issued Alternate Route Certificates by Year

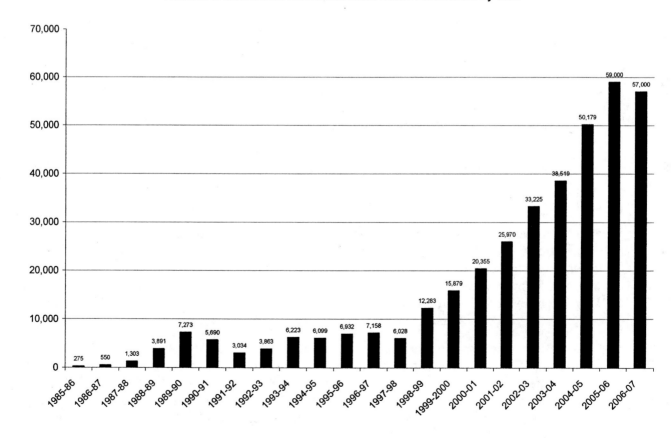

One- third of current state alternative routes to teacher certification have been created since 2000. More than half of them have been established in the last 15 years.

The fastest growth in alternative routes to teacher certification has occurred since 2000, with most of the new routes administered by colleges and universities. The operative term is "administered by." Most every alternative route to teacher certification is, in fact, collaboration among the state licensing authority, institutions of higher education and local school districts.

The states that first started alternate routes in the early 1980s are the most prolific alternate routes in terms of production of new teachers – per year, as well as total. They are: California, New Jersey, and Texas. New Jersey reports that about 40 percent of its new hires come through alternate routes. For Texas and California, about one-third of their states' new hires come through alternate routes.

Additional states where alternative routes to teacher certification are growing rapidly in producing more and more of the state's new teachers are: Alabama, Florida, Georgia, Kentucky, Louisiana, Mississippi, South Carolina, Tennessee, and Virginia.

Inner cities throughout the country – where the demand for teachers is greatest – are relying more and more on alternate routes to get the teachers they need.

A bit of history

To date, each state is the only entity that can issue licenses or certificates to teach or grant licensing authority. And, in order to teach in public schools in the United States, one has to have a license in the state in which one is teaching.

The variation in numbers and types of teaching certificates issued by states, as well as requirements for obtaining them through traditional college-based undergraduate teacher education program routes, has been huge. In addition, the certificates issued have been ever changing.

It is no different in the area of alternative routes to teacher certification (ARTC). As ARTCs have proliferated, so have the variations of them.

State teacher education and licensing officials, who are ultimately responsible for issuing teaching certificates, began calling any and every certificate they had been issuing to people who had not completed the traditional college approved teacher education program route, including emergency certificates, "alternative teacher certification."

In 1990, in an attempt to provide some order to the chaos, as well as to give some direction to the movement, states were asked to send NCEI original source documents – legislation, regulations, guidelines, brochures – whatever they had that was related to their alternative routes to teacher certification. We pored through these documents and created a format for describing each alternate route. In addition, we created a classification system to make clear the distinctions among these routes.

Beginning with the 1991 edition of this annual publication, *ALTERNATIVE TEACHER CERTIFICATION: A State-by-State Analysis,* NCEI began classifying and providing a detailed description of each alternate route to teacher certification in each state. State officials, legislators and policymakers regularly use the publication to guide their efforts in creating laws with provisions for alternative routes to teacher certification.

The 1980s were characterized by two rather divergent phenomena regarding alternative routes to teacher certification:

1. A focus in a few states to develop new and different ways of recruiting non-traditional candidates for teaching and the creation of new pathways for certifying them to teach.

2. A flurry in several states to re-name existing teacher certification routes, such as emergency or other forms of temporary certificates, "alternate routes."

The early to late 1990s saw formulation of a cohesive definition for alternate routes to certification. Common characteristics of nontraditional teacher certification routes emerged:

- Routes specifically designed to recruit, prepare and license talented individuals who already had at least a bachelor's degree -- and often other careers – in fields other than education.

- Rigorous screening processes, such as passing tests, interviews, and demonstrated mastery of content.

- Field-based programs.

- Coursework or equivalent experiences in professional education studies before and while teaching.

- Work with mentor teachers and/or other support personnel.

- High performance standards for completion of the programs.

Some states list four or five alternate routes, yet use them sparingly or not at all. From year to year, routes are added and routes are dropped by states.

What has been noteworthy as alternative routes have gained in notoriety is a shift away from emergency and other temporary routes to new routes designed specifically for non-traditional populations of post-baccalaureate candidates, many of whom come from other careers.

In February 2004, during the first annual conference of the National Center for Alternative Certification (NCAC), participants requested that a template be created for states to use to describe their alternate route programs, record basic data and share information about their programs in a uniform way across the country.

That template was designed with input from numerous state officials, providers of alternate route programs and researchers. It was made available for use online in June 2004 at NCAC's web site, www.teach-now.org. The program providers now access the information online through a user ID and password that they obtain from NCAC.

There is mounting evidence that alternative routes to teaching and the numbers of individuals using them to enter teaching are growing at an increasingly fast pace. Data and information that the National Center for Education Information has been tracking for more than two decades indicate that this trend will continue. A flurry of academic research is now underway to ascertain the effectiveness of the teachers entering teaching through these alternative routes. Please visit our web sites at *www.teach-now.org* and *www.ncei.com* to keep abreast of findings of these studies as well as any other information about alternative routes to teaching.

What we have documented in this annual publication since 1990 are the alternative routes to the traditional, approved college teacher education program for certifying teachers. Since the states have sole authority for certifying teachers, we rely on the data and information submitted by certification offices in each state.

This publication provides information and analyses to prospective teachers, as well as policy and decision-makers, about alternative routes to teacher certification, in the United States. This current edition, ***ALTERNATIVE TEACHER CERTIFICATION: A State-by-State Analysis 2008,*** is organized into eight parts:

    I. Introduction

   II. Overview of Alternate Routes to Teacher Certification

  III. How to Use This Manual

  IV. Reciprocity and Acceptance of Teaching Certificates Across States

   V. State Contacts for Alternative Teacher Certification Routes

  VI. Tables Including Results of 2006-07 NCEI State Survey of Alternative Teacher Certification

 VII. Classification system developed by NCEI to characterize different programs states identify as "alternative routes."

VIII. Profile and Classification of Each Alternative Teacher Certification Route in Each State

- A detailed description of each of the alternative teacher certification programs in each of the states.

- Lists of colleges and universities in each state that have developed alternative teacher preparation programs.

- Lists of colleges and universities in each state that have any type of teacher preparation program.

- Contact people within each state for alternative teacher certification and for finding a teaching job.

I wish to thank the many people who made this project possible -- the people in every state agency of education who answered our questions, who put up with our numerous telephone calls, e-mails, faxes and mailings and came through with the information that makes this manual so valuable. They have enabled us to tell this current and complete story of alternative routes to teacher certification in the United States.

Emily Feistritzer
February 28, 2008

HOW TO USE THIS MANUAL

This edition of *ALTERNATIVE TEACHER CERTIFICATION: A State-by-State Analysis* offers several aids to help readers locate the information they may need.

- First of all, what does "Alternative Teacher Certification" mean?

  Alternative teacher certification, alternative routes to teacher certification and alternate routes to teacher certification are used interchangeably in this publication. The terms refer to alternatives to the traditional state-approved college-based teacher education program routes for certifying teachers.

- Are all alternative routes to teacher certification the same?

  No. See Classification of Alternate Routes on page 30.

- What states have alternative routes to teacher certification? What type(s) of alternate routes do they have?

  See Table of Contents. Go to the Classification section on page 30 to find definitions of each class.

- What are the entry requirements and the program requirements for any given alternate route? How long does it take?

  Go to the Table of Contents at the beginning of this manual, see what Class of alternate route you are interested in, find specific routes by name and go to the page cited for a full description.

- What if I want only to participate in an alternate route that has been specifically designed for people who decide they want to teach after getting a non-education degree and want to begin teaching right away?

  Review the alternative routes described in Classes A and B.

- What if I want to participate in a program designed and controlled by a college or university?

  Review programs in Classes D and E.

- How can I find what colleges and universities have alternative teacher preparation programs?

  See this section at the end of each state you are interested in.

- What colleges and universities have any kind of teacher preparation program?

  See this section at the end of each state you are interested in.

- What if I want to ensure getting a Master's degree, as well as a teaching certificate?

  Review the routes classified as "E."

- What if I already have a teaching certificate and want to know if I can teach in another state?

  Check the states that have reciprocity with each other on page 14.

- How can I find out how many alternative teacher certificates any particular state issues?

  See Table 1 on page 21.

- How many new teachers does a state hire?

  See Table 2 on page 22.

- How do I contact the state(s) I am interested in getting more information from?

  Review the list of state contacts on pages 15-18.

- Where can I keep abreast of everything that is going on in the field of alternative teacher certification?

  Go to the National Center for Alternative Certification Web site at www.teach-now.org.

Reciprocity and Acceptance of Teaching Certificates Across State Lines

NASDTEC Interstate Contract – Most states, the District of Columbia, Guam, and Puerto Rico have signed the Interstate Contract for teacher certification, maintained by the National Association of State Directors of Teacher Education and Certification (NASDTEC). The NASDTEC Interstate Contract provides a vehicle to recognize training in state-approved programs, comparable licenses, and teaching experiences when teachers and other educators move from one state to another. Each state, however, determines comparability and reciprocity with each of the other participating states and teachers must still meet certain requirements before becoming certified in states other than the state that issued the initial license.

Regional Collaborations on Reciprocity:

Northeast Common Market: In 1988, eight states in the northeastern region: Connecticut, Maine, Massachusetts, New Hampshire, New York, Pennsylvania, Rhode Island, Vermont established a Northeast Common Market for educators. The participating states developed a regional credential that allows teachers with an initial license in one state to teach in another state for up to two years before meeting the latter state's licensing requirements. Educators can receive a regional credential only once.

Midwest Regional Exchange: Nine states (Illinois, Iowa, Kansas, Michigan, Missouri, Nebraska, Oklahoma, South Dakota and Wisconsin) have an exchange program that is similar to the Northeast Common Market. Teaching candidates or experienced teachers who complete a regionally accredited preparation program or hold a license from one of the participating states can obtain a two-year conditional license in any one of the other states. This agreement is based on the requirements for teacher preparation programs; candidates so licensed must still meet any additional grade point average, testing, coursework, or other requirements the receiving state demands to earn a regular license or certificate.

Mid-Atlantic Regional Teacher Project: In 1999, a meeting of the Council for Basic Education, the Maryland Department of Education, and the Mid-Atlantic Regional Educational Laboratory produced the Mid-Atlantic Regional Teacher Project (MARTP). MARTP is a regional partnership among Delaware, Maryland, Pennsylvania, and the District of Columbia to collectively address teacher supply and demand issues in the region, including common strategies for preparing, recruiting, hiring, and retaining new teachers.

Reciprocity for Advanced Certification:

NBPTS: The National Board for Professional Teaching Standards has developed standards for advanced certification and program accreditation in more than 30 fields. Some states and the District of Columbia automatically grant licenses to out-of-state teachers with national board certification. States still vary in the type of license they issue, and in some states teachers must meet additional requirements before they can earn a standard or advanced state license.

NCATE: Some states accept individuals who completed teacher preparation in another state at an institution of higher education whose teacher preparation program has been accredited by the National Council for Accreditation of Teacher Education (NCATE).

The American Board for Certification of Teacher Excellence (ABCTE), recently funded by the United States Department of Education, will provide a credential for teachers who pass rigorous content area examinations and document a history of student learning gains.

STATE CONTACTS FOR ALTERNATE ROUTES TO TEACHER CERTIFICATION

Alabama Dept. of Education
5215 Gordon Persons Bldg, 50 N. Ripley St.
P.O. Box 302101
Montgomery, AL 36130-2101
Attn.: Sarah P. Justice
(334) 242-9998
Fax: (334) 242-9998
email: tcert@alsde.edu

Alaska Dept. of Education and Early Dev.
Teacher Education and Certification
801 West Tenth St., Suite 200
Juneau, AK 99801-1984
Attn: Cynthia Curran, Administrator
(907) 465-2831
email: cynthia_curran@eed.state.ak.us

Arizona Dept. of Education
Teacher Certification Unit
1535 West Jefferson
Phoenix, AZ 85007
Attn: Patricia Hardy
(602) 542–3626
email: phardy@ade.az.gov

Arkansas Dept. of Education
ADE-Non-Traditional Licensure Program
501 Woodlane, Suite 220 C
Little Rock, AR 72201
Attn: Ann DeLoney, Program Advisor
(501) 371-1580 (direct)
(501) 682-5535 (main)
email: anndeloney@arkansas.gov

California Commission on Teacher Credentialing
1900 Capitol Avenue
Sacramento, CA 95814-4213
Attn: Michael McKibbin
(916) 445-4438
email: mmckibbin@ctc.ca.gov
Catherine Creegan
(916) 324 – 3054
CCreeggan@ctc.ca.gov
Web site: http://www.cde.ca.gov

Colorado Dept. of Education
Office of Professional Services
   and Educator Licensing
201 E. Colfax, Room 105
Denver, CO 80203
(303) 866-6628, press 0 (zero)
email: alternative.tir@cde.state.co.us

Connecticut Bureau of Certification
   and Preparation Development
P.O. Box 150471
Hartford, CT 06115-0471
Attn: Nancy L. Puglese
(860) 713-6708
email: teacher.cert@po.state.ct.us
Also, Anita Hastings
email: Anita.Hastings@po.state.ct.us
Edwin Anderson
Email: Edwin.Anderson@ct.gov

Delaware Department of Education
P.O. Box 1402Townsend Building
Dover, DE 19903
Contact: (302) 739-4686
Web site: www.doe.state.de.us.

Delaware Alternative Routes to Certification
Linda Hughes, Ph.D.
University of Delaware
Delaware Center for Teacher Education
Williard Hall
Newark, DE 19711
(302) 831-4598 or 831-1100
email: artc-de@udel.edu
Web site: www.udel.edu/artc

District of Columbia Dept. of Education
Ed. Credentialing and Standards Branch
Attn: Bridget Doyle
825 North Capitol Street, NE, Sixth Floor
Washington, DC 20002-4232
Phone: (202) 442-5377
email: Bridget.Doyle@dc.gov

Florida Department of Education
Bureau of Educator Certification
325 W. Gaines Street
Turlington Building Room 201
Tallahassee, FL 32399-0400
Attn: Eileen McDaniel/Tracy Brandenburg
(850) 245-0568
email: Eileen.mcdaniel@fldoe.org
tracy.blandenburg@fldoe.org
Web site: http://www.altcertflorida.org/

Georgia Professional Standards Commission
2 Peachtree Street, Suite 6000
Atlanta, GA 30303
Attn: Phyllis S. Payne
(404) 232-2650
email: Phyllis.Payne@GAPSC.com

Hawaii Teacher Standards Board
650 Iwilei Road, Suite 201
Honolulu, HI 96817
Attn: Lynn Hammonds
(808) 586-2619
email: LHammonds@htsb.org

Idaho Dept. of Education
Teacher Education/Professional Standards
P.O. Box 83720
Boise, ID 83720-0027
Attn: Larry Norton
(208) 332-6885or
Michael P. Stefanic
(208) 332-6800
email: MStefanic@sde.state.id.us

Illinois State Department of Education
Certification and Professional Development
100 North First Street, S-306
Springfield, IL 62777-0001
Attn: Martha A (Marti) Woelfle
Phone: (217) 782-7091
Fax: (217) 782-3687
email: profprep@isbe.net

Indiana Department of Education
Educator Licensing and Development
Attn: Debby Williams
251 W. Ohio St., Suite 300
Indianapolis, IN 46204-1953
(317) 232-9010
email: dwilliam@doe.in.gov

Iowa Board of Educational Examiners
Grimes State Office Bldg.
East 14th and Grand
Des Moines, IA 50319
Attn: George Maurer
(515) 281-3611
email: George.maurer@iowa.gov

Kansas Dept. of Education
Teacher Education and Licensure
120 East Tenth Ave.
Topeka, KS 66612-1182
Attn: Susan Helbert
Director of Teacher Education and Licensure
(785) 296-8012
email: shelbert@ksde.org

KY Education Professional Standards Bd
100 Airport Road, 3rd Fl
Frankfort, KY 40601
Attn: Michael Carr
(502) 564-4606
(888) 598-7667
Fax: (502) 564-7092
email: Mike,Carr@ky.gov

Louisiana Department of Education
Teacher Certification and Higher Education
P.O. Box 44064
Baton Rouge, LA 70804
Attn: Andrew Vaughn
(225) 342-3563
email: andrew.vaughn@la.gov

Maine Dept. of Education
Certification Office
23 State House Station
Augusta, ME 04333-0023
Attn: Nancy Ibarguen
(207) 624-6603
email: nancy.ibarguen@maine.gov

Maryland Dept. of Education
Teacher Education/Certification
200 W. Baltimore Street
Baltimore, MD 21201
Attn: Michelle Dunkle
Phone: (410) 767-0391
Fax: (410) 767-0390
email: mdunkle@msde.state.md.us

Massachusetts Dept. of Education
Bureau of Educator Certification
350 Main Street
Malden, MA 02148
Attn: Marion Gillon
Phone: (781) 338-6624
email: mgillon@doe.mass.edu
Web site: www.doe.mass.edu/educators

Michigan Dept. of Education
Office of Professional Preparation Services
P.O. Box 30008
Lansing, MI 48909
Attn: Frank Ciloski
Phone: (517) 373-6791
Fax: (517) 373-0542
email: ciloskif@michigan.gov

Minnesota Board of Teaching
1500 Highway 36
WestRoseville, MN 55113
Attn: Allen Hoffman
(651) 582-8833
email: Allen.Hoffman@state.mn.us

Mississippi Dept. of Education
Office of Educator Licensure
P. O. Box 771
Jackson, MS 39205
Attn: Cindy Coon, Director
(601) 359-3483
email: ccoon@mde.k12.ms.us

MO Department of Elementary and
  Secondary Education
Educator Preparation
P.O. Box 480
Jefferson City, MO 65102-0480
Attn: Gale "Hap" Hairston, Director
(573) 751-0371
email: Gale.Hairston@dese.mo.gov

Montana Teacher Education/Certification
Office of Public Instruction
P.O. Box 202501
Helena, MT 59620-2501
Attn: Elizabeth Keller
Phone: (406) 444-3150
Fax: (406) 444-2893
email: ekeller@state.mt.us

Nebraska Dept. of Education
Teacher Education/Certification
P. O. Box 94987
301 Centennial Mall Square
Lincoln, NE 68509
Attn: Demaris Grant
(402) 471-2496 or (402) 471-0739
Fax: (402) 471-9735
email: grantda@unk.edu

Nevada Department of Education
1820 E. Sahara #205
Las Vegas, NV 89104-3746
Attn: Dr. Jerry Barbee, Director Teacher
Licensing
(702) 486-6458
email: drbarbee@doe.nv.gov

New Hampshire Dept. of Education
Bureau of Credentialing
101 Pleasant Street
Concord, NH 03301-8157
Attn: Robin Warner
(603) 271-4196
email: RWarner@ed.state.nh.us

New Jersey Dept. of Education
Provisional Teacher Program
P.O. Box 500
Trenton, NJ 08625-0500
Attn: Betty Sue Zellner, Coordinator
(609) 984-6377
Email: Betty.Zellner@doe.state.nj.us

New Mexico Public Education Department
Professional Licensure Bureau
300 Don Gasper
Santa Fe, NM 87501-2786
Attn: Bernadette Bach
Phone: (505) 827-6587
Fax: (505) 827-4148
email: bernadette.bach@state.nm.us

New York Office of College
  and University Evaluation
5 N Mezzanine, Education Building
Albany, NY 12234
Attn: Ruth L. Pagerey
(518) 474-1914
email: rpagerey@mail.nysed.gov

North Carolina Dept. of Public Instruction
Division of Human Resource Management
6330 Mail Service Center
Raleigh, NC 27699-6330
Attn: Nadine Ejire
(919) 807-3310
email: nejire@dpi.state.nc.us
Danny Holloman(919) 807-3375
email: dholloman@dpi.state.nc.us

North Dakota Dept. of Education
Standards and Practices Board
2718 Gateway Ave., Suite 303
Bismarck, ND 58505-0585
Attn: Janet Placek Welk, Ex. Director
Deb Jensen, Asst. Director
Phone: (701) 328-1659
Fax: (701) 328-2815
email: jwelk@state.nd.us

Ohio Dept. of Education
Center for the Teaching Profession
Office of Certification/Licensure
25 S. Front St., Mail Stop 105
Columbus, OH 43215
Attn: Jennifer Kangas
(614) 466-3593
email: Jennifer.kangas@ode.state.oh.us

Oklahoma Dept. of Education
Professional Standards Section
Teacher Education/Certification
2500 N. Lincoln Blvd., Rm. 211
Oklahoma City, OK 73105
Attn: Paul Simon
Phone: (405) 521-2062
Fax: (405) 522-1520
email: paul.simon@sde.state.ok.us

Oregon Teacher Standards/Practices
465 Commercial Street, NE
Public Service Bldg., Suite 105
Salem, OR 97301
Attn: Keith Menk
(503) 378-3757
email: Keith.Menk@state.or.us

Pennsylvania Dept. of Education
Bureau of Certification
333 Market Street
Harrisburg, PA 17108
Attn: Marjorie Blaze
Phone: (717) 783-9252
Fax: (717) 783-6736
email: mblaze@state.pa.us

Rhode Island Dept. of Education
Office of Teacher Preparation, Certification
    and Professional Development
255 Westminster Street
Providence, RI 02903
Attn: Lisa.Foehr
(401) 222-8809
email: Lisa.Foehr@ride.ri.gov

South Carolina Dept. of Education
Division of Teacher Quality
Landmark II Office Building
3700 Forest Drive, Suite 500
Columbia, SC 29201
Attn: Falicia Harvey
(803) 734-5758
email: FHarvey@scteachers.org

South Dakota Dept. of Education
Office of Accreditation and Teacher Quality
700 Governors Drive
Pierre, SD 57501-2291
Attn: Melody Schopp
Phone: (605) 773-5232
Fax: (605) 773-6139
email: Melody.Schopp@state.sd.us

Tennessee Dept. of Education
Teacher Licensing
4th Floor, Andrew Johnson Tower
710 James Robertson Parkway
Nashville, TN 37243-0377
Attn: Vance Rugaard
(615) 532-4880
email: Vance.Rugaard@state.tn.us

Texas State Board for Educator Certification
1701 N. Congress Ave. 5th Floor
Austin, TX 78728
(512) 936-8304
Karen Loonam
email: Karen.Loonam@tea.state.tx.us

Utah State Office of Education
Alternate Routes to Licensure
250 East Fifth South
Salt Lake City, UT 84111
Attn: James F. Schindler, Coordinator
Phone: (801) 538-7730
email: James.schindler@schools.utah.gov

Vermont Dept. of Education
Educational Resources Unit
State Dept. of Education
120 State Street
Montpelier, VT 05602-2501
Attn: Linda Hendrickson
(802) 828-0449
email: lindahendrickson@education.state.vt.us

Virginia Dept. of Education
Div. of Teacher Education and Licensure
P.O. Box 2120
Richmond, VA 23218-2120
Attn: James W. Lanham
(804) 371-2471
email: James.lanham@doe.virginia.gov

Washington Professional Educator
   Standards Board
Old Capitol Building
P.O. Box 47236
Olympia, WA 98504-7200
Attn: Mea Moore
(360) 725-6276
email: mea.moore@k12.wa.us

West Virginia Dept. of Education
Office of Professional Preparation
1900 Kanawha Boulevard, East
Building #6, Room 252
Charleston, WV 25305-0330
Attn: Kellie Crawford or Scottie Ford
(304) 558-7010 or (800) 982-2378
email: kcrawford@access.k12.wv.us
or smford@access.k12.wv.us

Wisconsin Dept. of Public Instruction
Bureau of Teacher Education, Licensing
   and Placement
P.O. Box 7841
Madison, WI 53707-7841
Attn: Laurie Derse
(608) 266-1028
email: laurie.derse@dpi.state.wi.us

Wyoming Professional Teaching Standards Board
2300 Capitol Avenue
Hathaway Building, 2nd Floor
Cheyenne, WY 82002-0190
Attn: Linda Stowers
(307) 777-6261
email: lstowe@missc.state.wy.us

If you wish to purchase this report, which details all of the states' requirements and program descriptions for alternative routes toward certification, send $150, plus $10 for shipping and handling. If you are interested in only certain states, send $15 for the first state and $7 for each additional state to: NCEI, 4401A Connecticut Ave., N.W., PMB 212, Washington, DC 20008. For credit card orders (VISA and MasterCard), telephone (202) 822-8280 or order directly from our Web site: http://www.ncei.com.

NATIONAL CENTER FOR EDUCATION INFORMATION
4401A Connecticut Ave., N.W., PMB 212
Washington, DC 20008

202-822-8280

http://www.ncei.com

STATE STATISTICS REGARDING TEACHER PRODUCTION
1985–2007

Table 1. Number of Certificates Issued to Persons Entering Teaching Through an Alternative Route, by State: 1985-2007

STATE	1985-86	1986-87	1987-88	1988-89	1989-90	1990-91	1991-92	1992-93	1993-94	1994-95	1995-96	1996-97	1997-98	1998-99	1999-00	2000-01	2001-02	2002-03	2003-04	2004-05	2005-06	2006-07
Alabama				74	222	309	460	559	522	609	854	885	880	1,159	1,596	1,751	2,087	2,225	2,069	2,318	1,921	2,209
Alaska										2		0								0	0	0
Arizona					3	11	5	32				0					164	147	0	0	121	72
Arkansas					11	10	6	50		100									260	179	497	425
California						962	1,188	1,139	1,201	735	1,010	1,194		2,042	2,503	4,455	4,492	4,998	5,490	8,341	7,309	8,517
Colorado	50			50	50	50		41	44	65	48	60	88	155	171	238	462	723	695	517	761	810
Connecticut			100	100	100	100	38	59			90	108		159	219	199	213	300	249	888		245
Delaware													29	33	33	39	44	47	48	42	60	41
District of Columbia							46												82	N/A	187	62
Florida													79	147					650	847	1,502	2,052
Georgia	25	14						55	68	96	59	48	51	209	1,311	1,152	766	1,303	1,330	2,281	2,848**	
Hawaii			16	9	8	2								8	5	5	3	6	7	7	6	16
Idaho		16		9			4	8	7													
Illinois						6								24	21	157	274	491	302	369	337	277
Indiana																		2	137	322	278	278
Iowa																				9	8	12
Kansas						20				50											46	
Kentucky						20							14	40	33	380	282	1,386	821	961	1,972	2,126
Louisiana								355	441	389	432	414	484	478	438	728	612			992		
Maine																				1,250		
Maryland	8	23		45	57		109		149	78	71	45		55		17	15	140	91	125	350	314
Massachusetts																1,891	3,280	4,669	3,091	8,083	5,281	3,802
Michigan																40		6				
Minnesota													28	29	9			6		56	33	0
Mississippi		40		201	199	229							554		561		354	402	516	760	982	939
Missouri							25	23				4				28	29	151	184	194	210	
Montana													58	21								100
Nebraska						14	45			50						8		8	35			
Nevada																					70	
New Hampshire			508	595	488	187	301	312	338	392	308	288	298	210	123					357		
New Jersey	110	294	460	746	985	975		458	702	2,186	2,494	2,610	2,426	1,223	1,832	1,981	1,826	2,395	2,908	2,546	2,852	
New Mexico			9	9		80		77	115	89	85	78	65	73			60	71	102	110	319	
New York																	1,165	1,428	2,072	1,546	2,256	2,042
North Carolina		177	297	243	318	432	325	223										246	282	508	821	752
North Dakota															31	35						
Ohio																						
Oklahoma				2	1		1	54	241	413	342	468		661	533	255	599	657	625	965	1,395	
Oregon		0		0	0	0			0		0	0				0	0		0	0	0	0
Pennsylvania					265	178		351	259	201	310	197	231	308	296					14	16	0
Rhode Island															434				407	0		0
South Carolina	62			35	38	48	32	42		65	68	77	139	191	76			39	8	15	439	
South Dakota								3	3		1		26	80							65	64
Tennessee			575	793	1,032	1,278			1,649							611	680	1,223	2,132	2,613	2,944	
Texas														2,663	2,660	2,505	3,528	4,628	7,117	9,962	11,316	12,133
Utah	20	20	20	20	20	20			75		35	29	16	92	108	104	120	26	102	87	108	108
Vermont	20						20			50												
Virginia				458	650	750			390	458				1,980	2,746			6,142	5,206	4,324	6,447	5,993
Washington																		169	103	158	101	84
West Virginia													19			0	0	0	0		0	
Wisconsin																10			0	178	221	221
Wyoming													6	11	20	10	0	14	10	14		

**Georgia reported that 12,949 new teachers were hired in 2005-06 and that 22% of them came through alternate routes.

Source: *National Center for Education Information, Washington, D.C., 2007*

Table 2. Numbers of Newly Hired Teachers, by State: 1985 to 2007

STATE	1985-86	1986-87	1987-88	1988-89	1989-90	1990-91	1991-92	1992-93	1993-94	1994-95	1995-96	1996-97	1997-98	1998-99	1999-00	2000-01	2001-02	2002-03	2003-04	2004-05	2005-06	2006-07
Alabama																					2,808	
Alaska																					1,120	
Arizona								2,250										1,586	11,174	11,093		
Arkansas	1,377	1,182	1,307	1,147														1,214		2,053		
California	7,680	8,730				20,000	18,000	12,500			15,000		20,442	24,849	23,260	24,824	21,586	20,139	18,039	19,246	20,628	19,133
Colorado		543	1,181	958	2,273	2,195	1,526	2,384	2,619	3,063	1,611	1,832	2,315	2,535	7,922	8,288	9,420	7,922	5,438	5,522		
Connecticut	114	104	700	811					2,200	3,141	2,687	3,542	3,364	3,771	4,526	4,486	3,836	2,171	7,155	3,052	N/A	4,766
Delaware		312	160	86	205	418	1,010	302		350	263	405	606	474	927	863	904	938	989	897	998	861
District of Columbia	275																	381			1,357	896
Florida	4,864	5,129	5,251	5,710					9,236	9,265	7,833	9,385	10,689	11,169	13,442	14,624	14,411	15,388	19,317	20,010	23,033	21,143
Georgia	3,917	3,742	4,216	4,388										9,563	10,069	11,817	13,084	12,507	10,929	11,697	12,949*	
Hawaii	765	686	927	854	973	1,216	1,156	1,115	1,099	1,032			986	1,008				1,363	1,657	1,698	1,589	1,616
Idaho	534	445	497	510								1,583	1,468	1,893	1,755	1,928	1,478	1,739	1,898	2,413	2,461	937**
Illinois	2,729	2,883	2,641	2,613	2,984	4,137	1,848	8,162	10,487	14,930	9,975	9,645	10,448	11,759	13,305	14,397	13,090	13,575	13,168	9,961		
Indiana	1,488	985		849	1,932	1,660		1,049		1,529												
Iowa	1,018	890	811	795	792	850	850	932			920	1,014	1,133	1,258	1,616	1,660	1,443	1,104	1,256	1,362	1,442	1,522
Kansas	1,473		1,297	1,465	1,837	1,993	1,743	1,339		1,396	1,732	1,078	1,266	1,504	2,050	1,919	1,767	1,552	1,600	1,824	1,734	1,743
Kentucky		1,317						1,794	1,766	1,834	2,103	1,800	2,191	2,274	3,919	2,681	2,562	3,088	3,049	3,047	3,601	3,421
Louisiana	2,621		2,533	2,699	2,349	2,376	2,031	2,030	3,330		3,482	3,471	2,350	4,311	4,642	5,059	4,805	4,439	3,428	4,305		
Maine	346	369	476	475	661	661	700	700	700	700			800						675			
Maryland	801	898	1,184	2,435	2,594	2,692	2,802	3,120	2,955	3,774	3,623	4,588		6,033	7,329	7,649	7,385	7,445	5,929	6,617	8,046	7,917
Massachusetts		2,000	2,200	2,200	2,714	4,112								3,422						392		
Michigan	2,436	1,506	1,395	2,110	2,095	2,683	3,066	3,048	2,784	3,940	4,289	5,183	4,108	2,000								
Minnesota	1,586	681		1,482	1,554	1,685	1,700			1,700										2,165	2,253	2,343
Mississippi															2,048		2,010	2,200	2,790	2,012		
Missouri	1,978	1,819	2,066	2,275	2,349	2,376	2,031	2,030	3,330		3,482	3,471	2,350	1,956	4,642	5,059	4,805	4,439	3,428	4,305		
Montana																						
Nebraska			767	855	931								800			1,312	1,300	1,125	675			
Nevada						1,750	2,643															
New Hampshire		956																		392		
New Jersey	2,000	2,000	2,200	2,200	2,714	4,112						5,751	6,525	5,371	6,356	6,856	7,527	6,808	6,823	7,171	7,713	
New Mexico		552	552	667	1,483			571						2,000						2,411	2,805	
New York	5,233	4,735	4,888	5,652	4,732	5,651	7,400	5,775				5,751		6,338	11,145	10,173	10,287	12,247	11,771	11,833	11,257	11,235
North Carolina	1,178	2,225		7,170	6,373	5,940												8,780	9,316	9,997	10,181	9,843
North Dakota	251	232	271	282	266	257	266	266	206	245	193	217	232	250		285	273	306	289	339		
Ohio	7,343	6,970	6,703	4,133	4,068	4,231		5,800	5,845				8,500	9,500								
Oklahoma	1,850							2,035							5,121			5,169				
Oregon	878	910	850	840	1,027			1,250	803	950	951	1,667	2,420	3,406	1,816	1,684	1,699					
Pennsylvania	1,800	1,800	2,480	2,600	3,957	2,220	2,326	2,475	4,795	2,906	3,095	3,207	5,159	3,152	5,778	3,149	3,423	3,678	4,818			
Rhode Island																				N/A	N/A	
South Carolina		800							2,714			2,441		4,600							N/A	
South Dakota	471	334	385	409	365	414	432	576	641	611			536	507	436		6,553	374	304	351	409	367
Tennessee	9,400	9,632	9,625	10,000		10,000	2,881		2,714					4,600			5,299	5,169	4,828	5,912	8,101	
Texas	1,148							2,035		6,800		6,475	6,808	6,530	6,631	6,858				23,429		39,687
Utah		1,304	1,304	1,015	1,583									1,937	1,934	1,410	1,949	1,684	2,003	1,906	2,199	
Vermont																						
Virginia	2,000	2,000	2,200	2,200	2,714	2,800	~3,000	1,833	1,727	1,579	1,292	1,667	1,495	1,616	5,121	2,289	2,502	1,995	1,742	1,939	7,044	5,947
Washington	959	1,050	369	439	1,481	1,497	1,617	1,833	1,727	1,579	1,292			1,616	N/A	2,289	2,502	1,995	1,742	1,939	2,101	
West Virginia	1,608	1,817	1,274	1,400	2,168	1,005	585	183	209	204	201	294	229	415	584	300	292	415	430	621	493	
Wisconsin	1,403	1,563	1,584	1,688	1,014	1,484	2,503	3,167	2,877	3,802	2,198	1,980	2,309	2,530	2,631	3,095	2,760	1,029	2,370	3,193	3,203	3,449
Wyoming								200	200				200			378			unknown	unknown		

Blanks indicate "no data".
Source: *National Center for Education Information, Washington, D.C., 2007*
** Note: This number is the count of "new to the profession" teachers. The count for newly hired to Idaho is 1,343.

Table 3. Numbers of Total Teachers Employed by State: 1985-2007

STATE	1985-86	1986-87	1987-88	1988-89	1989-90	1990-91	1991-92	1992-93	1993-94	1994-95	1995-96	1996-97	1997-98	1998-99	1999-00	2000-01	2001-02	2002-03	2003-04	2004-05	2005-06	2006-07
Alabama	36,971	36,980	37,716	38,619	39,100	39,054		41,000	41,700	42,307	43,000	43,000	43,000	47,000	55,439	48,163	51,086	46,830	46,463	46,514	49,399	49,574
Alaska	6,120	6,448	6,225	6,319	6,319	7,818	7,672	8,599	8,792	8,725		9,365		9,438	7,945		8,325				8,484	8,856
Arizona	24,003	27,933	30,707	39,911														32,434	50,107	42,641		
Arkansas	24,003	24,476	25,572	28,495									23,500					32,222	32,155	32,155		
California	183,330	189,426	195,475	198,521	210,000	210,000	220,000	220,000			232,559		250,527	284,030	292,055	301,361	306,940	309,773	305,855	306,548	307,864	308,790
Colorado	29,895	30,705	31,168	31,398	31,954	32,341	33,093	33,419	33,661	34,571	35,388	36,398	37,840	39,439	40,583	43,470	45,628	46,895	46,660	46,797	44,305	52,549
Connecticut	37,063	37,506	35,050	35,800	43,003		41,733	41,197	41,324	42,457	43,261	47,307	45,326	46,478	47,800	50,261	45,307	52,370	50,165	47,759		
Delaware	5,746	5,883	5,951	5,897	5,928	5,908	6,046	6,630		6,366	6,417	6,593	6,849	7,023	7,311	7,466	7,515	7,713	7,577	7,833	7,920	7,938
District of Columbia	5,871	5,999	6,232	6,572	6,500	6,500	6,630												7,500	7,300	6,382	6,027
Florida	88,973	91,969	95,857	100,370	104,127	108,088	109,939	107,590	112,130	116,785	119,388	122,392	126,397	129,731	132,521	134,508	136,866	141,003	148,198	158,624	164,665	168,181
Georgia	60,666	60,423	62,825	64,947									86,262	88,757	91,467	94,689	99,470	103,350	104,845		110,135	
Hawaii	9,380	9,434	9,863	10,159	10,373	10,780	11,057	11,346	11,513	11,634	11,724	11,725	12,006	12,075				10,943	12,481	12,426	12,310	14,770*
Idaho	10,255	10,234	10,285	10,425	11,059	11,601		13,801	14,572					15,661	15,962	16,130	16,225	16,256	16,373	16,587	16,913	
Illinois	102,657	104,609	105,217	105,097	106,182	108,775		117,713	117,194	119,535	122,319	125,204	128,292	131,528	134,826	137,826	138,485	137,900	135,688	138,202	141,165	
Indiana	51,971	52,940	53,514	53,246	53,246	54,220	54,623	51,938					57,219	57,942	59,716	59,206	59,560	59,891	59,833	60,470	60,486	61,183
Iowa	30,652	30,729	30,955	30,568	30,912	31,000	31,000			32,503	31,193	31,629	31,954	32,307	32,970		33,878	33,425	33,668	33,661	34,175	34,444
Kansas	26,658	27,035	27,317	28,122	34,324	34,324	35,276	35,831		30,578	36,273	33,795	39,760	41,250	41,250	41,058	41,525	41,238	41,096	39,859	39,254	40,545
Kentucky	33,670	34,351	35,325	35,736	41,559	42,526	38,208	38,538	39,153	39,168	41,104	41,080	38,417	46,430	47,643	40,002	42,136	42,391	41,864	42,040	42,618	43,560
Louisiana	42,530	43,056	42,433	43,633	47,102	47,231		52,358	52,358	48,971	53,330	53,711	54,248	54,775	55,619	55,429	55,526				48,476	
Maine	14,311	14,706	14,204	14,556	16,802	16,802	13,027	14,000	15,351					15,086	17,538		17,623	17,274		16,592	16,684	
Maryland	38,475	39,542	40,086	40,644	41,317	55,278	43,665	48,707	45,187	52,404	53,726	53,846		51,077	52,302	66,187	55,021		56,961			
Massachusetts	56,825	53,489	59,517	60,395										59,320								
Michigan	76,166	77,013	80,081	90,928	90,250	92,592	92,332	92,509	101,871	96,368	98,250	87,374	92,651	101,623								52,796
Minnesota	40,857	41,445	42,133	42,752	43,101		43,753	43,753	46,686	46,686		49,845					52,873	55,862	56,142	52,266	52,255	
Mississippi	25,610	26,214	26,930	27,367	27,367	32,900	35,000						29,574	35,199	31,017		32,569		33,204			
Missouri	48,115	48,875	49,874	50,693	51,361	52,304	52,302	54,011	62,691		63,100	63,100	52,400	62,290	63,703	64,797	65,090	66,211	64,645	65,042	66,236	
Montana	9,706	9,820	9,659	9,584	10,258	10,295	9,883	10,135		10,086		10,349					10,362	10,362	10,300	10,463		
Nebraska	17,574	17,652	17,614	17,896		20,000			20,000	20,000			20,000			27,850	27,430	23,600	23,525			
Nevada	7,751	7,908	8,348	8,699	9,175	10,384	13,027	14,000	15,351				18,431									
New Hampshire	10,251	10,300	10,363	10,422	10,422	10,519	10,879	11,187	14,301	16,311	16,461	17,321	16,410	16,391	10,240		18,919		18,594	17,414		
New Jersey	62,714	63,557	59,928	60,530	67,433	79,886			101,871		98,250	87,374	91,236	85,844	94,415	98,072	102,723	105,561	107,646	109,576	111,256	29,412
New Mexico	14,693	14,597	15,175	15,669	16,157		17,155	17,412	19,396	18,997			21,374	23,416	25,934	27,092	25,827	21,815	21,122	23,000	23,090	
New York	173,393	174,471	171,521	174,216	172,400	186,205						202,976	207,938	209,007	216,452	220,865	212,495	225,021	221,982	223,000	224,216	227,171
North Carolina	57,638	58,063	59,718	66,877	67,528	68,492	75,102	74,065		73,000			80,949		88,000	88,600	88,845	88,881	91,568	93,123	95,597	97,246
North Dakota	8,837	8,697	8,594	8,666	8,707	8,454		8,766	8,186	8,268	8,270	8,402	8,430	8,007		8,886	8,845	8,830	6,598	6,538		
Ohio	98,274	98,894	99,641	100,829	113,711	110,411	111,900	110,921	112,370	104,081	106,028	107,610	107,500	111,500	112,563	112,545						
Oklahoma	40,889	39,708	34,515	34,707	35,590	36,822	43,069	44,000	44,862	45,399		46,882	47,656	46,658	47,877	48,356	48,882	47,836				
Oregon	24,604	24,615	24,912	25,147	25,630			26,744	26,488	26,208	26,680		26,757	27,152	27,802	28,094	32,146	27,669	27,192	27,658	28,472	29,412
Pennsylvania	101,665	102,986	103,307	104,379	105,415	101,345	101,540	101,984	102,405	104,081	106,028	107,610	109,156	109,691	115,673	115,639	117,158	117,115	118,683			
Rhode Island	8,755	8,740	8,947	8,931	9,391	9,479	10,285	10,450	12,336	12,321			11,200	11,067	11,118	11,550					12,040	
South Carolina	34,458	34,677	35,701	35,877	36,877	36,963	37,171	39,787					49,237						50,437	50,412	49,638	
South Dakota	8,152	8,002	8,338	8,235	8,600	8,773	9,454	8,767	9,557	9,985	9,625		9,282	9,570	9,262		9,532	9,532	9,109	9,296	10,819	9,316
Tennessee	41,103	41,483	42,660	43,330	43,330	43,051	43,640	43,693			55,951	57,496	61,653	53,924	55,361	56,588	57,355	57,654	58,577	59,274		
Texas	180,827	182,286	187,974	191,737	200,179							243,867	251,372	258,438	264,997	272,534	280,108	288,986	289,187	294,258	300,134	315,998
Utah	17,076	18,090	18,250	18,667	19,004			19,883				22,582	21,114	25,740	26,260	24,567	24,663	21,636	21,464	24,763	25,390	
Vermont	6,397	6,460	6,656	6,700	6,500	6,500	6,500			6,700					8,000	8,472	8,710	8,822	8,693	8,750	8,847	8,856
Virginia	62,714	63,557	59,928	60,530	67,433	73,000	73,000		73,000				80,949	88,000	88,000	88,600	88,609	95,705	98,419	98,419		99,231
Washington	36,200	37,118	37,949	38,827	40,271	41,767	44,360	45,874	45,456	48,063	48,573	49,996	50,819	51,583	52,125	52,964	54,641	55,283	52,847	52,470	52,487	
West Virginia	22,733	22,931	22,702	22,177	21,653	21,807	21,179	22,222	22,010	21,013	20,817	20,823	20,819	24,533	24,563	24,380	24,181	24,154	24,107	24,070	24,365	
Wisconsin	46,503	47,039	47,721	48,541	49,329	50,983	52,276	52,282	51,011	55,892	54,891	54,714	57,464	57,840	58,766	59,982	60,744	61,394	60,370	60,517	60,123	59,088
Wyoming	6,307	6,273	6,698	6,705	6,705	6,500	6,581	6,581			7,201	7,295	6,673	8,285	8,307					6,580		

Blanks indicate "no data".

Source: *National Center for Education Information, Washington, D.C., 2007*

* This count is for FTE positions only.

Table 4. Numbers of Persons Who Completed an Approved College Teacher Preparation Program, by State: 1985-2007

STATE	1985-86	1986-87	1987-88	1988-89	1989-90	1990-91	1991-92	1992-93	1993-94	1994-95	1995-96	1996-97	1997-98	1998-99	1999-00	2000-01	2001-02	2002-03	2003-04	2004-05	2005-06	2006-07
Alabama	4,127	4,888		5,387	7,855	10,535	4,828	5,541	5,600	6,000	7,000	7,000	6,000	8,000	15,839	14,653	15,448					
Alaska	6,000	6,000	6,500	6,500	7,000	8,599									587		261	293	472	190	254	
Arizona			2,078	2,611	3.00													2,928	4,655			
Arkansas	1,068	1,680												2,500				1,246	1,279			
California	9,562	10,072	11,819	13,809	19,000	18,000	16,191	15,873	12,130	15,155	16,718	19,200	16,993		17,555	18,397	23,225	21,649	27,150	24,149	22,419	20,752
Colorado	5,146	5,363	6,369	5,947	5,340	6,400		2,389	2,686	2,258	2,205			2,991	2,336	2,042	1,968	2,143	2,345	2,566	2,952	
Connecticut						749	817		3,981	3,981	6,975	7,467	4,169	6,459	7,912	5,502	7,184	3,317	6,125	N/A	N/A	4,587
Delaware							753															
District of Columbia																		428	346	327		
Florida	5,000	5,000	5,000	5,000		5,000								5,588	5,475	5,580	5,790	5,707	5,871	5,000	6,098	
Georgia															5,054	4,329	3,705	4,364	4,459	5,000		
Hawaii		1,500	1,600	2,700	2,200	1,040	763	698	636	557	994			542				764				
Idaho	5,089	5,417	5,432	4,860	4,284	1,501		7,034	6,062	6,821	7,952	8,007	8,437	9,622	1,347	1,182		1,562	1,413	1,611	1,655	1,026
Illinois	5,480	5,158	5,483	6,727	6,895		5,747					5,704	5,383	5,772	8,423	10,789	10,611	11,642	10,701	11,910		
Indiana	6,856	5,185	3,621	5,350			5,747		3,600		3,000	3,100	2,788	2,800	7,815	7,714	5,194	6,045				
Iowa	4,130	4,250	4,100	4,000	4,000	3,200	3,200	4,105			3,000	3,610			2,846	2,889	3,104	3,217	3,291	3,166	2,952	
Kansas	3,822	3,666	3,589	3,808	2,966	7,500	4,226	4,899	4,533	4,396	3,683	3,610			3,272	2,889		2,946	1,749	1,670	1,076	
Kentucky	6,000	6,200	6,500	6,800	7,000	7,500			2,000		5,439	5,754			2,403	2,324	2,248	2,388				
Louisiana	2,621	2,621	2,465	2,533	3,046	2,648		3,143	3,356	3,016	2,823	2,137	2,540	2,862	2,297	3,016	2,936					2,920
Maine					400																	
Maryland	1,024	1,072	1,262	1,357	1,335	1,501	1,695		865	2,395	2,179	2,566	2,241	2,546	2,550	2,354	2,332	2,300	2,319	2,854		2,716
Massachusetts	3,075	5,076		6,880	9,133	5,598		3,637	5,347													
Michigan				5,575	6,046	5,398	6,630	5,623	5,847	6,246	6,417	6,562	5,372	5,636	6,471		6,400	4,313	5,524		5,169	
Minnesota	5,110	6,627	4,510		4,769	5,926	5,638	5,903	6,000	5,755	5,074	4,793	5,325	5,416	5,841			1,476				
Mississippi	1,806	1,997	1,936	1,949	1,987	1,909							1,386		1,432		1,448					
Missouri	2,200	2,175	2,400	2,750	3,200	2,580	3,200		3,600		3,800	7,566	7,059	6,562	6,822	6,462	6,970	5,919	5,326	5,059	5,958	
Montana								2,000	2,000	2,000	2,000	2,000	2,000					1,212	551	854		
Nebraska			700	1,000	1,500	2,000	2,000	1,800	2,300							1,658	1,650	1,475				
Nevada																						
New Hampshire			1,645	2,092	2,031	2,134	983	1,750	2,104	2,461	1,040	1,475		1,749	1,224			4,369	6,982	996		
New Jersey		2,939	2,988	2,585	3,538	3,992					2,640	3,110		4,617	3,830	4,260	4,412			8,500	9,630	2,036
New Mexico					1,500											1,400	1,296			N/A	1,689	
New York	6,081	6,820	7,556	7,487	7,655	8,938						25,400	24,443	27,400	24,692	16,666	25,281	21,449	24,143	20,839	24,300	12,762
North Carolina	2,135	3,034	2,090	2,143	2,509	2,689		1,786							723	645	669	2,685	2,967	3,446	3,090	
North Dakota	700	900	1,050	1,000	1,000	950			980	943	902	677	790	731	723	645			532	810	690	
Ohio	5,400	7,547	7,300	6,600	7,300	7,547	7,804	8,011	7,759				7,600	7,700	7,050	7,680						
Oklahoma	19,418	24,453	18,934	21,883	22,510	21,036			3,410	3,690	3,623	3,674	3,604	3,306	2,968	1,569	1,929	2,325		2,237	2,870	
Oregon	2,500	3,000	3,500	3,750	4,000	3,850		1,360	2,835	1,355	1,388		1,342	1,490	1,500	1,579						
Pennsylvania	7,132	6,866	6,709	7,327	8,092			10,406	10,255	10,999	11,088	11,782	11,377	11,423	11,102	10,437	10,364	10,680	11,658			
Rhode Island					822	897	840	870	1,000	881	948	894	913	925	944	963		713	532	810	989	996
South Carolina	3,018	3,576	3,319	3,173	3,386	3,062	4,139	3,405		3,926	3,920	3,714	4,013	2,400	3,341			2,053		2,144		
South Dakota	1,100	1,100	1,100	1,100	1,100	1,174	1,342	1,349	1,000		1,197		1,222	1,213	930			713	532	810	690	
Tennessee							3,420	2,859					2,000		4,129	3,219	3,264	3,372	3,367	3,563	3,749	
Texas	7,651	5,751	4,922	3,902	6,441				9,523	9,602	9,446	9,428	8,960	9,102	10,178	8,143	9,118	9,290	9,645	8,857	10,482	12,762
Utah	2,161	2,107	1,856	1,676	1,754					2,348	2,551	2,550	2,734	2,793	2,697	2,268	2,330	2,580	2,840	2,980	2,901	
Vermont	303	397	360	487	550	560	600			500					522	548	511	454	518	495	536	
Virginia		1,750	1,800	1,702	1,698	1,800	1,800		3,731	3,939	4,249				2,813	2,861	2,646	2,712	3,196			
Washington	2.58	2,308	2,146	2,332	2,204	2,294	2,519	2,732	2,907	3,028	3,204	3,160	3,303	3,282	3,345	3,099	3,159	3,419	3,694	3,667	3,691	
West Virginia	1,338		1,912	1,499	1,913		1,929		1,770		1,928	1,659	1,267	1,339	1,266	1,635	1,674	1,853	1,973	2,213	2,106	
Wisconsin	9,203	7,089	7,280	7,613	8,066	9,379	5,640	5,654	5,024	5,001	5,281	4,929	4,807	4,724	4,445	4,313	4,182	4,715	6,911*	5,219*	5,404	
Wyoming		3,600	4,168	3,595	3,637			3,841	3,103	3,083			711	745	1,000			787	275			
Totals	143,625	167,164	149,499	165,602	177,894	141,664	78,676	101,127	113,744	105,330	121,670	150,918	123,786	164,008	172,001	135,538	142,161	142,133				

Blanks indicate "no data".

Source: National Center for Education Information, Washington, D.C., 2007

* Bubble due to new rules taking effect 9-12004

Table 5. Race/ Ethnicity and Gender of Alternative Teacher Certification Candidates 2007

	Question: What percent of your alternative teacher certification candidates are represented by each of the following ethnic/racial groups?							Question: What percent of your alternative teacher certification candidates are represented by each of the following gender groups?	
		Ethnicity/race						Gender	
	State does not have data	Asian	American Indian/ Alaskan Native	Black	White	Hispanic	Other	Male	Female
Alabama	x								
Alaska	x								
Arizona	No program								
Arkansas		<1	0	3	93	2	1	30	70
California		6.3	1	8.1	53.7	21.8	9.1	34.8	65.2
Colorado	x								
Connecticut		4	1	5	80	10	0	43	57
Delaware		0		29	69	2		44	56
District of Columbia	x							28	72
Florida		1.9	0.1	19.2	67.9	10.1	0.8	32.5	67.5
Georgia	10	1	0.4	16	66	1.2	3.1	22	68
Hawaii	x								
Idaho		Don't track						Don't track	
Illinois	x								
Indiana	x			Data not collected					
Iowa	x	Don't track							
Kansas	x								
Kentucky		0.4	0.1	8	85	2	4	38	62
Louisiana	x								
Maine	x								
Maryland	x								
Massachusetts	x								
Michigan		5	0	75	10	10	0	30	70
Minnesota	x								
Mississippi		5	4	40	31	20	0	45	55
Missouri		1.2	0.6	11.9	83	1.8	1.5	33.2	66.8
Montana		2	4		89		5	49	51
Nebraska	x							30	70
Nevada									
New Hampshire	x			Data not collected					
New Jersey	x								
New Mexico	x								
New York		7	--	20	55	16	2	32	68
North Carolina	1.1	1.6	1.1	22.2	71.3	1.6	1.2	28	72
North Dakota	No program								
Ohio	x								
Oklahoma	x							45	55
Oregon	No program							N/A	N/A
Pennsylvania	x							N/A	N/A
Rhode Island	x							75	25
South Carolina		1	0.32	36	60	2.5		34	66
South Dakota	x								
Tennessee	x								
Texas		1.98	0.37	16.4	49.31	29.94	1.99	28.87	71.13
Utah		1.6	0.6	0.6	71.4	3.4	22.3	37.4	62.6
Vermont									
Virginia	x							29.3	70
Washington		3		1	77	13	13	49	51
West Virginia	No completers								
Wisconsin	x								
Wyoming					100			43	57

Source: National Center for Education Information, Washington, D.C., 2007

Table 6. Age of Alternative Teacher Certification Candidates 2007

	Question: What do you estimate is the average age of students currently enrolled in your state's alternative teacher certification program(s)?		Question; What percent of your alternative teacher certification candidates are represented by the following age groups?						
	State does not have data	Average age	18-24 years	25-29 years	30-39 years	40-49 years	50+ years	Not sure
		In years	%	%	%	%	%	%
Alabama	x							
Alaska	x							
Arizona								
Arkansas		35	3	68		18	7	4
California		Not available	48.7		26.5	15.5	9.1	0.2
Colorado		Not available	11	24	28	24	13	0
Connecticut		38	3	23	27	34	13	0
Delaware		35	0	40	38	16	6	
District of Columbia	x							
Florida		36.8	4.2	30.9	33.2	20.4	11.3	
Georgia			1.5	19.2	32	17	10	20
Hawaii	x							
Idaho		Data not collected						
Illinois	x							
Indiana		Data not collected						
Iowa		Data not collected						
Kansas	x							
Kentucky		27	30	30	18	16	3	
Louisiana	x							
Maine								
Maryland		35		18	65	15	2	
Massachusetts	x							
Michigan		39	0	35	30	25	10	
Minnesota	x							
Mississippi		26	10	35	35	15	5	
Missouri		36	4	31	35	18	12	
Montana		35						
Nebraska	x							
Nevada								
New Hampshire		30						
New Jersey	x							
New Mexico	x							
New York		29	42	27	18	8	5	
North Carolina			0.5	32.6	35.4	19.5	11.3	0.7
North Dakota								
Ohio	x							
Oklahoma		25-55						x
Oregon		No Alternative Certification Program						
Pennsylvania	x	N/A						
Rhode Island	x							
South Carolina		35	3.5	36.6	41	10	8.8	
South Dakota	x							
Tennessee	x							
Texas		32.3	16.8	33.1	28.5	14.5	6.7	0.4
Utah		37	8	25	27	25	15	
Vermont								
Virginia	x							
Washington		34						
West Virginia								
Wisconsin	x							
Wyoming		32	7	29	50	70	0	

Source: National Center for Education Information, Washington, D.C., 2005

Table 7. Employment and Cost of Alternative Teacher Certification Programs

State	Question: What percent of those who enter alternative teacher certification routes in your state complete the program and get certified to teach?	Question: Are individuals in your alternative route program employed by a school district while participating in your program?		Question: If "Yes", are they employed full-time or part-time?		Question: How much does it cost to participate in your state's alternative teacher certification program?	Question: Who pays?
	%	Yes	No	Full-time	Part-time	Cost	Source
Alabama	N/A	x		x			
Alaska	Program not used						
Arizona	No data						
Arkansas	85	x		x		$800 per year, plus transportation, lodging, etc.	Candidates. Reimbursement and scholarship aid are available are available for qualified candidates.
California	95	x		90%	10%	$0 to $13,000	States $2,500 per year & $2,500 project match
Colorado	91	x		x		$2,000-$7,500	Candidates
Connecticut	90	x		x		$3625 plus books and supplies	Candidates
Delaware	80-85	x		x		About $3,000 tuition	Candidates. Reimbursement and scholarship aid are available for qualififed candidates.
District of Columbia	93	x		x		$11,000 - $13,000	Candidates, District & other partners help defray this cost.
Florida	Info not available	x**		x		From 0 to $2000+	Some districts absorb cost; others share with the candidate.
Georgia		x		x		Varies by program	Varies by program
Hawaii	N/A	x		x	x	N/A	State and Candidate
Idaho							
Illinois	N/A	x		N/A		Varies by institution	Varies by program
Indiana						Varies by program	Varies by program
Iowa	100	x		x		Tuition costs	Candidates
Kansas	New	x		x		Varies by program	Varies by program
Kentucky		x	x	x	x	Varies per program	Candidate
Louisiana	85	Usually		x	x	Varies by provider	Candidate
Maine	N/A	N/A		N/A		N/A	Individual
Maryland	90%	Yes		Full-time		Varies from $600 to $3000	District/Candidate share with some federal grant funding.
Massachusetts	N/A	N/A		N/A		N/A	N/A
Michigan	97	x		x	x	$9,000 - $12,000	Both the district and the candidate.
Minnesota	N/A	N/A		N/A		Varies by program	Candidates
Mississippi	90	x		x		Varies by institution	Candidate
Missouri	N/A	x		x		Varies by institution	Candidate
Montana	81	x		x		$6600 ($275/credit)	DOE-Federal Funds, Scholarships, or self pay.
Nebraska	N/A	x		x		Varies	Candidate usually
Nevada							
New Hampshire	80	x		x		Alt. 3- $300; Alt. 4 - $180; Alt. 5 - $180	Teacher Candidate
New Jersey	N/A	x		x	x	Varies by program	Candidate unless subsidized by district.
New Mexico	N/A	Most	N/A	x		Tuition costs	The candidate, and in some instances, the district.
New York	N/A	x		x		Varies by institution	Varies
North Carolina	N/A	x		x		Varies by institution	Candidate
North Dakota	No program						
Ohio	N/A					Varies	Candidate
Oklahoma	95	x		x	x	$140 ($40 for application; $100 for Teacher Competency Review Panel); $435 for testing	Applicant
Oregon	New	x		x		Tuition rates of institutions	Candidate or district; some federal funds.
Pennsylvania	N/A	x		x		Tuition fees/test fees	Candidate
Rhode Island							
South Carolina	N/A	x		x	x	Graduate tuition for three graduate courses.	Cost of lodging and graduate courses paid by individual. Loan forgiveness for teaching critical subjects or in critical districts.
South Dakota	N/A	x		x	x	Tuition plus expenses	Alternative certification teacher
Tennessee	N/A	x		x		Varies by institution	Candidate
Texas	N/A	x		x		$3,000-5,000	Student
Utah	95	x		x		Tuition, $75 for background checks and Provisional Certificate	Individual (TTT grant to 5 districts)
Vermont	90					$1,200	Candidate; School Districti; VT DOL
Virginia	N/A	x		x		Varies	Candidate. Some funding also by school divisions (districts) and state.
Washington	90		x			Varies	State and intern share cost.
West Virginia	No completers	Varies				Varies	Candidates
Wisconsin	N/A	N/A		N/A		N/A	N/A
Wyoming	N/A	Optional				Fee upon presenting portfolio - $645	Candidate

Source: National Center for Education Information, Washington, D.C., 2005

Table 8. Types of Communities Alternative Teacher Certification Participants Teach In

State	State does not have data	Types of communities			
		Inner-city	Small town	Suburban	Rural
		%	%	%	%
Alabama	x				
Alaska	x				
Arizona	No data				
Arkansas	x				
California		67	6	6	21
Colorado	x				
Connecticut		45	8	41	6
Delaware		30	25	30	15
District of Columbia		100			
Florida	x				
Georgia	x				
Hawaii	x				
Idaho					
Illinois	x				
Indiana	x				
Iowa	Don't track				
Kansas	x				
Kentucky	x				
Louisiana	x				
Maine	x				
Maryland		87	6	3	4
Massachusetts					
Michigan		100			
Minnesota	x				
Mississippi		30	25	30	15
Missouri	x				
Montana		0	0	28	72
Nebraska					
Nevada					
New Hampshire	x				
New Jersey	x				
New Mexico	x				
New York		95	3		2
North Carolina					
North Dakota	No program				
Ohio	x				
Oklahoma		27	30	29	14
Oregon		20	30	40	10
Pennsylvania	x				
Rhode Island					
South Carolina	x				
South Dakota	x				
Tennessee	x				
Texas		20.9	32.2	36.3	10.5
Utah		40	20	30	10
Vermont					
Virginia	x				
Washington	x				
West Virginia	x				
Wisconsin		x	x	x	x
Wyoming	x				100

Source: National Center for Education Information, Washington, D.C., 2005

Table 9. Primary Activity Prior to Entering Alternative Teacher Certification Routes 2007

Question: What do you estimate is the percent of individuals who enter your alternative teacher certification route(s) who were engaged in the following as their primary activity right before entering your teacher preparation program?

State	No	Professional	Other Occup.	Military	Retired Military	Other Retired	IHE in state	IHE out of state	Emer. Certif.	Teaching Occup.	Non-teaching Ed.	Other
Alabama	X											
Alaska	X											
Arizona	X											
Arkansas	X											
California		15.4	6.5	0.5			25.7		11.3	40.6		
Colorado	X	34	46	2	2	8	5	1	2	0	0	
Connecticut												
DC	X											
Delaware		40					20	5		22		13
Florida		37	12	1	1	0			0			15
Georgia***	38	43	43					14		18	21	
Hawaii	X											
Idaho							Data not collected					
Illinois	X											
Indiana							Data not collected					
Iowa							Data not collected					
Kansas	X											
Kentucky	X	0		1		10	10		20	10	20	38
Louisiana		0	30	5	10	10	0		40	5		
Maine	X	53	12.5	0.02	1	1						24.5
Maryland									10			
Massachusetts	X	1	1	1	1		1	5	0			
Michigan		1						5	0	70	20	1
Minnesota	X											
Mississippi		15	15	5	5	5	20	5	10	15	5	
Missouri		12		7	0	2						
Montana	X	12	26					11		15	18	9
Nebraska	X											
Nevada							Data not collected					
New Hampshire	X											
New Jersey	X											
New Mexico		35	25	0	0	0	30 - not separated by state		0	22 - not separated by occupation		0
New York**												
North Carolina		No program										
North Dakota												
Ohio	X											
Oklahoma		50	30	5	10	0	5	0	0	0	0	
Oregon		0	0	0	0	0	0	0	0	0	0	
Pennsylvania	X											
Rhode Island		Data not collected										
South Carolina		61.9	6.8	5				17.7				8.4
South Dakota	X											
Tennessee	X											
Texas	X		0	0	10	10	80	20	50	40		
Utah		80	0	0				20	50	40	0	0
Vermont												
Virginia	X								4		0	0
Washington	X											
West Virginia	X											
Wisconsin	X											
Wyoming		22	14						50	14		

* Connecticut -- 0%(ARCI); 50%(ARCII).
** Florida -- The data that Florida has collected on previous work experience does not align with these fields.
Refer to report: "Alternative Teacher Certification in Florida: Progress Report" - August 2003, Florida Department of Education
Previous experience included: 24% business, 9% science, 47% education-related, 16% other, 2% military, 2% no previous experience
*** Georgia -- The data presented here are the actual numbers for Georgia, not percentages.
**NY State data is from NYC Teaching Fellows Program, largest Alt Cert program in state, graduates approx. 1800 teachers annually.

Table 10. Teachers and Enrollment in Public Elementary and Secondary Schools, by State, Ranked by Number of Teachers: Fall 2003

Rank	State	Teachers		k-12 Enrollment		% of All Teachers	Cumulative % of All Teachers
	United States	3,048,549	\2\	48,540,725	\2\		
1	California	304,311	\2\	6,413,862	\2\	10.00%	
2	Texas	289,481		4,331,751		9.50%	
3	New York	216,116		2,864,775		4.80%	
4	Florida	144,955		2,587,628		4.80%	
5	Illinois	127,669		2,100,961		4.20%	33.20%
6	Ohio	121,735		1,845,428		4.00%	
7	Pennsylvania	119,889		1,821,146		3.90%	
8	New Jersey	109,077		1,380,753		3.60%	44.70%
9	Georgia	97,150		1,522,611		3.20%	
10	Michigan	97,014		1,757,604		3.20%	51.00%
11	Virginia	90,573		1,192,092		3.00%	
12	North Carolina	89,988		1,360,209		3.00%	
13	Massachusetts	72,062		980,459		2.40%	
14	Missouri	65,169		905,941		2.10%	
15	Indiana	59,924		1,011,130		2.00%	63.40%
16	Tennessee	59,584	\2\	936,681	\2\	2.00%	
17	Wisconsin	58,216		880,031		1.90%	
18	Alabama	58,070		731,220		1.90%	
19	Maryland	55,140		869,113		1.80%	
20	Washington	52,824		1,021,349		1.70%	
21	Minnesota	51,611		842,854		1.70%	
22	Louisiana	50,495		727,709		1.70%	
23	Arizona	47,507		1,012,068		1.60%	
24	South Carolina	45,830		699,198		1.50%	
25	Colorado	44,904		757,693		1.50%	
26	Connecticut	42,370		577,203		1.40%	82.00%
27	Kentucky	41,201		663,885		1.40%	
28	Oklahoma	39,253		626,160		1.30%	
29	Iowa	34,791		481,226		1.10%	
30	Mississippi	32,591		493,540		1.10%	
31	Kansas	32,589		470,490		1.10%	
32	Arkansas	30,876		454,523		1.00%	
33	Oregon	26,732		551,273		0.90%	
34	Utah	22,147		495,981		0.70%	
35	New Mexico	21,569		323,066		0.70%	
36	Nebraska	20,921		285,542		0.70%	
37	Nevada	20,234		385,401		0.70%	
38	West Virginia...................	20,020		281,215		0.70%	
39	Maine	17,621		202,084		0.60%	
40	New Hampshire	15,112		207,417		0.50%	
41	Idaho	14,049		252,120		0.50%	
42	Rhode Island	11,918		159,375		0.40%	
43	Hawaii	11,129		183,609		0.40%	
44	Montana	10,301		148,356		0.30%	
45	South Dakota	9,245		125,537		0.30%	
46	Vermont	8,749		99,103		0.30%	
47	North Dakota	8,037		102,233		0.30%	
48	Alaska	7,808		133,933		0.30%	
49	Delaware	7,749		117,668		0.30%	
50	Wyoming	6,567		87,462		0.20%	
51	District of Columbia	5,676		78,057		0.20%	

\2\Includes imputations for underreporting of prekindergarten teachers/enrollment.

SOURCE: Basic data from U.S. Department of Education, National Center for Education Statistics, The NCES Common Core of Data (CCD), "State Nonfiscal Survey of Public Elementary/Secondary Education," 2003-04 (latest data available as of Jan. 2007).

CLASSIFICATION OF STATE ALTERNATE ROUTES

The National Center for Education information, for the sake of consistency in reporting and analyzing what is going on in the field of alternate routes to teacher certification, developed the following classification system for categorizing the "alternate routes" to the approved college teacher education program route for certifying teachers submitted by the states.

CLASS A is the category reserved for those routes that meet the following criteria:

- The alternative teacher certification route has been designed for the explicit purpose of attracting talented individuals who already have at least a bachelor's degree in a field other than education into elementary and secondary school teaching.

- The alternate route is not restricted to shortages, secondary grade levels or subject areas.

- These alternative teacher certification routes involve teaching with a trained mentor, and any formal instruction that deals with the theory and practice of teaching during the school year -- and sometimes in the summer before and/or after.

CLASS B: Teacher certification routes that have been designed specifically to bring talented individuals who already have at least a bachelor's degree into teaching. These routes involve specially designed mentoring and some formal instruction. However, these routes either restrict the route to shortages and/or secondary grade levels and/or subject areas.

CLASS C: These routes entail review of academic and professional background, and transcript analysis of the candidate. They involve specially (individually) designed inservice and course-taking necessary to reach competencies required for certification, if applicable. The state and/or local school district have major responsibility for program design.

CLASS D: These routes entail review of academic and professional background, and transcript analysis. They involve specially (individually) designed inservice and course-taking necessary to reach competencies required for certification, if applicable. An institution of higher education has major responsibility for program design.

CLASS E: These post-baccalaureate programs are based at an institution of higher education.

CLASS F: These programs are basically emergency routes. The prospective teacher is issued some type of emergency certificate or waiver, which allows the individual to teach, usually without any on-site support or supervision, while taking the traditional teacher education courses requisite for full certification.

CLASS G: Programs in this class are for persons who have few requirements left to fulfill before becoming certified through the traditional approved college teacher education program route, e. g., persons certified in one state moving to another; or persons certified in one endorsement area seeking to become certified in another.

CLASS H: This class includes those routes that enable a person who has some "special" qualifications, such as a well-known author or Nobel prize winner, to teach certain subjects.

CLASS I: These states reported that they were not implementing alternatives to the approved college teacher education program route for licensing teachers, but provided other information.

CLASS J: These programs are designed to eliminate emergency routes. They prepare individuals who do not meet basic requirements to become qualified to enter an alternate route or a traditional route for teacher licensing.

CLASS K: These avenues to certification accommodate specific populations for teaching, e.g., Teach for America, Troops to Teachers and college professors who want to teach in K-12 schools.

TITLE: Alternative Baccalaureate-Level Approach

HISTORY: Created by the Alabama Legislature as part of the Alabama Education Improvement Act of 1991. The Act authorized the program for grades 9-12 subject areas and for grades K-8 in the subject areas of the fine arts and foreign languages. Approved by the Alabama State Board of Education in Feb. 1992; implemented in the 1992-93 school year; expanded by the State Board in 1993 to include special education for grades 9-12, and in 1997, to include grades 6-8 for special education, and in 2000, to include dance and theatre.

MOTIVATION: To increase the pool of applicants from which LEA superintendents and headmasters may select persons who appear qualified to fill vacancies.

GRADE LEVELS AND/OR SUBJECT AREA(S) COVERED:

K-8 -- art, music, foreign languages, physical education, dance, and theatre.

6-8 and 9-12 -- art, music, foreign languages, sciences, social sciences, English, English language arts, career/technical education, mathematics, health, driver education, physical education, dance, and theatre. English-as-a-second-language and all areas of special education are being phased out.

WHO OPERATES: LEA.

REQUIREMENTS TO ENTER PROGRAM:

The participant must hold an earned baccalaureate degree from a regionally accredited college or university.

A minimum of 32 semester hours (19 semester hours must be upper division level) earned credit in the field or an earned bachelor's or higher degree with a non- education major in the academic area in which certification is sought.

The participant must be a candidate for employment by a local board of education or a nonpublic school.

PROGRAM DESCRIPTION:

The participant must be employed with the same local board of education or nonpublic school for three consecutive scholastic years, and must teach a majority of the time in the area and at the grade level of the certificate.

The participant has a mentor each year.

The certificate issued is valid for one-year periods.

Prior to the issuance of the second one-year certificate, the participant must have earned a grade of "C" or above in two of the four areas of coursework of the specified 12 semester hours/18 quarter hours. Prior to issuance of the third one-year certificate, the participant must have earned a grade of "C" or above in the remaining two areas of coursework.

The participant must meet the requirements of the Alabama Prospective Teacher Testing Program (basic skills assessments and subject assessment).

At the end of year three, the participant applies for the Class B (baccalaureate level) professional teacher's certificate (the initial regular certificate in Alabama).

NUMBER OF CREDIT HOURS TO COMPLETE:

12 semester hours or 18 quarter hours in specified coursework.

WHO EVALUATES CANDIDATES?

The local superintendent (or headmaster of nonpublic school).

LENGTH OF TIME: Three scholastic years.

OTHER:

An individual may not be employed for more than three years while holding an Alternative Baccalaureate-Level Certificate, a Special Alternative Certificate, a Preliminary Certificate, or any combination thereof.

TITLE: Preliminary Certificate Approach

HISTORY: Approved by the Alabama State Board of Education in 1997; implemented in 1997.

MOTIVATION: To increase the pool of applicants from which LEA superintendents and headmasters may select persons who appear qualified to fill vacancies.

GRADE LEVELS AND/OR SUBJECT AREA(S) COVERED:

Speech and language impaired and any teaching field requested by a local superintendent.

WHO OPERATES: LEA

REQUIREMENTS TO ENTER PROGRAM:

A local superintendent may apply for a Preliminary Certificate in speech and language impaired and other teaching fields. A headmaster of a nonpublic school may apply for a Preliminary Certificate in speech and language impaired only (the nonpublic school must be accredited, state-approved and/or state-registered).

The individual must have at least an earned master's degree from a regionally accredited college or university in speech-language impaired. An earned bachelor's degree from a regionally accredited college or university will be considered for other teaching fields.

PROGRAM DESCRIPTION:

The holder of a Preliminary Certificate must teach a majority of the time in the teaching field endorsed on the certificate.

The holder is eligible for the professional educator certificate upon completion of two years of successful teaching while holding the Preliminary Certificate.

The participant must meet the requirements of the Alabama Prospective Teacher Testing Program (basic skills assessments and subject assessment).

NUMBER OF CREDIT HOURS TO COMPLETE: None

LENGTH OF TIME: The Preliminary Certificate is valid for two years and may be reissued one time with a one-year valid period.

OTHER: An individual may not be employed for more than three years while holding an Alternative Baccalaureate-Level Certificate, a Special Alternative Certificate, a Preliminary Certificate, or any combination thereof.

TITLE: **Alternative Fifth-Year Program**

HISTORY: Approved by the Alabama State Board of Education in 1986; implemented the same year; IHEs set up proposed programs.

MOTIVATION: To create a quality-controlled alternative route to teacher certification.

GRADE LEVELS AND/OR SUBJECT AREA(S) COVERED: All.

WHO OPERATES: IHE

REQUIREMENTS TO ENTER PROGRAM:

The individual must have an earned bachelor's degree from a regionally accredited college or university.

The participant must have a 2.5 grade point average (on a 4-point scale), submit a score on the GRE or MAT, and meet prerequisite coursework in general studies and the chosen teaching field.

PROGRAM DESCRIPTION:

The master's degree program requires:

A teaching field of at least one-third of the total number of graduate hours in the program.

Study in each of the following areas: curriculum and teaching; professional studies; special education; evaluation of teaching and learning; technology; and reading.

and

A full-time internship as a teacher in the teaching field for at least a full semester.

Upon completion of the program, the individual receives a regular certificate at a higher level than that issued to a graduate of a four-year teacher education program.

The participant must meet the requirements of the Alabama Prospective Teacher Testing Program (basic skills assessments and subject assessment).

The program does not require the participant to be employed as a teacher. If employed as a teacher, a one-year Special Alternative Certificate may be requested a maximum of three times by the local superintendent or headmaster of a nonpublic school (the nonpublic school must be accredited, State-approved and/or State-registered).

NUMBER OF CREDIT HOURS TO COMPLETE:

Determined by the institution.

LENGTH OF TIME: Determined by the participant and IHE regulations.

OTHER:

An individual may not be employed for more than three years while holding an Alternative Baccalaureate-Level Certificate, a Special Alternative Certificate, a Preliminary Certificate, or any combination thereof.

Institutions of higher education that have developed alternative teacher preparation programs leading to a teaching license:

Alabama A&M University
Alabama State University
Auburn University
Auburn University Montgomery
Faulkner University
Jacksonville State University
Samford University
Spring Hill College
Troy University
Troy University Dothan Campus

Tuskegee University
University of Alabama
University of Alabama at Birmingham
University of Alabama in Huntsville

University of Mobile
University of Montevallo
University of North Alabama
University of South Alabama
University of West Alabama

States with which the state has reciprocity of teacher licenses:

NASDTEC Interstate Contract with all states, except Iowa, Minnesota, Missouri, South Dakota and

Wisconsin ("but we can usually certify their teachers")

Institutions of higher education that have *any* teacher preparation programs leading to a license to teach.

Alabama A&M University
Alabama State University
Athens State University
Auburn University
Auburn University Montgomery
Birmingham-Southern College
Concordia College
Faulkner University
Huntington College
Jacksonville State University
Judson College
Miles College
Oakwood College
Samford University
Spring Hill College

Stillman College
Talladega College
Troy University
Troy University Dothan Campus
Troy University Montgomery Campus
Tuskegee University
University of Alabama
University of Alabama at Birmingham
University of Alabama in Huntsville
University of Mobile
University of Montevallo
University of North Alabama
University of South Alabama
University of West Alabama

Contact for persons interested in finding a teaching position in the state:

Dr. Debra G. Pierce
State Department of Education
P.O. Box 302101
Montgomery, AL 36130-2101
Phone: (334) 242-9935

Alaska received a five-year federally-funded Transition to Teaching Grant in 2007 to create and implement alternative pathways to teaching in Alaska. The state also, through SB86 allows those persons currently enrolled in an approved teacher preparation program to become initially certified, be employed as a teacher, and contribute to the Teacher's Retirement System as they complete their requirements.

Institutions of higher education that have developed alternative teacher preparation programs leading to a teaching license:

N/A

States with which the state has reciprocity of teacher licenses:

Alaska has signed the NASDTEC Interstate Contract with states that are NCATE Partnership States.

Institutions of higher education that have any teacher preparation programs leading to a license to teach:

Alaska Pacific University
Sheldon Jackson College
University of Alaska, Anchorage

University of Alaska, Fairbanks
University of Alaska Southeast, Juneau

Contact for persons interested in finding a teaching position in the state:

Cynthia Curran
AK Dept of Education & Early Development
801 W. 10th St., Suite 200
PO Box 110500
Juneau, AK 99811-0500

TITLE OF ALTERNATIVE ROUTE: Teacher Preparation Program

HISTORY: Transition to Teaching Funds were used to design and implement the Teacher Preparation Program (TPP).

MOTIVATION: Increase the pool of applicants in the core content areas identified by the No Child Left Behind federal legislation.

SUBJECT AREAS COVERED: Core academic areas identified by NCLB.

GRADES: Elementary, middle and special education

WHO OPERATES: This is a partnership between the Arizona Department of Education, the Offices of the county Superintendents, the Institutions of Higher Education and the local education agencies.

REQUIREMENTS TO ENTER PROGRAM:
Requirements for eligible participants are based on USC 6682 Sec. 2312

Additional requirements include:

- Bachelor's degree or higher from an accredited institution
- Passing Score on AEPA Content Exam
- Letter of Intent to Hire from the school district
- Letter documenting enrollment in teacher preparation program
- 2 year program
- State Board Approved Teacher Preparation program, coursework and student teaching
- Valid fingerprint clearance card issued by the Arizona Department of Public Safety and satisfactory completion of an interview
- Institutional Recommendation issued by Institution of higher education
- Passing score on AEPA Professional Knowledge exam

PROGRAM DESCRIPTION:

The Teacher Preparation Program is a two year program. It is a State Board approved teacher preparation program that allows candidates to participate in contracted student teaching. It is designed for elementary, middle grades, and special education candidates.

NUMBER OF CREDIT HOURS TO COMPLETE: Varies by program

WHO EVALUATES: The participant is evaluated by the assigned mentor, university supervisor and building level administrator.

LENGTH OF TIME: 2 years

OTHER:

The Teaching Intern Certificate lacks portability between school districts and states.

STATES WITH WHICH THE STATE HAS RECIPROCITY OF TEACHER LICENSES:

All other states

INSTITUTIONS OF HIGHER EDUCATION THAT HAVE *ANY* TEACHER PREPARATION PROGRAMS LEADING TO A LICENSE TO TEACH

ASU- Polytechnic
ASU at the Tempe Campus
ASU at the West Campus
Grand Canyon University
Northern Arizona University
Ottawa University
Pima College
Prescott College
Rio Salado College
Scottsdale Community College
Southwestern College
University of Arizona
University of Arizona – South
University of Phoenix

CONTACT INFORMATION FOR PERSONS INTERESTED IN FINDING A TEACHING POSITION IN THE STATE:

School District websites may be accessed at www.ade.az.gov

TITLE: Non-Traditional Licensure Program

HISTORY: In 1987 the Arkansas Department of Education developed the Non-Traditional Licensure Program (NTLP) to attract well-qualified individuals to the teaching profession. The NTLP prepares teachers in an attempt to help stem the growing teacher shortage in Arkansas. The NTLP is a program for persons who have a four-year degree or higher.

MOTIVATION: "The program is intended to attract and prepare qualified individuals with four year college degrees to fill teaching assignments in districts which have a history of difficulty in recruiting licensed teachers. The Department of Education is committed to assisting local school districts' efforts to identify, recruit and employ teachers."

GRADE LEVELS COVERED:

Early Childhood (P-4)
Middle Childhood (4-8)
Secondary (7-12)

SUBJECT AREAS COVERED

Early Childhood (P-4)
Middle Childhood (4-8)
Math- Science
English, Lang Arts/ Social Studies
Secondary (4-12)
Agriculture
Business Education
Family & Consumer Sciences
Industrial Technology
Marketing Technology
Secondary (7-12)
English
Life/Earth Science
Mathematics
Physical/ Earth Science
Social Studies
Preschool-12th grade
Art
Drama/ Speech
French
German
Music, Vocal and Instrumental
Physician Education, Wellness & Leisure
Spanish

Endorsements

Coaching (7-12)
English as a Second Language (ESL) P-12
Journalism (7-12)
Mandarin Chinese (7-12)

WHO OPERATES: Arkansas Department of Education

REQUIREMENTS TO ENTER PROGRAM:
- Bachelor's degree or higher from a regionally accredited Institution of Higher Education documenting a cumulative grade point average of 2.50 (or 2.75 in the last 60 hours of coursework completed)
- Transcript(s) showing completion of required Arkansas History course and Teaching Reading courses required for Early Childhood and Middle Childhood license areas
- Transcript(s) showing completion of required Arkansas History course required for secondary Social Studies license area
- Passing scores on all parts of the Praxis I: Basic Skills Exam (PPST)
- Passing score on all required Praxis II: Subject Area Content exam(s)
- Proof of starting process for Arkansas and FBI Background Check clearance
- NTLP online application and program fee payment

REQUIREMENTS TO RECEIVE NTLP PROVISIONAL LICENSE:

First Year

- Full enrollment in NTLP

- Verification of employment by an Arkansas School

- Mandatory attendance of all three (3) weeks of summer Instructional Modules

- Verification of passing grade for all summer Instructional Modules

- Arkansas and FBI Background Check clearance

Second Year
- Successful completion of all first year NTL Instructional Modules (Summer and Saturdays)
- Verification of employment by an Arkansas School
- NTLP online application and payment of the second year program fee
- Mandatory attendance of all three(3) weeks of summer Instructional Modules
- Verification of passing grade for all summer Instructional Modules

SELECTION OF SCHOOL DISTRICTS
All districts in Arkansas are eligible to participate.

PROGRAM DESCRIPTION:

The Non-Traditional Licensure Program (NTLP) includes 288 hours of intensive specialized best practice instructional delivery for teacher preparation and 50 hours of support and focused feedback from a site-based Pathwise trained mentor who guides the new teacher's professional growth. The NTLP teacher preparation modules include, but are not limited to, the following areas:

- Pathwise
- Arkansas current practices and issues
- Classroom management
- Positive classroom discipline
- Legal responsibilities of teachers
- Legal issues in the classroom (IDEA, 504, ESL)
- Instructional delivery strategies
- Diverse needs of learners, multiple intelligences, and learning styles
- Thinking skills strategies
- Writing across the curriculum
- Technology integration in instruction
- Organizing content knowledge for student learning
- Assessments/ performance tasks/ rubric development instruction
- Managing the learning environment for diverse learners
- Arkansas content standards and curriculum frameworks

To complete the program and receive an initial Arkansas Teaching License the participant must successfully complete all NTL instructional modules and teach full time as the teacher of record for a minimum each year and pass the Praxis II Principles of Learning and Teaching or the Praxis II pedagogy assessment in the participant's content area.

NUMBER OF CREDIT HOURS TO COMPLETE:

In general there is no credit hour requirement. However, three areas of licensure do require coursework. These are:

License Area	Course(s)	
	Arkansas History	Methods of Teaching Reading
Early Childhood	3 credit hours	6 credit hours
Middle Childhood	3 credit hours	6 credit hours
Secondary Social Studies	3 credit hours	

WHO EVALUATES: The NTLP instructional site directors, coordinators, and instructors regularly conduct performance evaluations.

LENGTH OF TIME: Two years.

Institutions of higher education that have developed alternative teacher preparation programs leading to a teaching license:

Henderson State University
Southern Arkansas University
University of Arkansas at Little Rock
University of Arkansas at Monticello
University of Arkansas at Pine Bluff
University of Central Arkansas

States with which the state has reciprocity of teacher licenses:

NASDTEC Interstate Contract.

Institutions of higher education that have *any* teacher preparation program(s) leading to a license to teach.

Arkansas State University
Arkansas Tech University
Harding University
Henderson State University
Hendrix College
John Brown University
Lyon College
Ouachita Baptist University
Philander Smith College

Southern Arkansas University
University of Arkansas at Fayetteville
University of Arkansas Fort Smith
University of Arkansas at Little Rock
University of Arkansas at Monticello
University of Arkansas at Pine Bluff
University of Central Arkansas
University of the Ozarks
Williams Baptist College

Contact information for persons interested in finding a teaching position in the state:

Teach Arkansas
ADE Non-Traditional Licensure Program
501 Woodlane
Little Rock, AR 72201
Ms. Ann DeLoney, Program Advisor
Phone: (501) 682-5535

TITLE: District Intern Certificate

HISTORY: Legislation passed in 1983 originally authorized the program for secondary school teachers only; the first interns were in place in 1984. The law was changed in 1987 to expand the program to include bilingual and elementary teachers and again in 2002 to include special education teachers.

MOTIVATION: Teacher supply and demand, but available in all grades and subject areas.

GRADE LEVELS AND/OR SUBJECT AREA(S) COVERED:

Originally for secondary only; later expanded to include bilingual and elementary and then special education teachers.

WHO OPERATES: LEA.

REQUIREMENTS TO ENTER:

A bachelor's degree.

Demonstration of basic skills

Subject matter competence demonstrated by completing an approved program of study (secondary only), or passing appropriate subject area portions of the state-approved subject matter exam.

Bilingual classroom teachers must pass oral language component of state exam.

Knowledge of U.S. Constitution.

Character Fitness (Fingerprints)

PROGRAM DESCRIPTION:

The school district must employ persons to provide guidance and assistance. Each intern must be supported by at least one mentor or other designated support person.

The school district must develop a professional development plan for intern -- including training (120 clock hours or equivalent pre-service component including child development and methods of teaching), and ongoing teacher preparation, support and assistance, and annual performance evaluation.

The intern will be eligible for a preliminary credential with the school district's recommendation, based on a performance assessment of successful teaching.

NUMBER OF CREDIT HOURS TO COMPLETE:

120 clock hours of initial, preservice professional development training and a professional development program (approximately 360 additional clock hours). Special education has an additional 120 clock hour requirement.

WHO EVALUATES: LEA evaluates candidates; state evaluates LEA programs.

LENGTH OF TIME: The Intern Credential is valid for two years of teaching and may be extended.

OTHER: 18 percent of the state's Intern teachers are teaching as district interns. Of these, about 33 percent are in Los Angeles Unified School District.

Four county offices of education have developed consortium programs for multiple districts in their respective service areas. There are four urban single district programs. $24.3 million has been allocated through the state's budget act for alternative certification (both University and District Intern programs). One charter school has begun a district intern program. A total of 8,081 Interns (both University and District) are teaching in 926 districts through 71 funded programs.

The retention rate of participating District Interns is approximately 84 percent after 3 years in the classroom and 80 percent after 5 years.

Interns receive full beginning teacher's salary and benefits.

The total number of District Interns in classrooms in 2006-07 was 1,451.

2003 Legislation deleted the 2 year service requirement and instead requires all programs to meet same standards and performance requirements as all teacher preparation programs in California.

TITLE: Early Completion Intern Option

HISTORY: Legislation passed and signed by the governor in 2001.

MOTIVATION: Provides fast-track options for:

a) Private school teachers who want to become public school teachers;

b) Well-qualified individuals who can demonstrate that pedagogical preparation or supervised field experience is unnecessary for them through passage of the Foundations in Teaching exam.

GRADE LEVELS AND/OR SUBJECT AREA(S) COVERED:

Multiple and Single Subject (K-12) teachers. Exams currently available in Multiple Subject, and in four single subject areas: Math, Science, English and Social Studies.

WHO OPERATES: District and University Internship Programs

REQUIREMENTS TO ENTER:

Early Completion Internship

1. Baccalaureate degree

2. Subject matter content proficiency (exam or coursework)

3. Character fitness (fingerprints)

4. Written assessment of teaching knowledge and subject matter pedagogy in the areas of:

   a. Special needs students and learning differences

   b. English learners

   c. Classroom management

   d. Subject matter pedagogy

   e. Assessment of pupil progress

PROGRAM DESCRIPTION:

Individuals who complete the prerequisites -- including the Foundations in Teaching exam -- may enter the Early Completion Option if they are offered a teaching position and are accepted into the internship program.

Once admitted into the Early Completion Internship Option, a candidate completes the California Teaching Performance Assessment or other authorized assessment of classroom performance. The candidate's performance is demonstrated with his or her students in the classroom. If the candidate passes all sections or elements of the performance assessment and other district requirements, he or she is eligible for a preliminary credential. Candidates must also demonstrate knowledge of reading and computer technology.

If the candidate does not pass all sections of the performance assessment, he or she continues in the intern program and receives an individualized program of study, based on the assessment results and any district or intern program requirements. Early Completion Option interns, as well as all interns, must pass the Teaching Performance Assessment at the end of the internship to be recommended for a preliminary credential. Candidates for a multiple-subject credential must also pass the Reading Instruction Competency Assessment for credential recommendation.

NUMBER OF CREDIT HOURS TO COMPLETE:

No set number of credit hours. Completion is determined by the candidate successfully passing the teaching foundations exam and performance assessment.

WHO EVALUATES: California Commission on Teacher Credentialing and participating internship program and districts.

LENGTH OF TIME: No time limit, but could be completed in as little as one semester.

OTHER: In addition to the Early Completion Option, the statute also allows private school teachers to achieve California credentials, and has an option for challenging the induction portion of teacher preparation.

The private school option allows teachers with six years of full-time teaching experience in a regionally accredited private school and two years of rigorous performance evaluations to seek a preliminary credential. The evaluations must address the effectiveness areas in the California Standards for Teacher Profession.

Private school teachers with three years of successful teaching and two years of successful evaluations under the same conditions as above may waive teacher preparation fieldwork.

Private school applicants also must demonstrate knowledge of basic skills, reading, the U.S. Constitution, and subject matter, and have fingerprint clearance.

The statute also requires development of a fast track method to complete the formative assessment of teaching performance portion of the professional clear teaching credential.

In August 2004 a special administration of the qualifying pedagogy (Teaching Foundations Exam) was offered in order to set a passing score for the exams. Sufficient persons took the exam to set passing scores in the multiple subject, English and Mathematics.

TITLE: University Intern Credential

HISTORY: Authorized by legislation in 1967, but issuance of the first such credentials dates back to the early 1950s.

MOTIVATION: In practice, its use is targeted at subject area shortages, although this is not required by law.

GRADE LEVELS AND/OR SUBJECT AREA(S) COVERED:

The state's fastest-growing route, especially in special education, but available for all types of credentials.

WHO OPERATES: IHE and LEA (must be collaborative programs).

REQUIREMENTS TO ENTER:

A bachelor's degree.

Demonstration of basic skills.

Subject matter competence demonstrated by completing an approved program of study (secondary only), or passing appropriate subject area portions of the state-approved subject matter exam.

Knowledge of U.S. Constitution.

The teacher's union for the local school district hiring the intern must sign-off on the application.

Character Fitness (Fingerprints).

PROGRAM DESCRIPTION:

Professional education courses in methods must be completed or formed during the time the individual is employed as an intern teacher.

The individual must demonstrate subject matter competencies through an approved program or equivalent exam. For elementary teachers, this means competencies in the seven subjects taught in elementary schools by exam; for secondary teachers, this means competency in the subject area to be taught, at the level equivalent to a major. The college may require completion of courses it deems necessary to achieve these competencies.

Admission requirements must take into account the accelerated responsibilities of interns. Applicants should have a high degree of maturity and previous experience with children.

120 clock hours (or equivalent) of pre-service training must be provided to ensure a minimum level of knowledge in the 13 Teaching Performance Expectations before becoming teacher of record. Programs emphasize blending theory and practice and frequently include professors and experienced teachers on the program's faculty.

The local school district must designate someone to provide support and evaluation for the intern. The university must also provide supervisors.

NUMBER OF CREDIT HOURS TO COMPLETE:

Coursework as required by the IHE to meet competencies (approximately 36 semester units usually spread over two years). Programs may be one to two years long with instruction dispersed throughout the prior summer through the end of the program.

WHO EVALUATES: Individuals are evaluated by the IHE. Evaluation must include a Teaching Performance Assessment.

IHE programs are subject to periodic review by the state.

LENGTH OF TIME: The intern may teach two years with the credential, which may be extended.

OTHER: University Internships are offered in elementary, secondary, administrative, pupil personnel, special education and bilingual credential programs. There are more than 180 intern programs available at California colleges and universities.

This program is operated on 22 campuses of the California State University System, 8 campuses of the University of California System, and 28 campuses of independent colleges and universities. A program operated by the California State University system (CalState Teach) provides a program throughout the state using distance learning, internet technology, and on-site support and assessment.

Interns receive full beginning teacher's salary and benefits.

$24.3 million has been allocated in the state's budget for alternative certification. Approximately 6,630 interns were in university internships in 2006-07.

TITLE: Eminence Credential

HISTORY: First available in the early 1950s.

MOTIVATION: To enable a local school district to employ an
                      individual from another profession who possesses
                      unique abilities.

GRADE LEVELS AND/OR SUBJECT AREA(S) COVERED: All.

WHO OPERATES: LEA.

REQUIREMENTS TO ENTER:

                     The local school district must nominate the individual for a specific
                     teaching assignment.

PROGRAM DESCRIPTION:

                     The individual must pass the CBEST basic skills test during the first
                     year of teaching.

                     The individual is eligible for a clear credential upon completion of five
                     years of successful teaching.

NUMBER OF CREDIT HOURS TO COMPLETE: Not applicable.

WHO EVALUATES: LEA.

LENGTH OF TIME: The credential is valid for two years and may be
                    renewed one time for a three-year period.

                    After five years of successful service, the individual is eligible to apply
                    for a professional clear teaching credential.

OTHER: Fewer than 10 such credentials are issued each
                     year, compared to 25,000 other first-time teaching
                     credentials issued.

TITLE: Sojourn Credential

HISTORY: Available for at least 20 years.

MOTIVATION: Currently used to provide native speakers of Spanish
to teach secondary Spanish courses or bilingual
classes.

GRADE LEVELS AND/OR SUBJECT AREA(S) COVERED:

Currently, Spanish and bilingual.

WHO OPERATES: LEA.

REQUIREMENTS TO ENTER:

LEA must nominate the individual.

PROGRAM DESCRIPTION:

The individual is allowed to teach without having earned a bachelor's
degree -- the only such program still in effect in California.

The individual must have completed 90 semester units of college study.

Holders of this credential are currently used to teach high school
Spanish and bilingual classes.

The individual must pass the CBEST basic skills tests within the first
year, in order to qualify for renewal.

The credential may be renewed if the individual completes an
additional 6 semester units of coursework each year toward completion
of an approved college teacher education program and a bachelor's
degree (if the individual has no degree).

NUMBER OF CREDIT HOURS TO COMPLETE:

6 semester units per year toward completion of an approved teacher
education program and bachelor's degree.

WHO EVALUATES: LEA.

LENGTH OF TIME: One year; renewable if the individual passes the CBEST and completes 6 semester units of coursework in an approved teacher education program.

OTHER: A state official said these individuals are largely recruited in Spain and Mexico, many teach for one year, do not complete the basic skills test or the required college coursework, and return to their home countries.

Institutions of higher education that have developed alternative teacher preparation programs leading to a teaching license:

Alliant International University
Azusa Pacific University
Biola University
California Baptist University
California Lutheran University
California Polytechnic State University, San Luis Obispo
California State Polytechnic University, Pomona
CalState TEACH
California State University Bakersfield
California State University Channel Islands
California State University Chico
California State University Dominguez Hills
California State University East Bay
California State University Fresno
California State University Fullerton
California State University Long Beach
California State University Los Angeles
California State University Monterey Bay
California State University Northridge
California State University Sacramento
California State University San Bernardino
California State University San Marcos
California State University Stanislaus
Chapman University
Claremont Graduate School
Concordia University
Dominican University of California
Fresno Pacific University
Holy Names College
Humboldt State University

John F. Kennedy University
La Sierra University
Loyola Marymount University
National Hispanic University
National University
Notre Dame De Namur University
Pacific Oaks College
Patten University
Pepperdine University
Point Loma Nazarene University
San Diego State University
San Francisco State University
San Jose State University
Santa Clara University
St. Mary's College
Sonoma State University
Touro University
University of California, Berkeley
University of California, Davis
University of California, Irvine
University of California, Los Angeles
University of California, Riverside
University of California, San Diego
University of California, Santa Barbara
University of California, Santa Cruz
University of Laverne
University of Phoenix
University of Redlands
Whittier College

School-District Based Alternative Programs

Compton School District
Elementary and Secondary Teaching Fellows Academy
Los Angeles Unified School District (LISTOS)
Ontario-Montclair School District Intern Academy
Orange County Dept. of Education
Project Pipeline
San Joaquin District Intern (IMPACT)
Stanislaus County Office of Education

Charter School Alternative Programs

High Tech High

Institutions of higher education that have *any* teacher preparation programs leading to a license to teach.

Antioch University of Southern California
Azusa Pacific University
Bethany Bible College
Biola University
California Baptist College
California Lutheran College
California Polytechnic State Univ.,
    San Luis Obispo
California State Polytechnic Univ., Pomona
Cal State Teach
California State University, Bakersfield
California State University, Chico
California State University, Dominguez Hills
California State University, Fresno
California State University, Fullerton
California State University, Hayward
California State University, Long Beach
California State University, Los Angeles
California State University, Monterey Bay
California State University, Northridge
California State University, Sacramento
California State University, San Bernardino
California State University, San Marcos
California State University, Stanislaus
Chapman College-Fort Ord
Chapman College-Orange
Christian Heritage College

Claremont Graduate School
College of Notre Dame
Concordia University
Dominican College of San Rafael
Fresno Pacific College
Holy Names College
Humboldt State University
John F. Kennedy University
La Sierra University
Loma Linda University
Loyola Marymount University
Masters College
Mills College
Mount St. Mary's College
National Hispanic University

National University
New College of California
Nova Southeastern University
Occidental College
Pacific Christian College
Pacific Oaks College
Pacific Union College
Patten College
Pepperdine University
Point Loma Nazarine College
Saint Mary's College
San Diego State University-Imperial Valley
San Diego State University-San Diego
San Francisco State University
San Jose State University
Santa Clara University
Simpson College
Sonoma State University
Southern California College
Stanford University
Alliant International University
University of California, Berkeley
University of California, Davis
University of California, Irvine
University of California, Los Angeles
University of California, Riverside
University of California, San Diego
University of California, Santa Barbara
University of California, Santa Cruz
University of LaVerne
University of Phoenix
University of Redlands
University of San Diego
University of San Francisco
University of Southern California
University of the Pacific
Westmont College
Whittier College

Contact information for persons interested in obtaining information on Teacher Preparation Programs in the state:
Michael McKibbin, California Commission on Teacher Credentialing, 1900 Capitol Avenue, Sacramento, CA 95811-4213, Phone: (916) 445-4438

TITLE: Teacher in Residence

HISTORY: The program was created in legislation (SB 99-154) in 1999.

MOTIVATION: The program was created to address teacher shortages and school districts'
                        inability to find qualified and fully-licensed individuals for teaching positions.
                        The legislation recognized that school districts have increased the use of
                        emergency authorizations to employ individuals who do not have licenses and
                        may not have received any former teacher preparation. The new policy further
                        recognized that persons with experience in areas other than teaching can help
                        alleviate teacher shortages faced by many school districts, provided these
                        persons receive adequate supervision and education in teaching.

GRADE LEVELS AND/OR SUBJECT AREA(S) COVERED:
                        Agriculture and Renewable Natural Resources
                        Art
                        Business
                        Business/Marketing
                        Drama
                        Early Childhood Education
                        Elementary Education
                        English
                        Family and Consumer Studies
                        Foreign Languages
                        Health
                        Instructional Technology (Computers)
                        Marketing
                        Mathematics
                        Music
                        Physical Education
                        Science
                        School Librarian
                        Social Studies
                        Special Education Generalist
                        Speech
                        Technology Education

WHO OPERATES: Programs are the primary responsibility of school
                        districts or Board of Cooperative Education Services
                        (BOCES), but must be planned and operated with an
                        institution of higher education that has an approved
                        teacher education program.

REQUIREMENTS TO ENTER:

Candidates interested in employment as a Teacher In Residence must:

- Hold a bachelor's degree from a regionally accredited college or university.

- Demonstrate subject matter knowledge necessary for teaching in an endorsement area through transcript review, equal to 30 semester hours.

- Pass a background check conducted by Colorado Department of Education, including fingerprinting.

- Pass the state's required assessment in the content (endorsement) area.

- Obtain a full-time teaching position in the selected endorsement area.

PROGRAM DESCRIPTION:

School districts or BOCES must submit a proposal for approval by the State Board of Education.

Within 30 days of employment, the Designated Agency must report the hiring of a Teacher in Residence to the Colorado Department of Education. An Authorization: Teacher in Residence is issued from the Colorado Department of Education while the Teacher In Residence is participating in the two-year program.

Designated Agencies are required to collaborate with an approved teacher education institution in the design and delivery of a teacher education program, based on performance-based standards adopted by the State Board of Education. These performance-based teacher education standards are the same standards used in the preparation of teachers in collegiate teacher education programs.

Teachers in Residence must have an assigned teacher mentor and supervisor.

Candidates must be observed and supervised for a minimum of 100 hours each year for the duration of the two-year program.

NUMBER OF CREDIT HOURS TO COMPLETE:

Credit hours or clock hours of training are not specified. Candidates must complete the teacher education program provided by the school district and/or institution of higher education. The program is performance based and districts must continually assess each Teacher in Residence's progress in meeting performance-based standards. Generally speaking, these programs include 30 semester hours of collegiate pedagogy.

WHO EVALUATES: The Designated Agency makes the recommendation for licensure in consultation with the cooperating institution of higher education and the school district, upon completion of the program.

LENGTH OF TIME: Two years.

OTHER: During the 2000-01 school year, 209 teachers in residence were enrolled in the first year of the two-year program.

During the 2001-02 school year, 378 Teachers In Residence were enrolled in the first year of the program and 180 in the second year.

Participants for the 2002-03 school year included 325 in their first year and 266 teachers in their second year.

Participants for the 2003-04 school year included 230 in their first year and 276 teachers in their second year. A new endorsement area added this year was Special Education: Generalist.

Participants for the 2004-05 school year included 206 in their first year and 201 teachers in their second year. New endorsement areas for 2004-05 include School Librarian and Instructional Technology.

TITLE: Alternative Teacher Program

HISTORY: Began Sept. 1, 1991

MOTIVATION: Programs are intended to attract talented individuals into public
                    education who are liberal arts graduates, non-public school teachers,
                    college professors, and/or successful individuals seeking career
                    changes.

GRADE LEVELS AND/OR SUBJECT AREA(S) COVERED:
                    Agriculture and Renewable Natural Resources
                    Art
                    Business
                    Business/Marketing
                    Drama
                    Early Childhood Education
                    Elementary Education
                    English
                    Family and Consumer Studies
                    Foreign Languages
                    Health
                    Instructional Technology (Computers)
                    Linguistically Diverse Education
                    Marketing
                    Mathematics
                    Music
                    Physical Education
                    Science
                    School Librarian
                    Social Studies
                    Special Education Generalist
                    Speech
                    Technology Education

WHO OPERATES: School districts, independent schools, charter
                    schools, boards of cooperative educational services
                    (BOCES), and/or institutions of higher education.

REQUIREMENTS TO ENTER:

                    Candidates interested in employment as an Alternative Teacher must:

                    Hold a bachelor's degree from a regionally accredited college or
                    university.

Pass the state's required assessment in the content (endorsement) area.

Demonstrate subject matter knowledge necessary for teaching in an endorsement area through transcript review, equal to 30 semester hours.

Pass a background check conducted by the Colorado Department of Education, including fingerprinting.

Obtain a full-time teaching position in the selected endorsement area.

PROGRAM DESCRIPTION:

Approved alternative teacher program sites provide a one-year program of teaching, training, and supervision for the alternative teacher. The program includes: 225 clock hours of professional education, based on performance-based standards adopted by the State Board of Education. These performance-based teacher education standards are the same standards used in preparation of teachers in collegiate teacher education programs.

Training may be modified by the support team, based on assessment of the alternative teacher's knowledge, skills, and ability.

Supervision and guidance by members of a support team, including a mentor teacher, principal, and representative of a higher education institution.

After successfully completing an approved alternative teacher program, the candidate is recommended by the approved agency for a Colorado Provisional Teaching License.

NUMBER OF CREDIT HOURS TO COMPLETE:

225 clock hours of professional education.

WHO EVALUATES: Evaluation for eligibility to participate in the program is done by the Colorado Department of Education; evaluation for employment is conducted by a Designated Agency.

LENGTH OF TIME: One year.

OTHER:

During the 2000-01 school year, 274 Alternative teachers were enrolled in the one-year program.

During the 2001-02 school year, 376 Alternative Teachers were enrolled in the program.

During the 2002-03 school year, 490 Alternative Teachers were enrolled in the program.

During the 2003-04 school year, 448 Alternative Teachers were enrolled in the program. A new endorsement area added this year was Special Education: Generalist.

During the 2004-05 school year, 383 Alternative Teachers were enrolled in the program. New endorsement areas for 2004-05 include Linguistically Diverse, School Librarian and Instructional Technology.

Institutions of higher education that have developed alternative teacher preparation programs leading to a teaching license:

For the Alternative Program:

Adams State College
Colorado Christian University
Colorado State University-Pueblo
Mesa State College
Metropolitan State College
Naropa University
Regis College
University of Colorado at Boulder
University of Colorado at Colorado Springs
University of Colorado at Denver
University of Denver

University of Northern Colorado
University of Phoenix
Western State College

For the Teacher In Residence Program:

Colorado State University-Pueblo
Metropolitan State University
University of Colorado at Colorado Springs
University of Colorado at Denver

States with which the state has reciprocity of teacher licenses:

NASDTEC Interstate Contract.

Institutions of higher education that have *any* teacher preparation programs leading to a license to teach.

Adams State College
Colorado Christian University
Colorado College
Colorado State University at Ft. Collins
Colorado State University at Pueblo
Fort Lewis College
Johnson and Wales University
Jones International University
Mesa State College
Metropolitan State College

Regis University
Rocky Mountain College of Art and Design
University of Colorado-Boulder
University of Colorado-Colorado Springs
University of Colorado-Denver
University of Denver
University of Northern Colorado
University of Phoenix
Western State College

Contact information for persons interested in finding a teaching position in the state:

Positions are handled through each local school district

CDE has established an new centralized website to post opportunities andfor candidates to apply for positions, located at www.teachinColorado.org

Colleges working with Designated Agencies for the Delivery of Alternative Licensure

For the Alternative Program:

IHE	Collaborating Agency
Adams State College	Centennial BOCES, Cesar Chavez Academy, Colorado Academy, East Central BOCES, Mountain BOCES, Northwest BOCES, San Luis BOCES, South Central BOCES
Colorado Christian University	Colorado Christian University
Colorado State University-Pueblo	Southeastern BOCES
Mesa State College	West Central Licensing Program
Metropolitan State College Denver Public Schools, Metro State College	Denver Arts & Technology Academy,
Naropa University	Naropa University
Regis College	Archdiocese of Denver
University of Colorado at Boulder	Eagle Rock School of Prof . Dev., Horizon's K-8 Alternative School
University of Colorado at Colo. Springs	Peak To Peak Charter School, University of Colorado at Colo. Springs
University of Colorado at Denver	The Boulder Journey School, Denver Public Schools, Friends' School, P.S. 1 Charter School, Stanley British Primary School
University of Denver	Denver Academy, Englewood Schools, Mapleton/Boettcher Program
University of Northern Colorado	Weld County RE-3(J) District
University of Phoenix	Cherry Creek School District, Douglas County
Western State College	Western State College

Colleges working with Designated Agencies for the Delivery of Alternative Licensure

For the Teacher In Residence Program:

Colorado State University-Pueblo   Pueblo District 60, Pueblo District 70

Metropolitan State University   Adams 12 Five Star Schools, Adams District 50, Adams-Arapahoe 28J, Brighton 27-J, Clear Creek School District RE-1, Denver District 1, Douglas County District RE-1, Jefferson County Schools, Littleton Public Schools, Sheridan District #2

University of Colorado at Colorado Springs   Pikes Peak BOCES

University of Colorado at Denver   Front Range BOCES

TITLE: Alternate Route to Teacher Certification

HISTORY: Created in 1986 as part of the Connecticut Education Enhancement Act. The first class (106 candidates) began the program June 20, 1988.

MOTIVATION: The state describes it as: "An innovative and exciting program to attract talented individuals from fields outside of education into teaching. . . . The program is intended for professionals from diverse fields such as industry, government, and the military or human services that wish to change careers. Individuals who have substituted, who have taught part-time, or who have experience as teachers in independent schools are also encouraged to apply."

SUBJECT AREAS/GRADE LEVELS COVERED:

Middle school grades 4 - 8 to teach specific subject areas in middle schools. The subject areas include English, history/social studies, earth science, general science or mathematics. A teacher endorsed in middle grades will only be able to teach in the subjects endorsed on the certificate.

Secondary grades 7 - 12 to teach specific subject areas. The subject areas include English, history/social studies, mathematics, and sciences (biology, chemistry, earth science, physics, and general science).

Pre-K-12 certification to teach art, music, world languages, bilingual education, family and consumer science, and technology education.

WHO OPERATES: The Connecticut Department of Higher Education conducts two Alternate Route to certification programs. Monitoring during the first two years of teaching is under the auspices of the Connecticut Department of Education.

REQUIREMENTS TO ENTER:

Minimum of a bachelor's degree from an accredited institution with a major in or closely related to, the intended teaching field. Prospective middle school teachers, secondary school teachers and special area (art and music) teachers must have the subject-area semester hours required for certification.

A minimum grade point average of "B" (3.00 on a 4.00 scale) in undergraduate studies or the same average in at least 24 semester hours of graduate study.

A passing score on Praxis I (PPST) or a passing score on an approved substitute exam.

A passing score on a subject area test, Praxis II or ACTFEL.

Experience in an educational environment with children of the age group the individual wishes to teach.

PROGRAM DESCRIPTION:

The Summer Alternate Route to Certification Program is an intensive eight-week, full time study in the summer. A three-week student teaching experience in a summer school setting is included in the eight-week program. The faculty consists of Connecticut public school teachers, teacher-educators from the state's public and private higher education institutions, and professionals from diverse public and non-public agencies. The curriculum is innovative and interdisciplinary, based on the Connecticut Teaching Competencies and utilizing teaching methods of demonstrated effectiveness.

The other Alternate Route to Certification Program is a weekend program which runs from October to May, and includes four weeks of student teaching. This program focuses on shortage areas: bilingual education, mathematics, science, world languages, family and consumer science, and technology education.

Employed Alternate Route teachers participate in the Beginning Educators Support and Training (BEST) Program of the State Department of Education. BEST includes a mentoring component and subject specific portfolio assessment.

Additionally, employing school districts must provide Alternate Route teachers with a special plan of supervision that may exceed that provided to other novice teachers.

NUMBER OF CREDIT HOURS TO COMPLETE:

The Alternate Route is a non-credit program.

WHO EVALUATES: State Department of Higher Education screens for eligibility and admission to the program. Admissions are competitive. Final decisions are made in conjunction with review of certification eligibility by the State Department of Education. Continued state certification of applicants is determined based upon their successful completion of the state's induction program. The Alternate Route to Certification Program (ARC) is evaluated on a five-year cycle, as are all teacher preparation programs in the state. Program approval is granted by the State Board of Education for a specified period of time.

LENGTH OF TIME: ARC I: Summer sessions: 8 weeks.
ARC II: Weekends October - May.

TITLE: Post Baccalaureate Certification

MOTIVATION: Students with a bachelor's degree may apply to a college or university and, upon acceptance, take the courses designed to meet certification or program requirements. Many institutions combine the certification/program courses with a master's degree.

SUBJECT AREAS/GRADE LEVELS COVERED:

Early childhood, elementary, middle grades areas, secondary academic areas, art, music, physical education, technology education, and special education.

WHO OPERATES: The following Institutions of Higher Education in the state:

Albertus Magnus College
Central Connecticut State University
Connecticut College
Eastern Connecticut State University
Fairfield University
Quinnipiac University
Sacred Heart University
Saint Joseph College
Southern Connecticut State University
University of Bridgeport
University of Connecticut
University of Hartford
University of New Haven
Yale University

REQUIREMENTS TO ENTER:

Bachelor's degree from an accredited institution.

B-grade point average.

Subject area major as required by Connecticut regulations.

Passing score on Praxis I PPST, or a passing score on an approved substitute exam.

PROGRAM DESCRIPTION:

Students complete a post baccalaureate level planned program, which includes, at a minimum, professional education courses in: foundations of education, educational psychology, curriculum and methods of teaching, student teaching, and special education.

NUMBER OF CREDIT HOURS TO COMPLETE:

The number of credits required to complete these post baccalaureate programs varies, depending upon whether or not the higher education institution requires that a master's degree also is completed.

WHO EVALUATES: All post baccalaureate planned programs have been approved by the Connecticut State Board of Education.

LENGTH OF TIME: The length of time required to complete these programs varies, depending upon whether or not the higher education institution requires that a master's degree also is completed.

TITLE: Connecticut Math Certification Program - Online

HISTORY: Quinnipiac University Division of Education offers this program for certified teachers to earn a mathematics cross-endorsement for middle grades or secondary education. The program is for teachers with Connecticut provisional educator certificates or professional educator certificates. Teachers only holding a certificate with endorsements in vocational technical areas do not qualify for admission.

MOTIVATION: To address the need for mathematics teachers, a shortage area, the State Department of Education and the Department of Higher Education have approved an alternate route program to be offered at Quinnipiac University for middles grades or secondary school mathematics.

SUBJECT AREAS/GRADE LEVELS COVERED:

Middle school endorsement for mathematics, grades 4-8; or Secondary school endorsement for mathematics, grades 7-12

WHO OPERATES: Quinnipiac University. Tel: 203-582-3510

REQUIREMENTS TO ENTER:

Each middle grades math candidate should submit the following:

- An online registration form;
- A copy of your academic transcript to verify completion of a college algebra course with a grade of B or better within the last few years;
- A copy of your provisional educator certificate (Connecticut) or professional educator certificate (Connecticut). Teachers only holding a certificate with endorsements in vocational technical areas do not qualify for admission, and;
- Tuition of $2,000.00.

Each secondary school math candidate should submit the following:

- An online registration form;
- A copy of your provisional educator certificate (Connecticut) or professional educator certificate (Connecticut). Teachers only holding a certificate with endorsements in vocational technical areas do not qualify for admission, and;
- A copy of your academic transcript to verify completion of a course in college calculus and statistics with a grade of B or better in each within the last few years;
- Tuition of $2,000.00.

In addition to standard technology requirements (computer/internet access), candidates must have graphic calculator (TI-83 Plus by Texas Instruments preferred) and a portfolio with problem sets, observation reports, reflective essays, teaching units, assessments and instructional technology material.

PROGRAM DESCRIPTION:

The program, upon successful completion of the appropriate Praxis II assessment, is designed to lead to a cross-endorsement to teach mathematics in the middles grades or the secondary schools. As an online program that is offered once a year, for six months (fall to spring), most of the instruction is online. However, the program includes three Saturday workshops on campus.

Students will develop lessons, assessments and performance tasks to integrate content with the internet, graphing calculators, Geometer's Sketchpad, Excel and PowerPoint.

The middle grade content focuses on the following:
- Data-driven mathematics;
- Solving problems using geometry, and
- Integrating algebraic concepts into a technology-rich discovery environment.

The secondary education content focuses on the following:
- Traditional and integrated curricula;
- Calculus, probability and statistics, and discrete math;
- Using a graphic calculator;
- Using Geometer's Sketchpad, and
- Computer-based laboratory probes

Information and applications are available at:
http://www.quinnipiac.edu/x1968.xml

Mail to:
Assistant Dean, Division of Education
Quinnipiac University
275 Mount Carmel Avenue
Hamden, CT 06518-1908
Phone: 203-582-3510
Fax: 203-582-3473

NUMBER OF CREDIT HOURS TO COMPLETE:

WHO EVALUATES: Quinnipiac University screens for eligibility and admission to the program. Admissions are competitive.

LENGTH OF TIME: Six months, fall (October 14, 2006) to spring (April 20, 2007).

TITLE: Cross Endorsement

MOTIVATION: Teachers who have Connecticut certification may become certified in another endorsement area by taking the required cross endorsement courses and achieving a passing score on the required Praxis II or ACTFL assessment. Individual courses may be taken at any higher education institution. Connecticut State Department of Education certification consultants review transcripts, to ensure that required courses have been taken.

SUBJECT AREAS/GRADE LEVELS COVERED:
Early childhood (requires completion of a planned program)
Elementary
Middle grades academic areas
Secondary academic areas
Art
Music
Physical education
Technology education
Special education
Health
Bilingual education – content specific – must hold a Connecticut certificate in elementary education or middle grade certificate or secondary subject and complete 18 semester credits at one college/university in areas identified in regulations.
     Also must complete assessments:
     a.) ACTFL OPI and WPT in native/bilingual language
     b.) ACTFL OPI for English
     c.) Praxis I PPST – Reading and Writing
Teaching English as a second language
Remedial reading and remedial language arts (require completion of a planned program)
School library media specialist

WHO OPERATES: The following IHEs in the state:

      Albertus Magnus College
      Central Connecticut State University
      Connecticut College
      Eastern Connecticut State University
      Fairfield University
      Mitchell College
      Quinnipiac University
      Sacred Heart University
      Saint Joseph College
      Southern Connecticut State University
      University of Bridgeport
      University of Connecticut
      University of Hartford
      University of New Haven
      Western Connecticut State University
      Yale University

REQUIREMENTS TO ENTER:

      Connecticut certification.

      Relevant academic or subject area major.

PROGRAM DESCRIPTION:

      Students complete the required courses for a cross endorsement. The courses may be taken at any of the higher education institutions in the state, which offer them.

NUMBER OF CREDIT HOURS TO COMPLETE:

      The number of credits required to complete cross endorsement requirements varies, depending on the specific endorsement area.

WHO EVALUATES: The college/university transcript(s) are evaluated by certification consultants in the Bureau of Educator Preparation, Certification, Support and Assessment.

LENGTH OF TIME: The length of time required to complete these programs varies, depending upon the number of credits required, and how many courses a student wishes to take at one time.

TITLE: **Advanced Alternative Preparation for Literacy Specialist in Reading/Language Arts Certification (AAP)**

HISTORY: Created in the Summer of 2005, the first cohort of twenty-four includes elementary and secondary teachers from across the state, including technical high schools, charter schools, and urban, suburban and rural districts. The program was developed over the past two years with assistance from the State Department of Education, the Department of Higher Education, professors in reading/language arts, and district reading consultants.

MOTIVATION: To address the need for reading specialists, the State Department of Education and the Department of Higher Education have joined with Albertus Magnus College to offer a new alternate route program to prepare reading specialists, a shortage area in Connecticut.

SUBJECT AREAS/GRADE LEVELS COVERED:

Remedial reading and remedial language arts.

WHO OPERATES: Albertus Magnus College. Tel: 203-773-8550

REQUIREMENTS TO ENTER:
Each candidate should:
- Hold a valid Connecticut certificate;
- Hold a master's degree;
- Have completed five years of recent teaching experience, and
- Document the support from his or her employing district.

PROGRAM DESCRIPTION:
The program commenced in the summer of 2005. Nine follow-up sessions are scheduled throughout the 2005-06 school year. Several practicums are scheduled up to the summer of 2006 for a final practicum and culminating project.

The program is a blend of the practical and theoretical, with a heavy concentration on practice in various settings

NUMBER OF CREDIT HOURS TO COMPLETE: This Alternate Route is a non-credit program

WHO EVALUATES: Albertus Magnus College screens for eligibility and admission to the program. Admissions are competitive. The program is evaluated by the State Department of Education.

LENGTH OF TIME: One year, summer to summer.

TITLE: Advanced Alternative Program for Certification of Teachers to Become Library Media Specialists

HISTORY: The Advanced Alternative Program for School library Media Specialists is an innovative and exciting program developed by the Connecticut State Department of Education, approved by the Department of Higher Education, accredited using the NCATE (National Council for Accreditation of Teacher Education) standards and administered by ACES to attract talented, successful Connecticut teachers to a new teaching career as school library media specialists.

MOTIVATION: To address the need for school library media specialists, the State Department of Education and the Department of Higher Education have joined with ACES to offer a new alternate route program to prepare school library media specialists, a shortage area in Connecticut.

SUBJECT AREAS/GRADE LEVELS COVERED:

School library media specialists.

WHO OPERATES: Area Cooperative Educational Services (ACES)

REQUIREMENTS TO ENTER:
Each candidate should submit the following:

- The three-page application form;
- A copy of your Connecticut certificate;
- Two letters of reference, including one for an administrator;
- Your resume;
- A non-refundable application fee of $75.00;
- Tuition of $4,100.00, and;
- Textbooks and supplies of approximately $500.00.

PROGRAM DESCRIPTION:

The program is an innovative and exciting program developed by the Connecticut State Department of Education, approved by the Department of Higher Education, accredited using the NCACTE (National Council for Accreditation of Teacher Education) standards and administered by ACES to attract talented, successful Connecticut teachers to a new teaching career as school library media specialists. The program consists of a school year with activities and seminars related to the role and structure of high-quality library media programs and a rigorous, two-week period of intensive, full time instruction in the July before the school year and a three-week program in the July following the school year.

Information and applications are available at:
http://www.acesk12.ct.us

NUMBER OF CREDIT HOURS TO COMPLETE:

The program is an alternate route to certification and is a non-credit program. Although the program does not carry college course credit, completion of the advanced preparation program results in cross-endorsement as a school library medial specialist.

WHO EVALUATES: Area Cooperative Educational Services screens for eligibility and admission to the program. Prior to establishment of the program, it was evaluated and approved by the State Department of Education

LENGTH OF TIME: One year, July to July.

CONNECTICUT

Institutions of higher education that have developed alternative teacher preparation programs leading to a teaching license:

See "Post baccalaureate certification" program.

States with which the state has reciprocity of teacher licenses:

NASDTEC Interstate Contract.

Institutions of higher education that have *any* teacher preparation programs leading to a license to teach.

Albertus Magnus College
Central Connecticut State University
Connecticut College
Eastern Connecticut State University
Fairfield University
Mitchell College
Quinnipiac University
Sacred Heart College
Saint Joseph College

Southern Connecticut State University
University of Bridgeport
University of Connecticut
University of Hartford
University of New Haven
Western Connecticut State University
Yale University

Contact information for persons interested in finding a teaching position in the state:

Connecticut State Department of Education
Bureau of Educator Preparation, Certification,
Support and Assessment
P.O. Box 150471
Hartford, CT 06115-0471
Attn: Nancy L. Pugliese, Chief
Phone: (860) 713-6708

TITLE: **Alternative Route Teacher Education Programs**

HISTORY:

The State Education Agency (SEA) operates state level educational functions serving all Local Education Agencies (LEA).

The public schools are operated by the Local Education Agency referred to as DCPS. There are two Public Charter Schools Boards. One is chartered by the DC Public Charter School Board and the other is chartered by the DCPS Board of Education. Each public charter school is considered their own Local Education Agency.

In addition the DC SEA provides educational credential and accreditation services to all District of Columbia schools including parochial, private and home school educational settings.

The Superintendent of Schools serves as the Chief State School Officer and as Superintendent for the DCPS LEA.

MOTIVATION:

Alternative Route Teacher Education Programs aim to attract the area's most outstanding young and mid-career professionals interested in transitioning into the teaching profession.

DC defines Alternative Route Teacher candidates as those who complete their teacher preparation while serving as the classroom teacher of record in a DC Local Education Agency.

Any teacher preparation program offered at a DC Institution of Higher Education, which is approved by the DC State Board of Education, can potentially produce alternative route teacher candidates.

The State Education Agency facilitates the credentialing of candidates in Alternative Route programs by issuing an Alternative Route Provisional License valid for three years. This provisional license meets the No Child Left Behind criteria and allows holders to be identified as High Qualified.

WHO OPERATES: The SEA Office of Academic Credentials and Standards issues an Alternative Route Provisional License to candidates enrolled in Alternative Route Teacher Education programs.

There are seven Institutions of Higher Education that prepare teachers for licensure in the District of Columbia. These universities have teacher education programs accredited by the DC State Board of Education.

Some of the universities sponsor Alternative Route programs while others assist in the delivery of alternative routes to teacher preparation. The seven universities are listed below.

American University   www.american.edu

Catholic University of America   http://education.cua.edu/

Gallaudet University   http://education.gallaudet.edu/

George Washington University   http://gsehd,gwuledu/gsejd/

Howard University   www.howard.edu/schooleducation/

Trinity University   www.trinitydc.edu/acadmemics/education/

University of the District of Columbia   www.unversityofdc.edu

TITLE: D.C. Teaching Fellows

HISTORY: Initiated in Fall 2001.

MOTIVATION: The mayor and school superintendent called on 100 of the area's most outstanding young and mid-career professionals to commit two years to teach in D.C. Public Schools. These professionals from a variety of careers bring their experience, knowledge, and record of achievement to positively impact the lives of students.

GRADE LEVELS AND/OR SUBJECT AREA(S) COVERED:

Elementary Education; Special Education (grades 1-6); English-as-a-Second Language (ESL)/Bilingual Education (1-6); Secondary Mathematics and Science.

WHO OPERATES: The New Teacher Project and D.C. Public Schools.

REQUIREMENTS TO ENTER:

Candidates must:

Possess a bachelor's degree from an accredited institution; and

Submit an application, cover letter and resume.

PROGRAM DESCRIPTION:

The D.C. Public Schools and the city's administration are calling on the area's most outstanding professionals to become Fellows and commit at least two years to teaching in D.C. Public Schools. They want professionals from a variety of careers to bring their experience, knowledge, and record of achievement to the classroom, and positively impact the lives of students.

Fellows are trained at a comprehensive instructional summer institute, and are provided with an extensive support network to ensure success in the classroom.

Fellows receive financial incentives toward completion of their teacher certification and/or master's degree.

NUMBER OF CREDIT HOURS TO COMPLETE:

24 - 32 semester credit hours.

WHO EVALUATES: D.C. Teacher Education and Certification Branch and local school administrators.

LENGTH OF TIME: Two-year program plus an additional third year of teaching in a D.C. public school.

TITLE: District of Columbia Alternative Certification Program: Teach for America

HISTORY:　　Implemented September 1992.

MOTIVATION:　　This national program was designed to attract talented college student graduates who have a strong desire to teach in urban/rural school districts.

GRADE LEVELS AND/OR SUBJECT AREA(S) COVERED:

Bilingual Education; Elementary Education; Special Education; Early Childhood Education; English-as-a-Second Language, Mathematics, Science, and Foreign Language.

WHO OPERATES:　Teach for America.

REQUIREMENTS TO ENTER:

Possess at least a BA degree from an accredited institution.

Through regional Teach for America Office.

Submit a completed application.

An interview by select school administrators.

PROGRAM DESCRIPTION:

This program was designed to increase the pool of eligible teacher applicants and to meet critical shortages in the areas of Bilingual Education, Early Childhood Education, Elementary Education; English-as-a-Second Language, and Special Education; Mathematics and Science.

The program consists of three basic components: professional education, field experience, and a support structure.

The field experience will be satisfied by one successful year of teaching in lieu of student teaching.

NUMBER OF CREDIT HOURS TO COMPLETE: 24 - 32 semester credit hours.

WHO EVALUATES: Teacher Education and Certification Branch; local school administrators.

LENGTH OF TIME: One year program but years of DC teaching responsibility may vary

TITLE: Transitions to Teaching

HISTORY: The U. S. Department of Education has awarded the District of
                      Columbia a Transitions to Teaching grant for Alternative Route
                      Programs. There are four program administrators for this grant.

- SEA via American University
- Howard University
- The University of the District to Columbia
- Friendship Edison Schools in conjunction with the Center for
  Student Support Services

For information on the Transitions to teaching grants please visit the
websites listed below.

SEA/American University - TOPS & AQUE programs can be accessed
via www.american.edu/cas/soe/partnerships

Howard University - T3 program – www.transitiontoteaching.org

University of the District of Columbia - www.unversityofdc.edu

The Friendship Edison Schools and Center for Student Support
Services programs can be accessed via www.csss.org

GRADE LEVELS AND/OR SUBJECT AREA(S) COVERED:

Below is a list of teaching subjects offered at the DC Institutions of
Higher Education that are DC State Board of Education approved for
state licensure.

Visit the SEA-OACS website for more program information at
www.k12.dc.us/dcsea/certification.

Art	Health and Physical Education
Bilingual Special Education	Music
Dance	Reading
Drama/Theatre	Secondary English and General Science
Early Childhood Education	Secondary Math and Physics
Early Childhood Special Education	Secondary Social Studies
Elementary Education	Special Education (Hearing Impaired)
English as a Second Language	Special Education (Learning Disabled)
Secondary Biology and Chemistry	Special Educatiaon (Multiple Disorders)
Special Education (Non-categorical)	Special Education (SED)

REQUIREMENTS TO ENTER:

Candidates must possess a bachelor's degree from an accredited institution of higher education; and submit an application, cover letter and resume directly to each Alternative Route Program/university.

PROGRAM DESCRIPTION:

Accepted Candidates must:

- Enroll in a state approved teacher education program at an accredited institution of higher education in a major course of study for the subject area of the teaching license being sought.

- Secure or contract employment as a new teacher in the subject area of the license being sought.

- Successfully complete all portions of the Praxis I and PreProfessional Skills exams (reading, writing and mathematics) and the applicable subject content portion test of the Praxis II exam. Praxis exams are administered by the Educational Testing Service; (www.ets.org)

TITLE: Delaware Alternative Route to Certification (ARTC)/Secondary Education

HISTORY: Program developed by Alternative Routes to Certification Consortium under the direction of the Delaware Professional Standards Council, 1995-96. Legislation was approved in 1996. Program was approved by the State Board of Education to operate in 1997.

MOTIVATION: The program developed out of the Professional Standards Council's "Educational Plan for Certification and Career Development." The desire was to develop a less traditional route (that meets the same standards as traditional routes) for talented individuals to enter the teaching profession more quickly while being trained as teachers. Currently the program serves primarily to help fill critical needs shortages in specific secondary school subject areas.

GRADE LEVELS AND/OR SUBJECT AREA(S) COVERED:

Secondary (middle and high school) content areas designated "critical needs areas" in Delaware – currently the sciences (including agricultural sciences), mathematics, foreign languages, English, business and technology education.

WHO OPERATES: A collaboration among the Department of Education, the University of Delaware, and Delaware public and charter schools. The Program Coordinator is housed at the University of Delaware campus in Newark and directs the program serving New Castle County school districts. The Assistant Coordinator is located at the UD campus in Georgetown and directs the program for Kent and Sussex County school districts.

REQUIREMENTS TO ENTER:

- A Bachelor's Degree or equivalent from an accredited college with a major in the field to be taught/certified.

- Passing scores on the state's basic skills tests (currently the Praxis I).

- Satisfactory health and criminal background checks.

- Employment in a Delaware public or charter secondary (middle or high) school as a teacher in the qualified content area.

PROGRAM DESCRIPTION:

Once a candidate has been hired in a teaching position for which they are content-area qualified, the school or district can request to enroll him or her in ARTC. The program consists of two interrelated components:

Each university center provides a state-approved program of 15 graduate credits in professional education: effective teaching strategies, adolescent development and classroom management, reading in the secondary content areas, classroom diversity (including multicultural education and special needs students), and methods in the specific teaching field. Candidates ideally begin with a Summer Institute of two courses in effective teaching (instructional design, planning, assessment and delivery) and classroom management. Later hires begin the program as new cohorts are formed.

The employing school agrees to provide intensive on-the-job mentoring and supervision by a school administrator during the period of ARTC training. The supervisor documents successful classroom performance as an internship in lieu of the student-teaching requirement for certification.

Certification requires satisfaction of the Praxis requirements and successful completion of both the professional education and internship components, including a recommendation from the school supervisor for initial certification. Occasionally individuals will also need to complete additional courses in the content area.

The program employs a cohort model, in which small groups of ARTC teachers enter the program and complete the entire course sequence together in specially designed classes. Courses and workshops are conducted by both university faculty and skilled practitioners experienced in the content areas covered by the program.

NUMBER OF CREDIT HOURS TO COMPLETE:

Candidates take the equivalent of 15 credit hours of professional education coursework within a period of approximately 12 to 18 months. Candidates who need additional courses in the subject area may take longer to complete certification requirements.

WHO EVALUATES: Delaware Department of Education.

LENGTH OF TIME: Twelve to eighteen months.

TITLE: Special Institute for Teacher Certification

HISTORY: Legislation approved in 1986.

MOTIVATION: The program was originally initiated in anticipation of projected teacher shortages, to recruit and support individuals seeking certification in areas identified as "critical needs."

GRADE LEVELS AND/OR SUBJECT AREA(S) COVERED:

All areas identified by the state as "critical needs": currently the sciences, mathematics, foreign languages, English, technology education, business education, library/media specialists, reading specialists and special education.

WHO OPERATES: Governed by the State Board of Education which makes the rules and regulations for the program, and the University of Delaware which administers the Institute.

REQUIREMENTS TO ENTER:

A bachelor's degree in a "critical needs" subject area and passing scores on Praxis I.

PROGRAM DESCRIPTION:

The state reimburses the tuition costs of participants taking courses required for teacher certification in designated "critical needs" areas. Includes a loan forgiveness provision for those who teach in Delaware upon completion of certification.

NUMBER OF CREDIT HOURS TO COMPLETE:

Depends on the requirements set by the graduate program the candidate is enrolled in; sometimes on transcript analysis completed by the Department of Education Office of Professional Standards and Certification.

WHO EVALUATES: Delaware Department of Education

LENGTH OF TIME: Varies according to number of credits needed for certification.

TITLE: Master's in Primary/K-4 or Middle Level/5-8 Education

HISTORY: Began in 1992.

MOTIVATION: Developed for individuals with bachelor's degrees who meet content prerequisites for entry and complete a state-approved, 36 semester hour master's degree program in Primary/K-4 or Middle Level/5-8 Education.

GRADE LEVELS AND/OR SUBJECT AREA(S) COVERED:

Primary/K-4 or Middle Level/5-8.

WHO OPERATES: IHE (Wilmington College); developed in conjunction with and approval of SEA.

REQUIREMENTS TO ENTER:

This program is designed for candidates who already have a bachelor's degree in any field, who come from a non-education background, and have an interest in teaching primary or middle-level age children.

PROGRAM DESCRIPTION:

The program offers an accelerated means to earn both a master's degree and state teacher certification in two years. It is designed to accommodate those who hold another job while training. The individual must complete:

36 semester hours of courses, given during evening hours, over about 18 months.

12-15-weeks of student teaching. Candidates who have jobs must be available full-time during daytime hours to complete this requirement.

Additional coursework the summer after student teaching.

A three-week intensive research project.

There is an Internship requirement in order to complete the program for State of Delaware certification.

NUMBER OF CREDIT HOURS TO COMPLETE:

36 semester hours.

WHO EVALUATES: IHE.

LENGTH OF TIME: Approximately two years.

TITLE: Master's in Secondary Education with Initial Certification

HISTORY: Established in 1996 at the request of the Delaware Department of
                      Education. Number served to date: 13; 100 percent employment.

MOTIVATION: Designed to provide individuals who hold a bachelor's degree from a
                      regionally-accredited college or university with the professional
                      education courses necessary to become certified in an approved
                      content area.

GRADE LEVELS AND/OR SUBJECT AREA(S) COVERED:

                      Grade levels: 7-12.

                      Subjects: Reading, English/Language Arts, Science, Mathematics,
                      Social Studies.

WHO OPERATES: IHE; developed in conjunction with and with approval of the Delaware
                      Department of Education.

REQUIREMENTS TO ENTER:

                      A bachelor's degree from a regionally-accredited IHE.

                      Overall undergraduate GPA of 2.75.

                      Content area GPA of 3.0.

                      Submission of scores for the Graduate Record Examination (GRE), and
                      scores from one subject test in the teaching field.

                      Completed written application which includes a statement of
                      professional goals.

                      One-page resume.

                      Two letters of recommendation, one of which must be from a college
                      instructor in their major discipline in an approved content area.

                      All supporting documentation must be received by July 30 of each
                      year. No coursework may be taken in this degree program until formal
                      acceptance into the program.

PROGRAM DESCRIPTION:

Candidates complete graduate university coursework, including: theories of learning; classroom management; models of curriculum and instruction design; and a student teaching experience.

NUMBER OF CREDIT HOURS TO COMPLETE:

30 graduate credits.

WHO EVALUATES: IHE.

LENGTH OF TIME: Full-time study: program can be completed in one year. Part-time: two years.

Institutions of higher education that have developed alternative teacher preparation programs leading to a teaching license:

Wilmington College (implemented 1992)
University of Delaware (implemented 1997)
Wesley College (implemented 1996)

States with which the state has reciprocity of teacher licenses:

NASDTEC Interstate Contract.

Institutions of higher education that have *any* teacher preparation programs leading to a license to teach.

Delaware State University
University of Delaware

Wesley College
Wilmington College

Contact information for persons interested in finding a teaching position in the state:

Employment is handled by local school districts.

Many districts post job openings and applications may be filed on-line at teachdelaware.com.

Candidates interested in the ARTC Program can be entered in a database of prospective teachers by filling out the "request form" under CONTACT US at www.udel.edu/artc.

TITLE: Alternative Certification Professional Preparation and Education Competence Program Via School Districts

HISTORY: In the 2002-03 school year, Florida initiated statewide implementation of competency-based school district alternative certification programs that satisfy the professional preparation requirement for a Florida Professional Teaching Certificate. As a result, qualified individuals may choose not to enroll in college or university courses to satisfy the professional preparation requirements for a Professional Certificate, but instead complete these requirements while employed as a full time classroom teacher in a state-approved district program.

GRADE LEVELS AND/OR SUBJECT AREAS COVERED:

All classroom-based subject areas.

WHO OPERATES: Florida Department of Education and Florida school districts.

REQUIREMENTS TO ENTER:

The individuals participating in the school district programs must qualify for and hold a valid nonrenewable three-year Temporary Certificate; therefore, subject area specialization requirements have been met.

Furthermore, in order to qualify for the five-year renewable Professional Certificate, district alternative certification program participants must pass the Florida Teacher Certification Examinations (tests of General Knowledge, Professional Knowledge, and Subject Area Knowledge);

and have their employing school district document their Professional Education Competence as a result of successful completion of a state-approved alternative certification program.

PROGRAM DESCRIPTION: All school districts are required to offer a competency-based alternative certification program, either the program developed by the state or one developed by the district and approved by the state. As of July 2005 all programs include competencies associated with teaching scientifically-based reading instruction and strategies that research has shown to be successful in improving reading among low-performing readers. Individual school districts implement and manage their programs with oversight from the Florida Department of Education. Several institutions of higher education are currently collaborating with school districts in the implementation of the approved district programs.

TITLE: Temporary Certificate (includes Alternate Route)

HISTORY: Authorized by legislation in 1988.

MOTIVATION: To address teacher shortages and to provide a mechanism for persons who are not teacher-trained to consider becoming a teacher.

GRADE LEVELS AND/OR SUBJECT AREAS COVERED: All

WHO OPERATES: Florida Department of Education.

REQUIREMENTS TO ENTER:

A bachelor's degree.

The individual must meet specialization requirements in a subject in which Florida offers certification.

The individual must have a 2.5 grade point average on a 4.0 scale in each subject shown on the certificate.

The individual must obtain employment in a Florida public school or in a private school with a state-approved system for demonstration of professional education competencies.

PROGRAM DESCRIPTION:

The Temporary Certificate may be issued when the individual obtains employment in a public school or in a private school with a state-approved system for demonstration of professional education competencies and when cleared fingerprint reports have been received.

The recipient then has three years to complete the requirements for the Professional Certificate, which are to:

• Satisfy professional education preparation requirements by either:

- Completion of 15 semester hours of college coursework in education and one year of practical teaching experience; and

- Demonstrate professional education competencies; OR

- Completion of a district's approved competency-based alternative preparation program or educator preparation institute via Florida postsecondary institutions. (See "Other" below and the next section, "Class E," for more information on educator preparation institutes.)

Attain:

A passing score on the Professional Education Subtest of the Florida Teacher Certification Examination.

A passing score on the General Knowledge Test.

A passing score on the subject area examination for each subject or field shown on the certificate.

Operating under required competencies set by the state, a local school district or educator preparation institute works with the candidate to achieve the competencies, then verifies to the state that these competencies have been demonstrated.

LENGTH OF TIME: Valid for three years; non-renewable.

WHO EVALUATES: Florida Department of Education.

OTHER: Each school district must offer a competency-based alternative certification program by which members of its instructional staff who have not been trained as teachers but who meet state requirements for specialization in a subject coverage area may satisfy the professional education preparation requirements. Instead of completing college courses, program participants complete training only in those competencies which are identified as deficient by the district. If the district chooses to develop its own program in lieu of implementing the program developed by the state, then the Department of Education must approve each district-developed program.

Educator Preparation Institutes may only be created at accredited or approved Florida postsecondary institutions (including community colleges) and each institute must receive approval from the Department of Education. As in the district programs, instruction for baccalaureate or higher degree holders who were not education majors is provided through competency-based alternative certification programs to provide yet another route to full certification in Florida.

TITLE: Alternative Certification Program Through Educator Preparation Institutes

HISTORY: The 2004 Florida Legislature established a statute which provided the opportunity for accredited or approved postsecondary institutions to create competency-based Educator Preparation Institutes (EPI). Upon approval from the Florida Department of Education, an EPI will provide instruction for baccalaureate degree holders to become certified teachers through competency-based alternative certification programs.

MOTIVATION: Educator Preparation Institutes were created in order to increase routes to the classroom for mid-career professionals who hold a baccalaureate degree and college graduates who were not education majors.

SUBJECT AREAS COVERED: All Classroom-based Subjects

WHO OPERATES: Accredited or approved postsecondary institutions, including community colleges and universities may choose to offer an Educator Preparation Institute; such programs must receive approval from the Florida Department of Education.

REQUIREMENTS TO ENTER:

Program participants must hold a bachelor's degree from an accredited or approved institution and meet all certification requirements pursuant to s. 1012.56(1), F.S., by obtaining a Statement of Status of Eligibility and meet the requirements of s. 1012.56(2)(a)-(f), F.S.

PROGRAM DESCRIPTION:

Instruction in Alternative Certification Programs within Educator Preparation Institutes must be provided in professional knowledge and subject matter content that includes educator-accomplished practices and competencies specified in State Board of Education rule and meets subject matter content requirements, professional competency testing requirements, and competencies associated with teaching scientifically-based reading instruction and strategies that research has shown to be successful in improving reading among low-performing readers.

Approved programs must also provide field experiences with supervision from qualified educators.

Furthermore, each participant must fully demonstrate his or her ability to teach the subject area for which he or she is seeking certification and demonstrate mastery of professional preparation and education competence by achievement of a passing score on the professional education competency examination required by state board rule prior to completion of the program.

Each program must also provide a certification ombudsman to facilitate the process and procedures required for participants who complete the program to meet any requirements related to the background screening and educator professional or temporary certification.

NUMBER OF CREDIT HOURS TO COMPLETE: Not applicable

WHO EVALUATES: Each approved institute submits annual performance evaluations that measure the effectiveness of the programs to the Florida Department of Education; FLDOE utilizes the evaluation for purposes of continued approval of an educator preparation institute's alternative certification program.

LENGTH OF TIME: Up to three years

OTHER:

TITLE: "Add-on Programs"

Florida also has offered what may qualify as a Class G program for teachers to add subjects to a Professional Certificate. These "Add-on Programs" have been approved by the Department of Education and implemented either by school districts, or the universities, or a combination of both. Teachers who complete an approved Add-on Program complete only the specialization (content) requirements they are lacking as part of the Program.

Until July 1, 2002, completion of the approved add-on program was required in combination with a passing score on the corresponding subject area test to establish eligibility for the additional coverage. Presently, a passing score on the appropriate subject area test is sufficient to establish eligibility for the coverages that do not require master's level training. A district may offer the training content of the add-on program as a means by which teachers can acquire the content knowledge and competencies that must be demonstrated on the subject area exam to qualify for the additional coverage.

States with which the state has reciprocity of teacher licenses:

Florida has signed NASDTEC Interstate Agreements with <u>all</u> other states. State Board of Education rules provide for additional consideration of out-of-state certificates and appropriate years of experience to satisfy some or all eligibility requirements (excluding the fingerprint requirement).

Institutions of higher education that have *any* teacher preparation program(s) leading to a license to teach.

Barry University
Bethune-Cookman College
Chipola College
Clearwater Christian College
Flagler College
Florida A&M University
Florida Atlantic University
Florida College
Florida Gulf Coast University
Florida Institute of Technology
Florida International University
Florida Memorial University
Florida Southern College
Florida State University
Jacksonville University
Lynn University
Miami-Dade College

Nova Southeastern University
Palm Beach Atlantic University
Rollins College
Saint Leo University
Southeastern College
St. Petersburg College
Saint Thomas University
Stetson University
University of Central Florida
University of Florida
University of Miami
University of North Florida
University of South Florida
University of Tampa
University of West Florida
Warner Southern College

CONTACT INFORMATION FOR PERSONS INTERESTED IN FINDING A TEACHING POSITION IN THE STATE:

Florida Department of Education
Bureau of Educator Recruitment, Development and Retention
1-800-832-2435
http://www.teachinflorida.com/

TITLE: Georgia Teacher Alternative Preparation Program (TAPP)

HISTORY: The Georgia Teacher Alternative Preparation Program began in 2000 as one solution to the shortage of teachers in Georgia.

MOTIVATION: The goal of the Georgia TAPP alternative preparation program is to provide a University, Regional Education Service Agencies (RESA), and Public Schools collaborative non-traditional option for prospective post-baccalaureate teacher candidates to acquire the critical and essential knowledge and skills necessary for successful entry into the classroom. Georgia TAPP seeks to equip teacher-candidates with the skills to ensure a reasonable expectation of initial success in their classrooms, and to put in place a supervised internship/induction program that will help them move toward subsequent mastery of teaching.

GRADE LEVELS/SUBJECT AREAS COVERED:
All.

WHO OPERATES: Agencies, including institutions of higher education (IHE's), or regional service agencies (RESAs), or local education agencies (LEAs), or independent school systems may seek approval from the Professional Standards Commission to provide Georgia TAPP.

REQUIREMENTS TO ENTER PROGRAM:

Bachelor's degree or higher from a regionally accredited college or university.

Graduate with an overall grade point average of 2.5 or higher.

Pass the GACE Basic Skills test requirements.

Pass the appropriate GACE Content Area test requirements

GA TAPP candidates must take and pass the appropriate GACE content test(s) to be Highly Qualified:

All Early Childhood Education candidates

Special education candidates who are assigned to teach core academic content as the teacher of record, and

Any middle grades and secondary teachers **who do not have a concentration or major** in the subject area(s) they are assigned to teach

Pass the Georgia GCIC criminal background check.

Job offer as a beginning teacher from a local school system.

PROGRAM DESCRIPTION:

Phase One -- An instructional phase offered as an introduction to teaching during the summer.

Phase Two -- A two-year classroom based induction training period completed while teaching.

Candidates who are required to pass the appropriate GACE content must do so to be accepted into the program. If the candidate is not in the Highly Qualified testing category and has not passed the appropriate GACE content examination, he or she will be required to take it during the first year of teaching. The test scores will be used to determine whether or not one needs to take additional content in the subject area one is teaching.

This model requires that teacher candidates complete an intensive performance-based preparation program of approximately four weeks during the summer prior to entering the classroom in the fall. Additionally, it requires intensive monitoring, supervision and mentoring during a two-year induction period. (The model could be adjusted to accommodate teachers hired on provisional status after the school year has begun. In this model, the time required for pre-assignment training will be shortened with training classes held after school hours.)

The Professional Education Unit unit including the teacher preparation unit of a college or university, an approved RESA, and/or and approved LEA work with the cooperating schools to implement the program and to recommend candidates for initial certification.

WHO EVALUATES: The approved Professional Education Unit: IHE, RESA and local school system.

LENGTH OF TIME: Two years.

TITLE: One Year Supervised Practicum

HISTORY: The One-Year Supervised Practicum standards were approved in 2004. It is one of the fastest growing alternative routes to certification.

MOTIVATION: A One-Year Supervised Practicum provides pedagogical preparation for individuals who need to fulfill such a requirement for renewable certification. This requirement may be applicable to individuals who are using the Professional Standards Commission (PSC) test-based option to meet the requirements for renewable certification as well as individuals who have completed all the requirements in a preparation program except student teaching.

GRADE LEVELS/SUBJECT AREAS COVERED: All.

WHO OPERATES: Agencies, including institutions of higher education (IHE's), or regional service agencies (RESAs), or local education agencies (LEAs), or independent school systems may seek approval from the Professional Standards Commission to provide the one-year supervised practicum.

REQUIREMENTS TO ENTER PROGRAM:

Bachelor's degree or higher in a related field from a regionally accredited college or university.

Graduate with an overall grade point average of 2.5 or higher.

Pass the GACE Basic Skills test requirements.

Pass the appropriate GACE Content Area test requirements:

Pass the GACE Pedagogy test

Pass the Georgia GCIC criminal background check.

Job offer as a beginning teacher from a local school system.

PROGRAM DESCRIPTION:

This model requires that during a one-year induction period, the candidate must experience intensive monitoring, supervision, and coaching/mentoring under the guidance and supervision of a qualified mentor and program supervisor. The beginning teacher must begin the one-year practicum as soon as they are hired by the school system.

WHO EVALUATES: The approved Professional Education Unit: IHE, RESA and LEA.

LENGTH OF TIME: One year.

TITLE: Post-Baccalaureate Non-Degree Preparation Programs

HISTORY: Available since 1950.

MOTIVATION: To attract talented individuals with non-education
                      degrees into the teaching profession.

GRADE LEVELS AND/OR SUBJECT AREA(S) COVERED: All.

WHO OPERATES: IHE.

REQUIREMENTS TO ENTER PROGRAM:

A baccalaureate or higher degree from a regionally accredited
institution.

A minimum grade point average of 2.5 on a 4.0 scale.

Other requirements determined by the IHE.

PROGRAM DESCRIPTION:

The program of study is developed by the IHE in fields in which it has
approved programs.

The candidate's educational and experiential background is analyzed,
and an individualized program is developed in the area in which
certification is sought.

IHEs have the authority and flexibility to determine the programs.

Candidates must achieve a minimum grade point average of 2.5 and
pass the required Praxis II Subject Assessment(s) to be recommended
to the Professional Standards Commission for certification.

Some preparation may be completed in staff development programs
offered by LEAs for those teaching on a Provisional Certificate.

NUMBER OF CREDIT HOURS TO COMPLETE: Varies by individual

WHO EVALUATES: IHE.

LENGTH OF TIME: Determined by candidate and IHE.

TITLE: Master's Degree Level Initial Preparation

HISTORY: Began July 1, 1993.

MOTIVATION: To offer opportunities for non-education
                     baccalaureate degree holders to earn a master's
                     degree in education, while at the same time
                     completing state certification requirements.

GRADE LEVELS AND/OR SUBJECT AREA(S) COVERED:

                     All.

WHO OPERATES: IHE.

REQUIREMENTS TO ENTER PROGRAM:

                     Determined by the IHE.

PROGRAM DESCRIPTION:

                     These programs are individually designed by each IHE, and meet state
                     initial preparation program standards. Programs are approved by the
                     Professional Standards Commission.

NUMBER OF CREDIT HOURS TO COMPLETE:

                     Programs are designed within a 60 quarter hour framework, unless
                     there are compelling reasons for a longer program.

WHO EVALUATES: IHE.

LENGTH OF TIME: Determined by IHE.

TITLE: Permitted Personnel

HISTORY: Effective July 1, 1992.

MOTIVATION: To enable recognized experts -- such as artists, native speakers of less commonly taught languages, etc. -- to bring their knowledge and expertise into public schools.

GRADE LEVELS AND/OR SUBJECT AREA(S): Teaching fields and superintendent.

WHO OPERATES: Professional Standards Commission.

REQUIREMENTS TO ENTER PROGRAM:

Established competence in field.

Three years experience in field.

Bachelors or higher degree from a regionally accredited institution, except performing arts.

Permits granted to teaching fields and superintendent only.

There must be verified circumstances; including verification that there are no acceptable certified personnel available to serve in this capacity.

PROGRAM DESCRIPTION:

There are no program requirements.

NUMBER OF CREDIT HOURS TO COMPLETE: None

WHO EVALUATES: LEA.

LENGTH OF TIME: Permits are issued annually and may be renewed if the LEA verifies implementation of mentor support, induction, and professional development during the validity period of the previous permit. Additionally, the required Praxis II Subject Assessment(s) must be passed if one is available in the field.

TITLE: Teach for America

HISTORY: Began July 1989.

MOTIVATION: Recognition of the high quality of individuals
                      recruited into this program, and the design and
                      delivery of professional preparation.

GRADE LEVELS AND/OR SUBJECT AREA(S) COVERED:

All subjects with shortages.

WHO OPERATES: IHE, LEA, and Teach for America.

REQUIREMENTS TO ENTER PROGRAM:

Determined by Teach for America.

PROGRAM DESCRIPTION:

Program design by Teach for America.

IHE collaborates and provides a path through its approved programs for
individuals to complete full professional certification in Georgia.

NUMBER OF CREDIT HOURS TO COMPLETE:

Varies and may not necessarily be based on credit hour generation.

WHO EVALUATES: Teach for America and IHE.

LENGTH OF TIME: Varies -- generally completed in two years.

TITLE: Post-Baccalaureate Non-Degree Preparation Programs for Transitioning Military Personnel

HISTORY: Began July 1, 1993.

MOTIVATION: Georgia has numerous military establishments, and the downsizing of the armed forces has made available a unique pool of talented individuals, covering a broad range of skills that could enhance the delivery system of education in Georgia.

GRADE LEVELS AND/OR SUBJECT AREA(S) COVERED: All.

WHO OPERATES: IHE.

REQUIREMENTS TO ENTER PROGRAM:

A baccalaureate or higher degree from a regionally accredited institution.

A minimum grade point average of 2.5 on a 4.0 scale.

Other requirements determined by the IHE.

PROGRAM DESCRIPTION:

The program of study is developed by the IHE in fields in which it has approved programs.

The candidate's educational and experiential background is analyzed, and an individualized program is developed in the area in which certification is sought.

IHEs have the authority and flexibility to determine the programs.

Candidates must achieve a minimum grade point average of 2.5 and pass the required Praxis II Subject Assessment(s) to be recommended to the Professional Standards Commission for certification.

Some preparation may be completed in staff development programs offered by LEAs for those teaching on a Provisional Certificate.

NUMBER OF CREDIT HOURS TO COMPLETE:

Varies individually.

WHO EVALUATES: IHE.

LENGTH OF TIME: Determined by candidate and IHE.

Institutions of higher education that have developed alternative teacher preparation programs leading to a teaching license:

Albany State University

Armstrong Atlantic State University

Augusta State University

Columbus State University

Georgia Southern University

Georgia State University

Kenneth State University

North Georgia College & State University

University of Georgia

State University of West Georgia

States with which the state has reciprocity of teacher licenses:

Georgia accepts all states' professional certificates, plus DODDS, NBPTS, Washington, D.C., and U.S. territory certificates. NASDTEC Interstate Contract.

Institutions of higher education that have *any* teacher preparation programs leading to a license to teach.

Agnes Scott College

Armstrong Atlantic State University

Albany State University

Augusta State University

Berry College

Breneau University

Brewton-Parker College

Clark Atlanta University

Clayton College & State University

Columbus State University

Covenant College

Emmanuel College

Emory University

Fort Valley State University

Georgia College & State University

Georgia Southwestern State University

Georgia Southern University

Georgia State University

Kennesaw State University

LaGrange College

Mercer University

North Georgia College & State University

Oglethorpe University

Paine College

Piedmont College

Reinhardt College

Shorter College

Spelman College

State University of West Georgia

Thomas College

Toccoa Falls College

University College of Mercer/Forsyth

University of Georgia

Valdosta State University

Wesleyan College

Home page for the Georgia Professional Standards Commission:

http://www.gapsc.com

For current information:

PRAXIS Testing

Certification rules/requirements

Application forms

TITLE: Alternative Basic Certification in Special Education (ABCSE)

HISTORY:	Began in 1991.

MOTIVATION: Response to a shortage of certified special education teachers in Hawaii.

GRADE LEVELS AND/OR SUBJECT AREAS COVERED:

Special Education, Pre-K through grade 12.

WHO OPERATES   Hawaii State Department of Education, with
Chaminade University of Honolulu.

REQUIREMENTS TO ENTER PROGRAM:

A baccalaureate degree from an accredited four-year college or
university.

Attendance at an "Alternative Routes" information session and
completion of an application packet

Acceptance into Chaminade University of Honolulu

Must attain contracted employment in a Hawaii public school in either
a half-time or full-time special education teaching position

Additional requirements include:

Responsible for planning and providing direct group instruction to at
least 4 special education students for a minimum of 3 periods per day
or 50% of the instructional week

PROGRAM DESCRIPTION:

A two-year route leading towards licensure in special education for candidates who have no
formal training in education (have not completed a state approved teacher education program).
Candidates complete 30 semester hours of education related graduate-level coursework through
Chaminade University, which includes a 15-week student teaching practicum. In addition,
candidates are assigned a mentor teacher throughout the program and participate in 12 all-day (8
hour) seminars conducted by the Hawaii State Department of Education. The seminars focus on
best practices in special education and pedagogy with candidates completing classroom-based
assignments addressing these areas.

Tuition fees and related program costs are the responsibility of the candidate, however, a tuition stipend (for 15 semester credits) is available for candidates who commit to teaching for a minimum of 3 years in a Hawaii public school special education position.

NUMBER OF CREDIT HOURS TO COMPLETE:

30 semester hours at Chaminade University of Honolulu. 12 required non-credit seminars (8 hours each) conducted by Hawaii State DOE.

WHO EVALUATES: Candidates are evaluated by faculty from Chaminade University as well as evaluators from the Hawaii State Department of Education.

LENGTH OF TIME: Two years.

TITLE: Alternative Program for Shortage Areas

HISTORY: Began in 1996.

MOTIVATION: To reduce the shortage of teachers in selected
                      teaching fields or in geographic areas that are
                      difficult to fill.

GRADE LEVELS AND/OR SUBJECT AREAS COVERED:

Hawaii Department of Education (HDOE) declared shortage fields.

WHO OPERATES   Brigham Young University-Hawaii (BYUH).

REQUIREMENTS TO ENTER PROGRAM:

Official transcript verifying the baccalaureate degree earned from an
accredited institution.

Minimum of two semesters of satisfactory full-time contracted HDOE
teaching experience in the content area for which licensing is sought.

Favorable letter of recommendation from applicant's principal as well
as the completed form for the "Principal's Recommendation for
Temporary Teacher."

Transcript evaluation to determine specific courses needed with a
minimum of 2.7 GPA (on a 4.0 scale) on the baccalaureate degree.

PROGRAM DESCRIPTION:

Upon meeting the requirements outlined above, candidates are
required to apply for admission to BYUH. Upon acceptance,
candidates need to register for one semester of student teaching.
Supervision during the semester will be the responsibility of BYUH.
However, the principal or his/her designee will serve as the school-
based mentor to fulfill the regular duties of a cooperating teacher in
providing supervision and staff development support as well as
working collaboratively with the BYUH supervisors.

Upon successful completion of the student teaching requirement, the applicant must complete prescribed professional education coursework with a GPA of 3.0 on a 4.0 scale.

Before licensing is recommended, applicants must show demonstrated competency in the following areas: Assessment and lesson planning; Technology usage; Special education issues and strategies; and School law. Special education applicants also need to demonstrate competency in writing individualized education programs (IEPs).

Upon successful completion of the program requirements, applicants must submit passing Praxis score reports for the appropriate tests to the Hawaii Department of Education.

NUMBER OF CREDIT HOURS TO COMPLETE:

To be established by BYUH in consultation with the principal and applicant.

WHO EVALUATES: BYUH.

LENGTH OF TIME: Varies, depending upon applicant's prescribed program.

TITLE: Respecialization in Special Education (RISE)

HISTORY: Began in 1990.

MOTIVATION: Response to a shortage of certified special education
                        teachers in Hawaii.

GRADE LEVELS AND/OR SUBJECT AREAS COVERED:

Special Education, Pre-K through grade 12.

WHO OPERATES: Hawaii State Department of Education.

REQUIREMENTS TO ENTER PROGRAM:

A baccalaureate degree from an accredited four-year college or
university

Completion of an undergraduate or graduate level state approved
teacher education program in an area other than special education

Attendance at an "Alternative Routes" information session and
completion of an application packet

Must attain contracted employment in a Hawaii public school in either
a half-time or full-time special education teaching position.

Additional requirements include:

Responsible for providing direct group instruction to at least 4 special
education students for a minimum of 3 periods per day or 50% of the
instructional week

PROGRAM DESCRIPTION:

A one-year program conducted by the Hawaii State Department of
Education, targeting candidates who have already completed a state
approved teacher education program in an area other than special
education. Candidates are assigned a mentor teacher throughout the
yearlong program; complete online coursework and classroom-based
assignments; and attend 12 all-day (8 hour) seminars focused on

special education issues. The seminars focus on best practices in special education and pedagogy with candidates completing classroom-based assignments addressing these areas.

Most costs of the program are covered by the Hawaii State Department of Education in return for a three-year commitment to teach special education students in a Hawaii public school.

NUMBER OF CREDIT HOURS TO COMPLETE:

12 required non-credit seminars (8 hours each

WHO EVALUATES: Hawaii State Department of Education evaluators

LENGTH OF TIME: One year.

TITLE: MAED/TED-Elementary, Secondary, Special Education

HISTORY: Started in 1998 with post-bac program; UoPH now provides three graduate programs that lead to licensure with the Hawaii DOE.

MOTIVATION: Appropriate for all graduate students, especially those interested in working full-time while completing the degree.

GRADE LEVELS AND/OR SUBJECT AREAS COVERED:
Elementary education; Secondary education (w/ licensure in English, math, social studies, and science); Special Education, K-12 mild-moderate disabilities.

WHO OPERATES: Faculty and administrative staff of University of Phoenix Hawaii campus College of Education

REQUIREMENTS TO ENTER PROGRAM:

Undergraduate degree from regionally accredited university

2.5 GPA in undergraduate

TOEFL or other test of English for international students

PROGRAM DESCRIPTION:

Graduate degree in one of three specializations; Elementary education, secondary education, or special education.

Requires coursework, 100 hours of field observation and a 13-week student teaching practicum. Students create an electronic portfolio and a Teacher Work Sample as a culminating project.

NUMBER OF CREDIT HOURS TO COMPLETE:
35 for Secondary; 41 for Elementary; 45 for Secondary

WHO EVALUATES: Faculty and Chair of College of Education

LENGTH OF TIME: 18 months to 30 months

Institutions of higher education that have developed alternative teacher preparation programs leading to a teaching license:

Chaminade University of Honolulu, in conjunction with Hawaii State Department of Education
Brigham Young University-Hawaii

States with which the state has reciprocity of teacher licenses:

NASDTEC Interstate Contract.

Institutions of higher education that have *any* teacher preparation programs leading to a license to teach.

Brigham Young University-Hawaii
Chaminade University of Honolulu

University of Hawaii at Manoa
University of Hawaii at Hilo
University of Phoenix - Hawaii

Contact information for persons interested in finding a teaching position in the state:

State of Hawaii
Department of Education
Teacher Recruitment
680 Iwilei Rd., Suite 490
Honolulu, HI 96817
1-800-305-5104
http://doe.k12.hi.us/personnel/teachers_applying.htm

TITLE: Alternative Authorization-Content Specialist

HISTORY: Effective July 1, 2006.

MOTIVATION: To offer an expedited route to certification for
                     individuals who are highly and uniquely qualified in
                     a subject area to teach in a district with an identified
                     need for teachers in that area. To provide an
                     alternative for individuals to become certificated
                     preK-12 teachers in Idaho without following a
                     standard teacher education program.

GRADE LEVELS AND/OR SUBJECT AREAS COVERED: Secondary only.

WHO OPERATES: Participating colleges and universities, the State
                     Department of Education, and the employing local
                     school district.

REQUIREMENTS TO ENTER PROGRAM:

              A. Prior to application, the prospective trainee must:

                  1. Hold a Bachelor's degree.

                  2. Apply for entry into the program through a cooperating
                  college/university teacher preparation program.

PROGRAM DESCRIPTION:

              A consortium composed of a designee from the college/university to be
              attended, and a representative from the school district, and the
              candidate shall determine the preparation needed to meet the Idaho
              Standards for Initial Certification of Professional School Personnel.
              The preparation mnust include mentoring and a minimum of one
              classroom observation per month until certified.

              Prior to entering the classroom, the candidate completes 8 to 16 weeks
              of accelerated study in education pedagogy.

              Candidate will work toward completion of the alternative route
              preparation program through a participating college/university, and
              the employing school district.

A teacher must attend, participate in, and successfully complete an individualized alternative route preparation program as one of the conditions to receive recommendation for full certification.

The participating college/university shall provide procedures to assess and credit equivalent knowledge, dispositions, and relevant life/work experiences.

Prior to entering the the classroom, the candidate shall meet or exceed the state qualifiying score on appropriate state-approved content, pedagogy, or performance assessment (e.g. Praxis II).

NUMBER OF CREDIT HOURS TO COMPLETE: Varies by individual.

WHO EVALUATES: Principals are to provide assistance to teacher trainees regarding the purpose, expectations, and procedures involved in the evaluation process and with whatever guidance may be needed. The principal shall formally evaluate the teacher trainee at least once each quarter of the school year.

LENGTH OF TIME: Up to three years..

OTHER: Qualified applicants begin contracted employment earlier and will be admitted to the program using criteria that are different from existing programs but more appropriate for the circumstances.

TITLE: Computer-Based Alternate Routes to Idaho Certification

HISTORY: Rule IDAPA 08, Title 02, Cahp.02; 045, Section
015, March 12, 2004

MOTIVATION: To increase the pool of qualified teachers.

GRADE LEVELS AND/OR SUBJECT AREAS COVERED: May be used for initial
certification, subsequent certificates, and additional endorsements.

WHO OPERATES: State Board of Education.

REQUIREMENTS TO ENTER PROGRAM:

The State Board of Education must approve any computer-based alternative route to
teacher certification. The program mus include, at a minimum, the following components:

1. Pre-assessment of teaching content knowledge;

2. An academic advisor with knowledge of the prescribed instrution area;

3. Exams of pedagogy and content knowledge.

Candidate Eligibility: Individuals ho possess a bachelor's degree or higher from an
institution of higerh education may utilize this alternative route to an interim Idaho teacher
certificate.

PROGRAM DESCRIPTION:

To complete this alternate route, the individual must:

1. Complete a Board-approved program;

2. Pass the Board-approved pedagogy and content knowledge exams;

3. Complete the Idaho Department of Education criminal history check.

Upon completion of the computer-based certification process, the individual receives an interim certificate, good for three years.

- During the first two years of interim certification, teaching by the individual must be done through a teacher mentoring program.

- Continued teaching shall be subject to successful completion of the 2-year mentoring program.

NUMBER OF CREDIT HOURS TO COMPLETE: Varies by Board-approved computer-based program.

WHO EVALUATES:

LENGTH OF TIME: Up to 3 years.

OTHER: Individual is responsible for obtaining a full Idaho certificate during the 3-year initial certification term

The State Board of Education approved IDAPA 08.02.02.045.06 as a temporary rule on March 10, 2005, to clarify that currently certified teachers may add additional certificates or endorsements through computer-based routes..

TITLE: American Board for the Certification of Teacher Excellence (ABCTE)

HISTORY:

MOTIVATION: ABCTE is a "passport to teaching." This alternate routes to Idaoho certification is designed to be used to enter the teaching profession or to add additional certificates or endorsements to an already existing teaching certificate.

GRADE LEVELS AND/OR SUBJECT AREAS COVERED

WHO OPERATES: ABCTE and State Department of Education

REQUIREMENTS TO ENTER PROGRAM:

An individual with an ABCTE certificate applying for Idaho certification must submit an application packet including:

1. An original ABCTE certificate or notarized photocopy of the ABCTE certificate;

2. A completed application for Idaho certification;

3. Official college/university transcripts;

4. Required application fees;

5. Completed State Department of Education-approved fingerprint card.

PROGRAM DESCRIPTION:

A. Upon receiving a completed application, the applicant will be issued a 3-year Idaho interim certificate, allowing time to meet the following Idaho standards and qualify for a standard Idaho teaching certificate:

1. Complete a 2-year mentoring program (The program may be either the ABCTE mentoring program or the mentoring program provided in districts according to Idaho statute);

2. Meet the idaho Comprehensive Literacy requirements as provided in statute;

3. Meet one of the State Board-approved Idaho Teachnology Competence Assessments as required by State Board of Education Rule.

B. Subsequent to meeting these requirements during the 3-year interim certificate, the candidate may apply for a standard Idaho teaching certificate.

NUMBER OF CREDIT HOURS TO COMPLETE: N/A

WHO EVALUATES: ABCTE and State Department of Education

LENGTH OF TIME: Up to 3 years.

OTHER: Individual is responsible for obtaining a full Idaho certificate during the 3-year initial certification term.

For further information, refer to the ABCTE web site at www.abcte.org

Institutions of higher education that have developed alternative teacher preparation programs leading to a teaching license:

Albertson College of Idaho
Boise State University
Brigham Young University – Idaho
Idaho State University

Lewis-Clark State College
Northwest Nazarene College
University of Idaho

States with which the state has reciprocity of teacher licenses:

NASDTEC Interstate Contract.

Institutions of higher education that have *any* teacher preparation programs leading to a license to teach.

Albertson College of Idaho
Boise State University
Brigham Young University - Idaho
Idaho State University

Lewis-Clark State College
Northwest Nazarene College
University of Idaho

Contact information for persons interested in finding a teaching position in the state:

Each Idaho school district advertises its own vacancies and maintains its own employment procedures. District vacancies are often listed with college or university placement centers or with the Idaho Department of Employment. Questions about openings and salaries should be addressed to school districts.

Contact the following Idaho Teacher Placement Centers:

Teacher Placement Service, Employment Programs Section
State Department of Education
317 Main Street
Boise, ID 83735-0001
Phone: (208) 334-6137

Special Education Hotline
telephone toll-free (800) 247-0193

Albertson College of Idaho
Teacher Placement Service
Caldwell, ID 83686
(208) 459-5534

Lewis-Clark State College
Career Planning & Placement Center
Lewiston, ID 83501
(208) 799-2313

Boise State University
Career Planning & Placement
1910 University Drive
Boise, ID 83725
(208) 385-1747

Northwest Nazarene College
Teacher Placement
Nampa, ID 83686
(208) 476-8258

Idaho State University
Career Planning & Placement Center
Campus Box 8108
Pocatello, ID 83209 - Tel (208) 236-2380

University of Idaho
Career Planning & Placement Center
Moscow, ID 83843
(208) 995-6121

TITLE: **Alternative Teacher Certification**

HISTORY: Illinois School code: 105 ILCS 5/21-5b Effective
                    December 1999.

MOTIVATION: To provide alternative routes for certifying teachers
                    in Illinois.

GRADE LEVELS AND/OR SUBJECT AREAS COVERED: All.

WHO OPERATES: The program must be provided by a partnership that
                    includes an approved teacher preparation
                    institution, which offers baccalaureate and master's
                    degree programs, and one or more not-for-profit
                    organizations. The individual programs are limited
                    to 260 participants per year.

REQUIREMENTS TO ENTER:

                    An applicant must meet the following criteria:

                         Graduated from an accredited college or university with a
                         bachelor's degree.

                         Employed for at least five years in an area requiring
                         application of the participant's education. (Work experience is
                         not required for programs serving the city of Chicago.)

                         Passed the Illinois Basic Skills Test.

PROGRAM DESCRIPTION:

                    The alternative teacher certification program must include the content
                    and skills of the institution's approved preparation program and must
                    be approved by the State Board of Education.

                    Phase I:

                    Pass the Illinois Content-Area Test.

Successful completion of an intensive course of study in education theory, instructional methods, and practice teaching.

A one-year <u>nonrenewable provisional alternative teaching certificate</u> will be issued when the participant meets the requirements of Phase I.

Phase II:

Full-time teaching position with one school year with the advice and assistance of a mentor teacher.

Phase III:

A comprehensive assessment of the participant's teaching performance by school officials and program participants and recommendation for certification by the higher education institution.

A <u>nonrenewable Initial Alternative Teaching Certificate</u>, valid for four years, will be issued following completion of the three phases and successful completion of the State's Assessment of Professional Teaching. After completing four years of teaching, individuals may apply for <u>the Standard Teaching Certificate</u>.

NUMBER OF CREDIT HOURS TO COMPLETE:

Determined by IHE.

LENGTH OF TIME: Varies (one to three years).

WHO EVALUATES: State Board of Education.

TITLE: Alternative Route to Teacher Certification

HISTORY: Illinois School code: 105 ILCS 5/21-5c Effective
December 1999.

MOTIVATION: To provide alternative routes for certifying teachers
in Illinois.

GRADE LEVELS AND/OR SUBJECT AREAS COVERED: All.

WHO OPERATES: The program must be provided by an approved
teacher preparation institution and may be offered
in conjunction with one or more not-for-profit
organizations.

REQUIREMENTS TO ENTER:

An applicant must meet the following criteria:

Graduated from an accredited college or university with a
bachelor's degree.

Employed for at least five years in an area requiring
application of the participant's education.

Passed the Illinois Basic Skills Test.

PROGRAM DESCRIPTION:

The alternative teacher certification program must include the content
and skills of the institution's approved preparation program and must
be approved by the State Board of Education.

Phase I:

Successful completion of an intensive course of study in education
theory, instructional methods, and practice teaching.

Passed the Illinois Content-Area Test.

A one-year <u>nonrenewable provisional alternative teaching certificate</u> will be issued when the participant meets the requirements of Phase I.

Phase II:

Full-time teaching position with one school year with the advice and assistance of a mentor teacher.

Phase III:

A comprehensive assessment of the participant's teaching performance by school officials and program participants and recommendation for certification by the higher education institution.

A <u>nonrenewable Initial Teaching Certificate</u>, valid for four years, will be issued following completion of the three phases and successful completion of the State's Assessment of Professional Teaching. After completing four years of teaching, individuals may apply for <u>the Standard Teaching Certificate</u>.

NUMBER OF CREDIT HOURS TO COMPLETE:

Determined by IHE.

LENGTH OF TIME: Varies (one to three years).

WHO EVALUATES: State Board of Education.

Institutions of higher education that have developed alternative teacher preparation programs leading to a teaching license:

Aurora University
Benedictine University
Chicago State University
Concordia University
Dominican University
DePaul University
Eastern Illinois University
Governors State University
Illinois State University
McKendree College
National-Louis University
Northern Illinois University
Northwestern University
Southern Illinois University Carbondale
University of Illinois at Chicago

For current information on Illinois' alternative certification programs, contact:

Martha (Marti) A. Woelfle
Illinois State Board of Education
Certification and Professional Development
100 N. First Street
Springfield, IL 62777
Phone: (217) 782-7091
http://www.isbe.net/profprep/alternative.htm

States with which the state has reciprocity of teacher licenses:

None :
Individuals seeking a teaching certificate must provide evidence that they have completed a state approved program at a recognized higher education institution and meet the state certification testing requirements.

Institutions of higher education that have *any* teacher preparation program(s) leading to a license to teach.

Augustana College	McKendree College
Aurora University	Millikin University
Benedictine University	Monmouth College
Blackburn College	National-Louis University
Bradley University	North Central University
Chicago State University	Northeastern Illinois University
Columbia College	Northern Illinois University
Concordia University	North Park University
DePaul University	Northwestern University
Dominican University	Olivet Nazarene University
Eastern Illinois University	Principia College
Elmhurst College	Quincy University

Erikson Institute
Eureka College
Governors State University
Greenville College
Hebrew Theological College
Illinois College
Illinois Institute of Technology
Illinois State University
Illinois Wesleyan University
Judson College
Keller Graduate School of Management
Kendall College
Knox College
Lake Forest College
Lewis University
Loyola University-Chicago
MacMurray College

Rockford College
Roosevelt University
St. Xavier University
School of the Art Institute of Chicago
Southern Illinois University Carbondale
Southern Illinois University Edwardsville
Trinity Christian College
Trinity International University
University of Chicago
University of Illinois at Chicago
University of Illinois at Springfield
University of Illinois at Urbana-Champaign
University of St. Francis
VanderCook College of Music
Western Illinois University
Wheaton College

Contact information for persons interested in finding a teaching position in the state:

Illinois State Board of Education
Certification and Professional Development
100 N. First Street
Springfield, IL 62777
Phone: 1-800-845-8749
http://www.isbe.net/teachers/certification/default.htm

TITLE: Teacher Intern License

HISTORY: Authorized in 2002

GRADE LEVELS AND/OR SUBJECT AREAS COVERED:

Middle school, junior high school, or high school.

WHO OPERATES: State Board of Education.

REQUIREMENTS TO ENTER PROGRAM:

The prospective intern must:

1. Hold a baccalaureate from an accredited institution with a minimum cumulative grade point average of 2.5 on a 4.0 scale.

2. Be admitted to a teacher intern program, which has been approved by the state board of education.

3. Meet the requirements of at least one of the board's secondary endorsement areas.

4. Possess a minimum of three years of post-baccalaureate work experience (an authorized official at a college or university with an approved teacher intern program will evaluate this experience).

6. Meet all non-academic requirements of the state, including fingerprinting and state and national criminal investigation background checks.

PROGRAM DESCRIPTION:

The Teacher Intern must successfully complete:

1. An introductory program of at least 12 semester hours of the teacher intern program prior to fall employment. The following areas shall be integrated into the introductory teacher intern program for delivery, and it is intended that the program shall be developed further throughout the year of internship and during the summer following the internship year:

- Learning environment/classroom management;

- Instructional planning;

- Instructional strategies;

- Student learning;

- Diverse learners;

- Collaboration, ethics, and relationships;

- Assessment;

- Integrated field experience.

2. Four semester hours of a teacher intern seminar during the teacher internship year. These seminars are intended to provide continued support for the teacher intern and provide an extension of the coursework taken during the first summer prior to employment.

3. 12 additional semester hours during the summer after the teacher intern year and in the following areas:

Foundations, reflection, and professional development;

Communication;

Exceptional learner program;

Preparation in the integration of reading strategies into the content area;

Computer technology related to instruction;

An advanced study of items 1 through 7 listed above.

After completing these requirements, the Teacher Intern may apply for issuance of an Initial License with the following:

1. Verification from a licensed evaluator that the teacher intern served successfully as a teacher intern for a minimum of 160 days.

2. Verification from a licensed evaluator that the teacher intern was deemed competent by means of a comprehensive evaluation.

3. Recommendation for an initial license by a college or university offering an approved teacher intern program. This recommendation includes the successful completion of the second summer coursework consisting of 12 semester hours.

At the request of the state board of education, the teacher intern shall provide to the board information regarding, but not limited to, the teacher intern selection and preparation programs, institutional support, local school district mentor, and local school district support.

The teacher intern year will count as one of the years needed to move from the initial license to the standard license if the above conditions are met.

NUMBER OF CREDIT HOURS TO COMPLETE: 24 semester hours.

WHO EVALUATES: Participating local school district and college or university offering an approved teacher intern program.

LENGTH OF TIME: One year.

Institutions of higher education that have developed alternative teacher preparation programs leading to a teaching license:

Kaplan University

States with which the state has reciprocity of teacher licenses:

No reciprocity with any state.

Iowa has a regional exchange agreement with six other states -- the Central States agreement, which links Missouri, Oklahoma, Iowa, Nebraska, Kansas, South Dakota, Illinois, Michigan, and Wisconsin. Through this agreement, each state's respective minimum standards are protected, but the applicant is guaranteed an initial two-year license in the receiving state.

Institutions of higher education that have *any* teacher preparation programs leading to a license to teach.

Briar Cliff University
Buena Vista University
Central College
Clarke College
Coe College
Cornell College
Dordt College
Drake University
Emmaus Bible College
Faith Baptist Bible College
Iowa State University
University of Dubuque
Graceland College
Grand View College
Grinnell College
Iowa Wesleyan College
Loras College
Luther College
Maharishi University of Management
Morningside College
Mt. Mercy College
Northwestern College
St. Ambrose University
Simpson College
University of Iowa
University of Northern Iowa
Upper Iowa University
Wartburg College
William Penn University
Ashford University
Kaplan University

Contact information for persons interested in finding a teaching position in the state:

www.iowaeducationsjobs.com

TITLE: Restricted Teaching License

HISTORY: Available after July 1, 2002. Proposed and designed as part of
                        a total redesign of teacher preparation and licensure in Kansas
                        that was initiated in 1992. The State Board of Education
                        adopted the new licensure regulations in the summer of 2000.

MOTIVATION: Response to shortage of teachers in certain secondary teaching
                        fields and the need to allow immediate access to practice to
                        individuals who already hold degrees in the content field that
                        they would teach.

GRADE LEVELS AND/OR SUBJECT AREA(S) COVERED:

                        Any middle/secondary content teaching area for which the
                        participating higher education institution has an approved teacher
                        preparation program.

WHO OPERATES: The teacher education institution in cooperation
                        with the local school district.

REQUIREMENTS TO ENTER:

                        1. An undergraduate or graduate degree in the content area or with
                            equivalent coursework in the area for which the restricted license is
                            sought.

                        2. 2.5 grade point average (GPA).

                        3. Offer of employment from a local school district.

PROGRAM DESCRIPTION:

                        If the candidate meets the above content, degree and GPA
                        requirements and has an offer of employment, he/she may contact a
                        Kansas teacher education institution for a plan of study that will
                        qualify him/her for full licensure in the content area.

                        The plan must allow for completion of the approved teacher education
                        program in not more than three years and must show specific
                        requirements to be completed each year.

The teacher education institution provides the program through an alternative delivery system and supports the applicant on-site.

A federal Transition to Teaching Grant resulted in 12 teacher education institutions working together to develop an on-line sequence of professional education courses. The grant also allows funding of program costs to restricted license holders working in identified high needs districts. It also provides some monetary support to those districts to help with costs for supporting the restricted license holders. The grant work is with its final cohort.

The local hiring district must collaborate with the teacher education institution on delivery of the program.

The school district must assign a mentor teacher with three or more years of experience to provide support to the individual.

The local district and the teacher education institution must submit a yearly progress report.

The individual is issued a three-year restricted teaching license while they are completing program requirements.

NUMBER OF CREDIT HOURS TO COMPLETE:

Will vary with individuals, the institutions they are working with and the program areas they are completing. The online coursework consists of 18 credit hours; one course each semester and during each summer.

WHO EVALUATES: The teacher education institution, in cooperation with the local district, will evaluate and assess the individual as he/she progress through the program. Individuals will be required to complete all licensure assessments during and after completion of the program and prior to issuance of a conditional license.

LENGTH OF TIME: Three years under the restricted license will be allowed to complete the approved program requirements.

OTHER: Individuals who complete a program under a restricted license will be required to complete a content and pedagogy assessment to qualify for an initial conditional license. During the conditional licensing period, they will complete a performance assessment to move to a professional license.

Alternative License, State Board of Education Visiting Scholar License

Currently, Kansas bases licensure on the completion of state-approved programs. Kansas
does not base licensure on a transcript analysis and is a member of the Central States
Exchange Agreement (Illinois, Iowa, Kansas, Michigan, Missouri, Nebraska, Oklahoma,
South Dakota, and Wisconsin).

The State Board has adopted the following:

Alternative License, State Board of Education Visiting Scholar License -- This program
would seek to tap the human resources found at the state's 22 IHEs, several military bases,
and technology-based industries, targeting individuals with exceptional talent and/or
outstanding distinction in an academic field. If an LEA identified an individual or the
individual expressed an interest, the LEA could submit supporting documentation to the
Commissioner of Education. Documentation includes an advanced course of study or
extensive training in the area of licensure requested; outstanding distinction or exceptional
talent in the field of licensure requested; significant recent occupational experience which is
related to the field of licensure. After review, the Commissioner could order issuance of a
special license, valid for one year, specifying subjects the holder would be authorized to
teach.

Institutions of higher education participating in the Transition to Teaching program that supports the restricted license:

Baker University
Emporia State University
Fort Hays State University
Friends University
Kansas State University
Mid America Nazarene University
Newman University

Pittsburg State University
Southwestern College
University of Saint Mary

Washburn University
Wichita State University
University of Kansas

States with which the state has reciprocity of teacher licenses:

Kansas is a signatory of the NASDTEC Interstate Contract Agreement

Kansas is a signatory of the Central States Exchange regional agreement.

Institutions of higher education that have *any* teacher preparation programs leading to a license to teach.

Baker University
Benedictine College
Bethany College
Bethel College
Emporia State University
Ft. Hays State University
Friends University
Haskell Indian Nations University
Kansas State University
Kansas Wesleyan University
McPherson College

Mid-America Nazarene University
Newman University
Ottawa University
Pittsburg State University
St. Mary College
Southwestern College
Sterling College
Tabor College
University of Kansas
Washburn University
Wichita State University

Contact information for persons interested in finding a teaching position in the state:

Visit the Web site at: http://www.kansasteachingjobs.com

TITLE: Alternative Route --- Local District Certification Option

HISTORY: Legislation enacted in 1990.

MOTIVATION: Legislative response to the growing number of adults who already have a bachelor's degree in a field other than education who want to become licensed to teach.

GRADE LEVELS AND/OR SUBJECT AREAS COVERED:

All, except special education.

WHO OPERATES: School district, which must show that it has sought collaboration with an IHE.

REQUIREMENTS TO ENTER PROGRAM:

To participate, a candidate must:

(a) Have a baccalaureate degree;

(b) Have a grade point average (GPA) of 2.5 overall (on a 4.0 scale), or a GPA of 2.0 with "exceptional life experience" related to teaching;

(c) Pass written tests of knowledge in the specific teaching field (must have completed a 30-hour major/minor, or have five years' experience in the field);

(d) Have been offered employment in a school district which has an alternative certification program approved by the state's Education Professional Standards Board (EPSB).

Upon completion of these requirements, the candidate shall be issued a one-year Provisional Certificate.

PROGRAM DESCRIPTION:

The candidate shall be issued a Professional Certificate upon satisfactory completion of:

    (a) The program;

    (b) The PRAXIS exam(s); and

    (c) The teacher internship.

The candidate shall be placed on the local district salary schedule for the rank corresponding to the degree held.

Each local district alternative training program shall include:

    (a) A full-time seminar and practicum of no less than eight weeks duration prior to the time the candidate assumes responsibility for a classroom;

    (b) An 18-week period of classroom supervision, while the candidate assumes responsibility on a half-time basis for the classroom, including weekly visits by the professional support team, and three formal evaluations;

    (c) An 18-week period of supervision, while the candidate assumes full responsibility for the classroom, including monthly visits and at least two evaluations by the professional support team;

    (d) At least 250 hours of formal instruction;

    (e) A comprehensive evaluation report by the support team, including a recommendation as to whether the candidate should be issued a one-year certificate of eligibility to complete the internship.

The district plan for operating an alternative certification program must include:

    (a) Written evidence that the district has sought sponsorship of the program with an accredited college;

    (b) The four-member professional support team (school principal, experienced teacher, instructional supervisor, and college/university faculty member);

(c) The persons who will provide the 250 hours of formal instruction;

(d) The training program for the support team;

(e) The training program for the candidate;

(f) A budget, not to exceed five years duration;

(g) A program director;

(h) An appeals process for the candidate; and

(i) Roles and expectations for the professional support team.

NUMBER OF CREDIT HOURS TO COMPLETE:

250 contact hours of direct instruction.

WHO EVALUATES: Professional support team.

LENGTH OF TIME Total of 44 weeks: eight weeks full-time seminar and practicum; 18 weeks half-time teaching; 18 weeks full-time teaching.

TITLE: University-Based Alternative Teacher Certification

HISTORY: Enacted in legislation by the General Assembly in 2000.

MOTIVATION: Designed to relieve overall teacher shortages and provide a mechanism for recruitment of mid-career professionals into teaching.

GRADE LEVELS AND/OR SUBJECT AREAS COVERED: All.

WHO OPERATES: IHE.

REQUIREMENTS TO ENTER PROGRAM:

- Bachelor's or master's degree;

- Meet minimum teacher education admissions standards.

PROGRAM DESCRIPTION:

Allows completion of the teacher preparation program with concurrent employment in a school district.

After obtaining employment, the candidate is issued a Temporary Provisional Certificate.

Participates in the Kentucky Teacher Internship Program (KTIP).

The candidate must complete all requirements within three years and pass all required assessments.

The candidate then receives the Professional Certificate.

NOTE: Kentucky has two university-based options, Option 6 (described above) and Option 7, which operated similarly but relies only on a one summer-long institute before the teacher enters the classroom. Operated on a limited basis, details on Option 7 may be found at http://kyepsb.net/certification/optionVII.asp.

NUMBER OF CREDIT HOURS TO COMPLETE: N/A.

WHO EVALUATES: IHE.

LENGTH OF TIME Not more than three years.

TITLE: Alternative Route --- Adjunct Instructor Certification Option

HISTORY: Legislation enacted in 1984.

MOTIVATION: To allow entry into part-time K-12 teaching for
                      persons with training or expertise in specialty
                      area(s).

GRADE LEVELS AND/OR SUBJECT AREAS COVERED:

                      All.

WHO OPERATES: State (Education Professional Standards Board).

REQUIREMENTS TO ENTER PROGRAM:

                      Adjunct instructors:

                      (a) Shall be "of good moral character" and be at least 18 years of age;

                      (b) If employed for departmentalized instruction in grades 7-12, shall
                          hold a bachelor's degree from a regionally-accredited institution
                          with an overall minimum grade point average (GPA) of 2.5 (on a 4.0
                          scale), and a major, minor, or area of concentration in the subject
                          to be taught with a minimum GPA of 2.5;

                      (c) If employed for vocational education, shall be a high school
                          graduate, and have at least four years of appropriate occupational
                          experience (or its equivalent, as approved by the Division of
                          Secondary Vocational Education) for the specialty to be taught.

                      (d) If employed for teaching elementary or birth to primary, shall hold
                          a bachelor's degree from a regionally-accredited institution with an
                          overall 2.5 GPA (on a 4.0 scale) with a planned program in child
                          development or a related area.

PROGRAM DESCRIPTION:

                      Adjunct instructors are those persons who:

                      (a) Have training or experience in a specific subject area;

                      (b) Are employed in a part-time position on an *annual contract basis*
                          and shall not be eligible for continuing service status or retirement
                          provisions;

(c) May contract with local school boards for part-time services on an hourly, daily, or other periodic basis;

(d) Shall not fill positions that will result in the displacement of qualified teachers with regular certificates who are already employed in the district;

(e) Shall be provided an orientation program developed and implemented for adjunct instructors by the local school board; and

(f) Shall be placed on the local district salary schedule for the rank corresponding to the degree held by the teacher.

NUMBER OF CREDIT HOURS TO COMPLETE:

N/A

TITLE: Alternative Route --- Exceptional Work Experience Certification Option

HISTORY: Legislation enacted in 1998.

MOTIVATION: To bring into secondary school classrooms individuals who already have exceptional work experience in the field(s) in which they will teach.

GRADE LEVELS AND/OR SUBJECT AREAS COVERED:

Grades P-12

WHO OPERATES: School district with candidate approval by EPSB.

REQUIREMENTS TO ENTER PROGRAM:

An individual who has been offered employment at the secondary level (grades 8-12) in a local school district shall be issued a one-year Provisional Certificate, if he/she has:

Documented 10 years' exceptional work experience in the area for which certification is being sought;

A bachelor's degree, with a GPA of at least 2.5 on a 4.0 scale;

An academic major in the content area for which certification is sought or a passing score on the applicable academic content assessment(s) designated by the EPSB; and

Submit an application, jointly with the employing school district, to the state's Education Professional Standards Board (EPSB).

PROGRAM DESCRIPTION:

"Exceptional experience" is defined as "recognized superiority as compared with others in rank, status, and attainment."

Verification shall include:

Detailed, multi-page resume documenting exceptional work experience;

Documentation that the state's New Teacher Standards have been addressed; and

Professional recommendations.

Upon meeting the requirements, the candidate shall be issued a one-year Provisional Certificate. The Professional Certificate shall be issued upon satisfactory completion of the teacher internship. The candidate shall be placed on the local district salary schedule for the rank corresponding to the degree held.

NUMBER OF CREDIT HOURS TO COMPLETE:

No additional credit hours. See description of Alternative Certification Program for detailed information on the required internship program.

WHO EVALUATES: EPSB evaluates candidate's initial application. Internship committee assesses first-year performance.

TITLE: Alternative Route --- College Faculty Certification Option

HISTORY: Legislation enacted in 1996.

MOTIVATION: To allow entry into secondary school classrooms for
                     persons with experience teaching in colleges or
                     universities.

GRADE LEVELS AND/OR SUBJECT AREAS COVERED:

                     Grades P-12

WHO OPERATES: State (EPSB).

REQUIREMENTS TO ENTER PROGRAM:

                     To participate, a candidate must:

                     (a) Hold a master's or doctoral degree in the academic subject area for
                         which certification is sought; and

                     (b) Have a minimum of five years of full-time teaching experience (or
                         its equivalent of at least 90 semester credit hours taught) in the
                         academic subject area for which certification is sought, in a
                         regionally- or nationally-accredited IHE.

PROGRAM DESCRIPTION:

                     College faculty members applying for certification:

                     (a) Shall, contingent upon meeting the requirements, be issued a
                         Statement of Eligibility, valid for five years;

                     (b) Shall, contingent upon confirmation of employment, be issued a
                         Provisional Teaching Certificate for participation in the internship
                         program;

                     (c) Shall, contingent upon successful completion of the teacher
                         internship program, be issued the Professional Certificate, valid for
                         an additional four years, and may renew the Professional
                         Certificate for additional five-year periods, contingent upon three

years of successful teaching experience or six semester hours of additional graduate credit.

(d) The candidate shall be placed on the local district salary schedule for the rank corresponding to the degree held.

NUMBER OF CREDIT HOURS TO COMPLETE:

No additional credit hours. See description of Alternative Certification Program for detailed information on the required internship program.

WHO EVALUATES: Internship committee assesses first year performance.

TITLE: Minority Recruitment

HISTORY: Enacted in legislation by the General Assembly in
                      1990.

MOTIVATION: To bring minorities into teaching.

GRADE LEVELS AND/OR SUBJECT AREAS COVERED:

           All.

WHO OPERATES: IHEs.

REQUIREMENTS TO ENTER PROGRAM:

           Varies by program.

PROGRAM DESCRIPTION:

           Institutions may develop programs in accord with the alternative
           certification legislation or on an experimental basis to "identify, recruit,
           and prepare as teachers minority persons who already have earned
           college degrees in other job fields."

NUMBER OF CREDIT HOURS TO COMPLETE:

           Determined by IHE.

WHO EVALUATES: IHE.

TITLE: Veterans of the Armed Forces

HISTORY: Enacted in legislation by the General Assembly in
2000.

MOTIVATION: Designed to:

(a) Help relieve overall teacher shortages, especially
in the areas of math, science, special education,
and vocational technology; and

(b) Improve the quality of education by attracting
mature, highly-experienced personnel to the
classroom.

GRADE LEVELS AND/OR SUBJECT AREAS COVERED:

All.

WHO OPERATES: State (EPSB).

REQUIREMENTS TO ENTER PROGRAM:

Candidates for this route must have:

• Been discharged or released from active duty under honorable
conditions after six years of active duty immediately before the
discharge or release;

• A bachelor's degree in the subject matter or related area for which
certification is sought;

• A grade point average (GPA) of 2.5 (on a 4.0 scale) for a bachelor's
degree or hold an advanced degree; and

• Passing scores on EPSB-approved subject matter assessments.

PROGRAM DESCRIPTION:

A candidate meeting the above requirements receives a Statement of Eligibility.

After obtaining employment, the candidate is issued a one-year Provisional Certificate.

Upon successful completion of a Kentucky Teacher Internship Program (KTIP) during the first year of teaching, the teacher receives the Professional Certificate.

NUMBER OF CREDIT HOURS TO COMPLETE: N/A.

WHO EVALUATES: N/A.

Institutions of higher education that have developed alternative teacher preparation programs leading to a teaching license:

Asbury College
Bellarmine University
Campbellsville University
Cumberland College
Eastern Kentucky University
Georgetown College
Kentucky State University
Morehead State University
Murray State University

Northern Kentucky University
Spalding University
Union College
University of Kentucky
University of Louisville
Western Kentucky University

States with which the state has reciprocity of teacher licenses:

NASDTEC Interstate Contract.

Institutions of higher education that have *any* teacher preparation programs leading to a license to teach:

Alice Lloyd College
Asbury College
Bellarmine University
Berea College
Brescia University
Campbellsville University
Centre College
Cumberland College
Eastern Kentucky University
Georgetown College
Kentucky Christian College
Kentucky State University
Kentucky Wesleyan College
Lincoln Memorial University

Lindsey Wilson College
Mid-Continent College
Midway College
Morehead State University
Murray State University
Northern Kentucky University
Pikeville College
Spalding University
Thomas More College
Transylvania University
Union College
University of Kentucky
University of Louisville
Western Kentucky University

Contact information for persons interested in finding a teaching position in the state:

Natasha Murray
Kentucky Department of Education
Educator Recruitment & Retention
CPT 500 Mero Street, 17th Floor
Frankfort, KY 40601
Phone: (502) 564-1479

TITLE: Alternative Teacher Certification Program: Practitioner Teacher Program

HISTORY: Began as a pilot 2001-02, with nine approved
                     providers. Fully implemented in Summer 2002
                     with twelve approved providers.

MOTIVATION: Blue Ribbon commission Initiative -- a fast-track
                     alternate option for certifying teachers.

GRADE LEVELS AND/OR SUBJECT AREAS COVERED:

                     Elementary (grades 1-5), Middle School (grades 4-8), Secondary
                     (grades 6-12; vary by provider), and Special Education Mild/Moderate.

WHO OPERATES: Universities and approved private providers.

REQUIREMENTS TO ENTER PROGRAM:

                     Submission of an official transcript for evaluation to a Louisiana
                     college or university with an approved teacher education program or to
                     a state-approved private practitioner program provider.

                     Baccalaureate degree from a regionally accredited university.

                     Have a 2.5 GPA on undergraduate work. Appropriate, successful work
                     experience can be substituted for the required GPA, at the discretion of
                     the program provider. However, in no case, may the GPA be less that
                     2.2. (Note: State law requires that upon completion of the program
                     the teacher candidate has a 2.5 GPA for certification).

                     Pass the Pre-Professional Skills Test (e.g. reading, writing, and
                     mathematics) on the PRAXIS. (An exclusion from this requirement can
                     be granted for a candidate who has an earned Master's Degree.)

                     Pass the content specific examinations for the PRAXIS

                     • Candidates for Grades 1-5 (regular and special education) pass the
                       Elementary Education: Content Knowledge specialty examination;

                     • Candidates for Grades 4-8 (regular and special education): pass
                       the subject specific licensing examination;

                     • Candidates for Grades 6-12 (regular and special education): pass
                       the content specialty examination(s) (e.g. English, mathematics,
                       etc.) on the PRAXIS and in the content area(s) in which they intend
                       to teach.

                     Meet the other non-course requirements established by the college or
                     university.

PROGRAM DESCRIPTION:

1. Teaching Preparation (Summer)   9 credit hours (or equivalent 135 contact hours)

   - Grades 1-5, 4-8 and 6-12 practitioner teachers will complete courses (or equivalent contact hours) pertaining to child-adolescent development/psychology, the diverse learner, classroom management, assessment, instructional design, and instructional strategies before starting their teaching positions.

   - Mild/moderate special education teachers will take courses (or equivalent contact hours) that focus upon the special needs of the mild/moderate exceptional child, classroom management, behavioral management, assessment and evaluation, methods/materials for mild/moderate exceptional children, and vocational and transition services for students with disabilities.

2. Teaching Internship and First-Year Teaching   12 credit hours (or equivalent contact hours)

   Practitioner teachers will assume full-time teaching positions in school districts.

   Participate in two seminars (one during the fall and one in the spring) that address immediate needs of the Practitioner Teacher program teachers.

   Receive one-on-one supervision through an internship program provided by the program providers.

   The Practitioner Teacher will also receive support from school-based mentor teachers (provided by the Louisiana Teacher Assistance and Assessment Program) and principals.

3. Teacher Performance Review (end of first year).

   Program providers, principals, mentors and practitioner teachers will form teams to review the first year teaching performance or practitioner teachers and determine the extent of to which the practitioner teachers have demonstrated teaching proficiency.

If additional assistance is needed, prescriptive plans that require from 1 to 12 credit hours (or equivalent 15 - 180 equivalent contact hours) of instruction will be developed for practitioner teachers.

Prescriptive Plan Implementation   1-9 credit hours (15-135 contact hours)

Practitioner teachers who demonstrate areas of need will complete prescriptive plans.

If there is no need for remediation, the candidate will be recommended for a Level 1 Certificate.

4. Louisiana Assessment Program

Practitioner teachers will be assessed during the fall or spring of the second year of teaching depending upon their teaching proficiencies.

5. PRAXIS Review

Program providers will offer review sessions to prepare practitioner teachers to pass remaining components of the PRAXIS.

NUMBER OF CREDIT HOURS TO COMPLETE:

21-30 (Varies)

WHO EVALUATES: Private providers and colleges or universities.

LENGTH OF TIME: Not specified

TITLE: Non-Master's/Certification-Only Program

HISTORY: Summer 2003

MOTIVATION: Blue Ribbon Commission Initiative for alternative
certification.

GRADE LEVELS AND/OR SUBJECT AREAS COVERED: Early Childhood (PK-3),
Elementary (grades 1-5), Middle School (grades 4-8), Secondary (grades 6-12; secondary
areas vary by provider), and Special Education Mild/Moderate.

WHO OPERATES: Approved University providers.

REQUIREMENTS TO ENTER PROGRAM:

Baccalaureate degree from a regionally accredited university.

Have a minimum of 2.20 GPA on undergraduate work. (Note: State
law requires that upon completion of the program the teacher
candidate has a 2.5 GPA for certification).

Pass the Pre-Professional Skills Test (e.g. reading, writing, and
mathematics) on the PRAXIS.

Pass the content specific examinations for the PRAXIS.

- Candidates for PK-3 (regular and special education): pass the
  Elementary Education: Content Knowledge specialty examination.

- Candidates for Grades 1-5 (regular and special education) pass the
  Elementary Education: Content Knowledge specialty examination.

- Candidates for Grades 4-8 (regular and special education): pass
  the Middle School subject-specific examination.

- Candidates for Grades 6-12 (regular and special education): pass
  the subject-specific examination(s) (e.g. English, Mathematics, etc.)
  on the PRAXIS and in the content area(s) in which they intend to
  teach.

PROGRAM DESCRIPTION:

1. Knowledge of Learner and the Learning Environment: 12 credit hours.

   - Grades PK-3, 1-5, 4-8 and 6-12: Child-adolescent development/psychology, the diverse learner, classroom management and organization, assessment, instructional design, and reading/instructional strategies.

   - Mild/moderate special education 1-12 (We have proposed changing the grade levels for special education from 1-12 to Grades PK-3, 1-5, 4-8 and 6-12. These changes have been approved by the Board and are out for Notice of Intent): Special needs of the mild/moderate exceptional child, classroom management, behavioral management, assessment and evaluation including IEP and ESYP, reading instruction, and vocational/transition services for students with disabilities.

2. Methodology and Teaching -- Methods courses and field experiences: 6 credit hours

   - Methods courses, to include case studies and field experiences.

3. Student Teaching or Internship: 6 credit hours

NUMBER OF CREDIT HOURS TO COMPLETE: 24- 33 credit hours

WHO EVALUATES: Colleges or universities.

LENGTH OF TIME: Varies with individual candidates.

TITLE: Master's Degree Program

HISTORY: Summer 2002

MOTIVATION: Blue Ribbon Commission Initiative for alternative
                      certification.

GRADE LEVELS AND/OR SUBJECT AREAS COVERED: Early Childhood (PK-3),
Elementary (grades 1-5), Middle School (grades 4-8), Secondary (grades 6-12, secondary
areas vary by provider), and Special Education Mild/Moderate.

WHO OPERATES: Approved University providers.

REQUIREMENTS TO ENTER PROGRAM:

Baccalaureate degree from a regionally accredited university.

Have a 2.5 GPA on undergraduate work.

Pass the Pre-Professional Skills Test (e.g. reading, writing, and
mathematics) on the PRAXIS. (An exclusion from this requirement can
be granted for a candidate who has an earned Master's Degree.)

Pass the content specific examinations for the PRAXIS.

- Candidates for PK-3 (regular and special education): pass the
  Elementary Education: Content Knowledge specialty examination.

- Candidates for Grades 1-5 (regular and special education) pass the
  Elementary Education: Content Knowledge specialty examination.

- Candidates for Grades 4-8 (regular and special education): pass
  the Middle School subject-specific examination.

- Candidates for Grades 6-12 (regular and special education): pass
  the content specialty examination(s) (e.g. English, Mathematics,
  etc.) on the PRAXIS and in the content area(s) in which they intend
  to teach.

Meet the other non-course requirements established by the college or
university.

PROGRAM DESCRIPTION:

1. Knowledge of Learner and the Learning Environment: 15 credit hours.

    - Grades PK-3, 1-5, 4-8 and 6-12: Child-adolescent development/psychology, the diverse learner, classroom management, assessment, instructional design, and instructional strategies.

    - Mild/moderate special education 1-12 (We have proposed changing the grade levels for special education from 1-12 to Grades PK-3, 1-5, and 6-12. These changes have been approved by the Board and are out for Notice of Intent): Special needs of the mild/moderate exceptional child, classroom management, behavioral management, assessment and evaluation, methods and materials for mild/moderate exceptional children, and vocational and transition services for students with disabilities.

2. Methodology and Teaching -- Methods courses and field experiences: 12-15 credit hours.

3. Student Teaching or Internship: 6-9 credit hours.

NUMBER OF CREDIT HOURS TO COMPLETE: 33-39 credit hours.

WHO EVALUATES: Colleges or universities.

LENGTH OF TIME: Not specified.

**TITLE: Alternate Post-Baccalaureate Certification Program – Elementary Education
(Grades 1-8)**

HISTORY: March 1995 (Mandatory September 1, 2000).

MOTIVATION: Teacher shortage.

GRADE LEVELS AND/OR SUBJECT AREAS COVERED: Grades 1-8.

WHO OPERATES: IHE.

REQUIREMENTS TO ENTER PROGRAM:

A bachelor's degree.

An overall grade point average of 2.5 on a 4.0 scale.

PROGRAM DESCRIPTION:

This program provides opportunities for individuals with non-education
degrees to become certified public school teachers.

Certification requirements are:

General education -- The general education component of the
candidate's baccalaureate degree must meet the state minimum
requirements.

Specialized Academic Education -- The candidate must have a degree
with the major in the area of certification or meet the state minimum
requirements. A baccalaureate degree from a regionally accredited
institution will satisfy six hours of the specialized academic education
requirements of Bulletin 746.

Professional Education -- 24 semester hours of coursework in pedagogy
(professional education) as prescribed by the
school/department/college of education. The professional education
component should include courses in theories of teaching and
learning, student achievement and evaluation, human growth and
development, methods of instruction, reading diagnosis and
remediation, and expectations of children or at-risk children.

Student teaching or a one-year internship in the area(s) of certification with supervision provided by faculty in the College of Education.

The applicant must have attained scores on the Praxis/NTE (National Teacher Examinations) that meet state requirements for certification.

NUMBER OF CREDIT HOURS TO COMPLETE:

Varies individually.

WHO EVALUATES: IHE.

LENGTH OF TIME: Not specified.

OTHER: NOTE: No final grade below a "C" will be accepted for student teaching or any professional or specialized academic education course which is required for certification. In addition, no final grade below a "C" will be accepted for any other course specified as a deficiency under this plan.

The State Department of Education, Certification, and Higher Education unit has the authority to waive the student teaching upon verification of three years of successful teaching experience in the area of certification.

TITLE: Alternate Post-Baccalaureate Certification Program -- Secondary

HISTORY: March 1990.

MOTIVATION: Teacher shortage.

GRADE LEVELS AND/OR SUBJECT AREAS COVERED: Secondary (grades 7-12).

WHO OPERATES: IHE.

REQUIREMENTS TO ENTER PROGRAM:

A bachelor's degree.

An overall grade point average of 2.5 on a 4.0 scale.

PROGRAM DESCRIPTION:

This program provides opportunities for individuals with non-education degrees to become certified public school teachers.

Certification requirements are:

General education -- A baccalaureate degree will fulfill the general education requirements.

Specialized Academic Education -- The candidate must have a degree with the major in the area of certification or meet the state minimum requirements.

Professional Education -- 18 semester hours of coursework in pedagogy (professional education) appropriate to the level of certification as prescribed by the IHE teacher education program. The professional education component should include courses in theories of teaching and learning, student achievement and evaluation, human growth and development, and methods of instruction.

Student teaching or a one-year internship in the area(s) of certification with supervision provided by faculty in the College of Education.

The applicant must have attained scores on the Praxis/NTE, which meet state requirements for certification.

NUMBER OF CREDIT HOURS TO COMPLETE:

Varies individually.

WHO EVALUATES: IHE.

LENGTH OF TIME: Not specified.

OTHER:

NOTE: No final grade below a "C" will be accepted for student teaching or any professional or specialized academic education course which is required for certification. In addition, no final grade below a "C" will be accepted for any other course specified as a deficiency under this plan.

The State Department of Education, Certification, and Higher Education unit has the authority to waive the student teaching upon verification of three years of successful teaching experience in the area of certification.

TITLE: Alternate Post-Baccalaureate Certification Program -- Special Education

HISTORY: March 1990.

MOTIVATION: Teacher shortage.

GRADE LEVELS AND/OR SUBJECT AREA (S) COVERED: Special education areas.

WHO OPERATES: IHE.

REQUIREMENTS TO ENTER:

> A bachelor's degree.

> An overall grade point average of 2.5 on a 4.0 scale.

PROGRAM DESCRIPTION:

> This program provides opportunities for individuals with non-education degrees to become certified public school teachers.

> Certification requirements are:

>> General Education -- A baccalaureate degree will fulfill the general education requirements.

>> Specialized Academic Education -- The candidate must have a degree with a major in the area of certification or meet the state minimum requirements.

>> Professional Education -- 18 semester hours of coursework in pedagogy (professional education) appropriate to the level of certification as prescribed by the IHE teacher education program. The professional education component should include courses in theories of teaching and learning, student achievement and evaluation, human growth and development, and methods of instruction.

>> Student teaching or a one-year internship in the area(s) of certification with supervision provided by faculty in the College of Education.

The applicant must have attained scores on the Praxis/NTE (National Teacher Examinations) which meet the state requirements for certification.

NUMBER OF CREDIT HOURS TO COMPLETE:

Varies individually.

WHO EVALUATES: IHE.

LENGTH OF TIME: Not specified.

OTHER: NOTE: No final grade below a "C" will be accepted for student teaching or any professional or specialized academic education course which is required for certification. In addition, no final grade below a "C" will be accepted for any other course specified as a deficiency under this plan.

The State Department of Education, Certification and Higher Education unit has the authority to waive the student teaching upon verification of three years of successful teaching experience in the area of certification.

Institutions of higher education that have developed alternative teacher preparation programs leading to a teaching license:

Centenary College
Dillard University
Grambling State University
Louisiana College
Louisiana State University, Baton Rouge
Louisiana State University-Shreveport
Louisiana Tech University
Loyola University
McNeese State University
Nicholls State University

Northeast Louisiana University
Northwestern State University
Our Lady of Holy Cross College
Southeastern Louisiana University
Southern University, Baton Rouge
Southern University in New Orleans
Tulane University*
University of New Orleans
University of Southwestern Louisiana
Xavier University

States with which the state has reciprocity of teacher licenses:

NASDTEC Interstate Contract.

Institutions of higher education that have *any* teacher preparation programs leading to a license to teach.

Centenary College
Dillard University
Grambling State University
Louisiana College
Louisiana State University, Baton Rouge
Louisiana State University-Shreveport
Louisiana Tech University
Loyola University
McNeese State University
Nicholls State University

Northeast Louisiana University
Northwestern State University
Our Lady of Holy Cross College
Southeastern Louisiana University
Southern University, Baton Rouge
Southern University in New Orleans
Tulane University*
University of New Orleans
University of Southwestern Louisiana
Xavier University

Tulane University discontinued <u>new</u> enrollment into teacher preparation in October 1996.

Contact information for persons interested in finding a teaching position in the state:

Certification and Higher Education
P.O. Box 94064
Baton Rouge, LA 70804
Phone: (504) 342-3490

TITLE: Transcript Analysis

HISTORY: In effect for many years.

MOTIVATION: Shortage, to fill the needs of school districts, since only about
                     20 percent of newly hired teachers come through approved
                     teacher education programs in Maine.

GRADE LEVELS AND/OR SUBJECT AREAS COVERED: All.

WHO OPERATES: State.

REQUIREMENTS TO ENTER:

In applying for transcript analysis, an individual must provide official
undergraduate and/or graduate transcripts. These must show the
individual's social security number and all courses for which credit has
been received, the registrar's signature, embossed seal, and the date
that degrees were awarded. Continuing education units and teacher
recertification credits are not acceptable for initial certification.

An applicant for a Conditional Certificate must have met the academic
content area requirements and must complete needed coursework and
meet passing scores on the PPST during the initial term of the
certificate; must meet passing scores a PRAXIS content or PLT during
the second conditional; and meet all requirements during the third
conditional as a prerequisite for renewal, further renewal, or issuance
of a Provisional Certificate.

If the individual is certified to teach in another state, he or she must
submit a copy of out-of-state teaching certificate.

In order for a Conditional Certificate to be awarded, the local school
district must have actively sought to employ a Provisional or
Professional Certificate holder, but has been unable to do so.

PROGRAM DESCRIPTION:

If the state has determined, through transcript analysis, that the
individual is eligible for a Conditional Certificate, he or she must
complete all requirements for full certification while teaching under the
Conditional credential. The transcript analysis determines which
coursework deficiencies must be completed to qualify for full
certification.

To renew the Conditional Certificate, the individual must demonstrate that he or she has annually completed the amount of approved study ordinarily required for renewal. Approved study must consist of courses unless the Department gives advance approval for in-service training in lieu of courses, in whole or in part.

The individual's support system recommends that the Conditional Certificate be renewed or that a Provisional or Professional Certificate be issued.

NUMBER OF CREDIT HOURS TO COMPLETE:

EDUCATION COURSE WORK:

For secondary level -- 6 semester hours of education coursework plus student teaching; for elementary level -- 18 semester hours plus student teaching.

WHO EVALUATES: State.

LENGTH OF TIME: The Conditional Certificate may be renewed for not more than two additional one-year terms.

OTHER: Transcript analysis is used for teachers coming from out of state, Maine teachers seeking additional endorsements to teach out of their subject areas, and for career changers.

Institutions of higher education that have developed alternative teacher preparation programs leading to a teaching license:

N/A

States with which the state has reciprocity of teacher licenses:

NASDTEC Interstate Contract.

Note: Although Maine has an Interstate Agreement with the NASDTEC Interstate Contract states, this does NOT mean that someone certified in one of these states is automatically certified in Maine. There are conditions to certification.

Institutions of higher education that have *any* teacher preparation programs leading to a license to teach.

Bates College
Bowdin College
Colby College
College of the Atlantic
Husson College
Saint Joseph's College
Thomas College

University of Maine at Farmington
University of Maine at Fort Kent
University of Maine - Machias
University of Maine - Orono
University of Maine - Presque Isle
University of New England
University of Southern Maine

Contact information for persons interested in finding a teaching position in the state:

Nancy Ibarguen
Department of Education
23 State House Station
Augusta, ME 04333-0023
Phone: (207) 624-6603

TITLE: Resident Teacher Certificate

HISTORY: A revision of the Code of Maryland Regulation 113A.12.01.07, which permits school systems to hire liberal arts graduates for teaching assignments, was passed by the State Board of Education on October 25, 2005 and became effective on January 1, 2007. The regulation and its policy guidelines guide and frame Maryland Approved Alternative Preparation Programs (MAAPP). The MAAPP utilizes the Resident Teacher Certificate, considered to denote a Highly Qualified Teacher.

MOTIVATION: To increase the pool of Highly Qualified (NCLB) and effective professional educators.

GRADE LEVELS AND/OR SUBJECT AREAS COVERED: Secondary subjects, elementary education and special education.

WHO OPERATES: Local School System alone or in partnership with a provider.

REQUIREMENTS TO ENTER:

A liberal arts bachelor's degree for the certification area of elementary education or a bachelor's degree in the subject to be taught at the secondary level.

2.75 grade point average in the major to be taught.

Qualifying scores on the Praxis I and II tests. The professional education test is postponed until the end of the first year of teaching.

PROGRAM DESCRIPTION:

A school system or partnership that includes a school system may offer a Maryland Approved Alternative Preparation Program (MAAPP) requiring a minimum of 90 hours of study, a four-to eight-week supervised internship prior to employment, and a mentored residency of up to two years during which time the candidate is employed as the teacher of record.

The Resident Teacher will be mentored by a certificated teacher.

Upon completion of the MAAPP requirements, the local superintendent may recommend that the Resident Teacher be issued the Standard Professional Certificate.

NUMBER OF CREDIT HOURS TO COMPLETE: 90 clock hours before employment.

WHO EVALUATES: MAAPP Partnership

LENGTH OF TIME: The Resident Teacher Certificate will be valid for two years.

OTHER: As of September 2001, 16 MAAPP programs exist in nine local school systems with partnerships that include two-year and four-year colleges and/universities, Teach for America and The New Teacher Project.

Institutions of higher education that have developed <u>post-baccalaureate</u> teacher preparation programs leading to a teaching license:

Bowie State University
College of Notre Dame of MD
Frostburg State University
Goucher College
Hood College
Loyola College in MD
McDaniel College
Morgan State University

Mount Saint Mary's University
Salisbury State University
Towson University
University of Maryland, Baltimore County
University of Maryland College Park
University of Maryland, Eastern Shore
University of Maryland, University College

States with which the state has reciprocity of teacher licenses:

NASDTEC Interstate Contract.

Institutions of higher education that have *any* teacher preparation programs leading to a license to teach.

Bowie State University
College of Notre Dame of MD
Columbia Union College
Coppin State College
Frostburg State University
Goucher College
Hood College
Johns Hopkins University
Loyola College in Maryland
Maryland Institute College of Art
McDaniel College
Morgan State University

Mount St. Mary's University
Peabody Institute
St. Mary's College of Maryland
Salisbury State University
Towson University
University of Maryland, Baltimore County
University of Maryland, College Park
University of Maryland, Eastern Shore
University of Maryland, University College
Villa Julie College
Washington College

Contact information for persons interested in finding a teaching position in the state:

Office of Maryland Approved Alternative Preparation Programs
Program Approval and Assessment Branch
Maryland State Department of Education
200 West. Baltimore St.
Baltimore, MD 21202
Phone: (410) 767-5654

TITLE: The Performance Review Program for Initial Licensure

HISTORY: In August 2003, Class Measures was contracted by the
Massachusetts Department of Education's Office of Educator Quality
to provide a Performance Review Program for Initial Licensure
(PRPIL). This program is in response to the Board of Education's new
Regulations for Educator Licensure and Preparation Program
Approval that was adopted in October 2001 and is Route Four in the
DOE regulations.

MOTIVATION: The Performance Review Program for Initial Licensure is the
alternative licensure process for teacher candidates who (1) hold a
Preliminary license, (2) are hired as teachers of record, and (3) are
working in a district that does not have an approved program for the
Initial license.

GRADE LEVELS AND/OR SUBJECT AREA(S) COVERED:

All subject areas except for the following teacher and specialist
teacher licenses: early childhood, elementary, library, teacher of
students with moderate disabilities, teacher of students with severe
disabilities, teacher of the deaf and hard-of-hearing, teacher of the
visually impaired, academically advanced, reading, and
speech/language/hearing disorders.

WHO OPERATES: Class Measures, contracted vendor

REQUIREMENTS TO ENTER PROGRAM:

Candidates seeking licensure under this process shall meet the
following eligibility requirements:

- Possession of a Preliminary license in the field and at the level of
  the license sought.

- At least three full years of employment in the role of the
  Preliminary license.

- Documentation of seminars, courses, and experience relevant to
  the Professional Standards for Teachers.

- A recommendation from the principal of each school where the
  candidate was employed under the Preliminary license or in the
  role of the license sought.

- A competency review for those license fields that have no subject
  matter knowledge test for which not all the subject matter
  knowledge required for the license is measured by the test.

PROGRAM DESCRIPTION:

The program will be delivered through two key players who will work closely with the candidate throughout the process. They are the Instructional Consultant recruited and trained by Class Measures, and a mentor from the candidate's district, who is an experienced teacher, holds at least an initial license in the same field as the candidate, and who will provide support and guidance.

The candidates selected to enroll in the program will participate in the first four stages.

- *Stage One:* Submit a portfolio of work to Instructional Consultant

- *Stage Two:* Candidate will be observed in his/her classroom three times over a course of 12 weeks by the Instructional Consultant and Mentor. (observations can happen at different times)

- *Stage Three:* Resubmit portfolio with revisions or additions that reflect what was learned in Stage Two

- *Stage Four:* Candidate undergoes an interview with consultant and mentor as an assessment of his/her knowledge

The consultant and mentor will review the portfolio submitted in Stage One and provide written feedback.

In Stage Two a pre-observation meeting and post-observation meeting will take place between the Instructional Consultant and candidate and written feedback will be given after the observation.

In Stage Four of the review process, the instructional consultant and mentor will review the candidate's overall performance using the Department of Education's Preservice Performance Assessment and make a decision on the status of their initial licensure.

NUMBER of CREDIT HOURS to COMPLETE:

N/A

TITLE: The Preliminary License

HISTORY:
The April 1995 Regulations for the Certification of Educational Personnel in Massachusetts established the Provisional Certificate, which was available to candidates who had not completed an educator preparation program, but who had a bachelor's degree in the arts and sciences appropriate to the instructional field of the certificate, and passed the subject matter knowledge test and the Communication and Literacy Skills test.

In October, 2001 the regulations were revised and the Provisional Certificate became the Preliminary License, and it is available to any candidate who holds any bachelor's degree and passes the subject matter knowledge test for the field licensure sought and the Communication and Literacy Skills test. It is good for five years of employment in Massachusetts Public Schools

MOTIVATION:
To provide an easy route for candidates to become teachers.

GRADE LEVELS and/or SUBJECT AREAS:
All teaching areas.

WHO OPERATES:
The Commonwealth of Massachusetts.

REQUIREMENTS TO ENTER:
A bachelor's degree.

PROGRAM DESCRIPTION:
The Preliminary License is the first stage of a three-stage licensure system. Candidates must only document knowledge of the subject matter to be issued the license. School districts that hire teachers who hold only a Preliminary license must provide support and a mentor.

NUMBER of CREDIT HOURS to COMPLETE:
N/A

LENGTH OF TIME: Five years of employment.

TITLE: The Licensure Waiver

HISTORY: In existence since the 1950s.

MOTIVATION: A waiver allows an unlicensed person to teach for one year when a local school district, after a bona fide effort, has b been unable to fill a position with a certified and qualified candidate. The unlicensed teacher must make substantial progress towards meeting the requirements for licensure during that year to be issued a subsequent one-year waiver.

GRADE LEVELS AND/OR SUBJECT AREA(S) COVERED:

All teaching areas and grade levels.

WHO OPERATES: The Commonwealth of Massachusetts

REQUIREMENTS TO ENTER PROGRAM:

Bachelor's degree;

Waiver request by the local school district;

Licensure application for the teacher on file with the Office of Educator Licensure.

PROGRAM DESCRIPTION:

The teacher is issued a waiver, but not a teaching credential.

The Office of Educator Licensure specifies requirements which must be completed, based on its review of the applicant's education transcripts.

The teacher must make continuous progress towards completion of regular licensure requirements in order to continue in this program.

NUMBER OF CREDIT HOURS TO COMPLETE:

N/A

Institutions of higher education that have developed alternative teacher preparation programs leading to a teaching license:

N/A

States with which the state has reciprocity of teacher licenses:

NASDTEC Interstate Contract.

Institutions of higher education that have any teacher preparation programs leading to a license to teach.

EARLY CHILDHOOD

American International College
Anna Maria College
Atlantic Union College
Bay Path College
Becker College
Boston College
Boston University
Bridgewater State College
Eastern Nazarene College
Elms College
Endicott College
Fitchburg State College
Gordon College
Lasell College
Lesley College
Mount Holyoke College
Mount Ida College
North Adams State College
Northeastern University
Pine Manor College
Salem State College
Shady Hill School
Simmons College
Smith College
Springfield College
Stonehill College
Tufts University
University of Massachusetts/Amherst
University of Massachusetts/Boston
University of Massachusetts/Lowell
Westfield State College
Wheaton College

Wheelock College
Worcester State College

ELEMENTARY

American International College
Anna Maria College
Assumption
Atlantic Union College
Bay Path College
Becker College
Boston College
Boston University
Bradford College
Brandeis University
Bridgewater State College
Cambridge College
Clark University
Curry College
Eastern Nazarene College
Elms College
Emmanuel College
Endicott College
Fitchburg State College
Framingham State College
Gordon College
Hellenic College
Lasell College
Lesley College
Merrimack College
Mount Holyoke College
North Adams State College
Northeastern University
Pine Manor College
Regis College
Salem State College
Shady Hill School
Simmons College
Smith College
Springfield College
Stonehill College
Suffolk University
University of Massachusetts/Amherst
University of Massachusetts/Boston
University of Massachusetts/Dartmouth
University of Massachusetts/Lowell
Westfield State College
Wheaton College
Wheelock College
Worcester State College

MIDDLE SCHOOL

Bridgewater State College
Eastern Nazarene College
Fitchburg State College
Gordon College
Lesley College
North Adams College
Salem State College
Shady Hill School
University of Massachusetts/Boston
University of Massachusetts/Lowell
Westfield State College

STUDENTS WITH SPECIAL NEEDS

American International College
Assumption College
Boston College
Boston University
Bridgewater State College
Curry College
Eastern Nazarene College
Elms College
Fitchburg State College
Framingham State College
Gordon College
Lesley College
North Adams State College
Northeastern University
Salem State College
Simmons College
University of Massachusetts/Amherst
University of Massachusetts/Boston
Westfield State College
Wheelock College

STUDENTS WITH INTENSIVE
SPECIAL NEEDS

Boston College
Boston University
Fitchburg State College
Lesley College
Northeastern University
Simmons College
Westfield State College

For other areas, please contact the Massachusetts Department of Education/Bureau of Educator Certification and Licensure, Phone (781) 338-3000, Web site: http://www.doe.mass.edu/educators

Contact information for persons interested in finding a teaching position in the state:

Note: Positions are handled through each local school district.

TITLE: Michigan's Alternative Routes to Teacher Certification (MARTC)

HISTORY: In May 1993, the State Board of Education
                      approved "A Model Process and Standards for
                      Alternative Routes to Teacher Certification"
                      (MARTC).

MOTIVATION: MARTC is designed to address local/regional teacher
                      shortages (1) in specific grade levels, (2) in subjects
                      or geographic settings, (3) and to promote diversity
                      of culture and gender by expanding the pool of
                      minority and underrepresented teacher candidates.
                      It will allow Michigan citizens who have been
                      professionally active in specialized areas and who
                      are interested in teaching to come into the teaching
                      profession in non-traditional ways.

GRADE LEVELS AND/OR SUBJECT AREAS COVERED:

                      All grade levels, Pre K-12, and all teacher certification endorsement
                      areas where there is a critical need, identified by: an LEA or
                      consortium of LEAs and verified by the appropriate teacher bargaining
                      organization(s) to assure that there is no existing pool of appropriately
                      certified teachers; an approved teacher preparation institution or
                      consortium of such IHEs; and the Michigan Department of Education;
                      as approved by the State Board of Education.

WHO OPERATES: Collaborative: SEA, IHEs, LEAs, teachers' unions.

REQUIREMENTS TO ENTER PROGRAM:

                      The MARTC program is a system through which an individual -- who
                      (a) possesses a bachelor's degree from a regionally or nationally
                      accredited IHE, and (b) has a major or a graduate degree in the field of
                      specialization in which he or she will teach -- may become certified to
                      teach to address local/regional teacher shortages (1) in specific grade
                      levels, (2) in subject areas or geographic settings, and (3) in order to
                      expand the pool of minority and underrepresented teacher candidates
                      to promote diversity of culture and gender.

                      For grades 6-12, the candidate must have a major or graduate degree
                      in the field of specialization in which he or she wishes to teach.

For grades Pre K-5, he or she must have a major in the liberal arts, the humanities, the social sciences, the mathematical and natural sciences, the arts, or sciences, and in addition to such major, a minor of at least 20 semester hours in another field deemed appropriate for elementary education.

The individual must:

Have awareness that Michigan's constitution and laws guarantee the right to equal educational opportunity without discrimination because of race, religion, color, national origin or ancestry, age, gender, sexual orientation, marital status, or handicap.

Have an overall 2.5 grade point average and a 2.5 grade point in the major and/or minor or graduate program on a 4.0 scale or the equivalent.

Pass both the basic skills examination and the comprehensive elementary examination for elementary candidates, or the appropriate subject area examinations for secondary candidates, offered through the Michigan Test for Teacher Certification (MTTC) program.

Pass a criminal history check.

Be employed by a qualified LEA, with a letter of acknowledgment issued by the State Department of Education.

Except in the case of persons engaged to teach a foreign language, have not less than two years of occupational experience within the last five years in the field of specialization in which he or she will teach.

For elementary, have documented relevant work experience (voluntary or paid), or experience with children of elementary school age.

Participate in a structured interview used for screening or diagnostic purposes.

Meet all cost obligations related to participation in the MARTC program.

PROGRAM DESCRIPTION:

The individual will become certified by successfully completing required coursework and supervised practical experience offered under conditions which vary from the traditional state approved teacher preparation program.

Alternative routes may also be used to enable currently certified teachers to acquire additional endorsements in areas of <u>critical</u> needs.

Those with no Pre K-12 teaching experience must successfully complete appropriate initial pedagogy coursework prior to classroom placement.

Those certified candidates seeking an additional certificate or endorsement, and who do not possess a teachable major or minor, must successfully complete appropriate subject area coursework prior to classroom placement.

NUMBER OF CREDIT HOURS TO COMPLETE: Not specified.

WHO EVALUATES: LEA and IHE.

LENGTH OF TIME: Six months to two years.

TITLE: Limited License to Instruct (General Model)

HISTORY: Authorized for pilot to assist a large urban
                       district.

MOTIVATION: Developed to assist in reducing the number of
                       uncertified teachers employed and for recruiting
                       individuals with significant academic and
                       occupational experience into teaching.

GRADE LEVELS AND/OR SUBJECT AREAS COVERED:

                       Secondary, especially Science and Mathematics.

WHO OPERATES: Collaborative among state, school district and
                       university.

REQUIREMENTS TO ENTER PROGRAM:

                       An applicant must:

                       1. Possess a bachelor's or higher degree from a regionally or
                           nationally accredited college or university.*

                           Note: * Except in the case of an applicant to teach foreign language,
                           have completed the program of study/degree in the field of
                           specialization within the last 5 years or have at least 2 years of
                           occupational experience in the field of specialization within the last
                           5 years.

                       2. Have completed a major and/or a minor or a graduate degree in the
                           field of specialization in which the applicant wishes to instruct or
                           has one year of occupational experience in that specialization field.

                       <u>OR</u>

                       Have completed at least 120 semester hours of satisfactory college
                       credit in an approved teacher preparation program, including a major
                       and a minor or the equivalent and at least 15 semester hour credits in
                       professional education.**

                       Note: ** Professional education credit is coursework that is part of the
                       professional education sequence of a K-12 teacher preparation
                       program. Counselor education courses, educational leadership
                       courses, and psychology courses that are not required, as part of an
                       approved teacher education program may not be counted as
                       professional education credit.

3. Have an overall 2.5 grade point average and a 2.5 grade point in the major and/or minor, on a 4.0 scale or the equivalent or is between 2.0 - 2.5 grade point average and passes the MTCC test in the area of specialization by the second request for renewal.

4. Pass a criminal history check.

PROGRAM DESCRIPTION:

Validity period: The initial Limited License to Instruct (LLI) is valid for one academic year and will expire on June 30th of the academic year during which it was issued.

Renewal Requirements:

1. The initial LLI can only be renewed through the recommendation of the employing district/school.

2. Have taken the MTTC Basic Skills examination, including reading, writing and mathematics and passed one of the three within Year One. To receive consideration for a second renewal must have passed 2/3. To receive consideration for a third renewal, must pass 3/3.

3. Have taken and passed the appropriate teacher certification examination(s) for the field(s) of specialization for which the LLI was issued, by the second request for renewal.

4. Have received a rating no less than "satisfactory" on the Annual Performance Evaluation, based on at least 2 observations of classroom teaching.

5. Must have on file with the employing district evidence of admission to the partner University and an approved plan of work for earning a Michigan Provisional certificate, which may include the completion of an MDE-approved fast track teacher preparation program.*

    Note: A licensee who has completed all by the student/practice teaching experience for a Michigan Provisional certificate is exempt from this requirement.

6. Have successfully completed a professional orientation to teaching offered by the local district/school or ISD in collaboration with a teacher preparation college or university.

7. Annual renewals up to 3 additional academic years may be
    recommended at the discretion of the employing district/school if
    the licensee provides evidence of annual progress towards
    completion of the Individual Development Plan, and progress on
    the approved university plan of work.

NUMBER OF CREDIT HOURS TO COMPLETE:

Determined on a case-by-case basis, depending on
academic/experience background.

WHO EVALUATES: LEA and IHE.

LENGTH OF TIME: 1-3 years with successful completion resulting in a
Michigan Provisional teaching certificate.

TITLE: Limited License to Instruct (Mid-career Model)

HISTORY: Authorized for pilot to support the outplacement of retired or released business and industry personnel.

MOTIVATION: Especially developed to assist the entry of mid-career changers into teaching.

GRADE LEVELS AND/OR SUBJECT AREAS COVERED:

Initially, secondary level Mathematics and Science, then all levels and subject areas as needed.

WHO OPERATES: Collaborative among state, school district and university.

REQUIREMENTS TO ENTER PROGRAM:

Base requirements include at least a bachelor's degree from an accredited institution with a major or graduate degree in the field of specialization to be taught (Foreign language, Chemistry, Engineering, Robotics, Physics, Music).

Have, within the past 5 years, at least 2 years of occupational experience in the field of specialization to be taught. Those who will teach in the area of Foreign Language are exempted from this requirement.

PROGRAM DESCRIPTION:

A qualified individual must complete a Michigan Department of Education (MDE) approved orientation (4-8 week) after which he/she may be employed for one year with no additional academic requirements.

During years 2-5, an individual may continue to be employed on this restricted license track based on annual recommendation of the employing district. If the person remains on this track, he or she becomes unemployable under this license unless they convert to a regular certificate track leading to Michigan's initial Provisional certificate.

WHO EVALUATES: Employing district/school.

LENGTH OF TIME: 4-8 weeks.

Institutions of higher education that have developed alternative teacher preparation programs leading to a teaching license:

Oakland University
Wayne State University
University of Michigan - Dearborn Campus

Saginaw Valley State University
Western Michigan University

States with which the state has reciprocity of teacher licenses:

Michigan will certify a holder of a valid teaching certificate from any state to teach in comparable grade levels and endorsement areas. Those with less than three years of teaching experience and/or do not meet the academic requirements for certificate advance must take and pass the Michigan Test for Teacher Certification.

Institutions of higher education that have *any* teacher preparation programs leading to a license to teach.

Adrian College
Albion College
Alma College
Andrews University
Aquinas College
Calvin College
Central Michigan University
Concordia College
Cornerstone College
Eastern Michigan University
Ferris State University
Grand Valley State University
Hillsdale College
Hope College
Kalamazoo College
Lake Superior State University

Madonna University
Marygrove College
Michigan State University
Michigan Tech University
Northern Michigan University
Oakland University
Olivet College
Saginaw Valley State University
Siena Heights College
Spring Arbor College
University of Detroit Mercy
University of Michigan, Ann Arbor
University of Michigan-Dearborn
University of Michigan-Flint
Wayne State University
Western Michigan University

Contact information for persons interested in finding a teaching position in the state:

Note: There are 555 local districts in Michigan and 171 Public School Academies (charter schools). Therefore, the State Department of Education does not provide employment services.

TITLE: Teacher Licensure Candidate Assessment Alternatives (Licensure via Portfolio)

HISTORY: Authorized during the 2004 legislative session and implemented in Fall of 2004.

MOTIVATION: To provide a state licensure process to assess the level of knowledge, skills, and competencies of applicants who have not completed a regionally accredited and state approved college/university teacher preparation program in the licensure field being sought. The process is based on current licensure standards and procedures, which assess teacher competence and includes new provisions for flexibility and accessibility.

SUBJECT AREAS COVERED: All

WHO OPERATES: Minnesota Board of Teaching and Minnesota Department of Education

REQUIREMENTS TO ENTER:

A minimum of a bachelor's degree and teaching or other related experiences in the content area for which licensure is desired.

PROGRAM DESCRIPTION:

Licensure via Portfolio is a standards-based process based on meeting standards of professional knowledge and subject matter, identified in Minnesota Board of Teaching Rules. Individuals who believe they have the knowledge, skills and competencies required for a specific field of licensure may use this evaluation process to be recommended for a professional teaching license in Minnesota. This process utilizes documentation of professional, educational, and life experiences, toward demonstrating compliance with Minnesota licensure standards.

WHO EVALUATES: Minnesota Board of Teaching & Minnesota Department of Education

LENGTH OF TIME: Varies for applicants.
OTHER: Licensure via Portfolio may be used to add a field to a current Minnesota teaching license or to obtain an initial Minnesota teaching license.

TITLE: Alternative Preparation to Teacher Licensure Program (This program is not current operating).

HISTORY: The 1990 Legislature authorized the Board of Teaching to establish this program. This program is not currently operating.

MOTIVATION: 1) To augment the current high quality teacher corps with individuals whose backgrounds would be especially relevant in today's classrooms, but who might not otherwise seek the preparation needed to be licensed; especially individuals of color.

2) Foster closer relationships between school districts and colleges with teacher preparation programs.

GRADE LEVELS AND/OR SUBJECT AREAS COVERED:

Grades K-6. plus 5-8 specialty in science, math, communication arts and literature, or social studies

WHO OPERATES: The Minnesota Board of Teaching approves all alternative preparation programs. A school district, group of schools, or an educational district must be affiliated with a postsecondary institution to offer an alternative preparation program.

REQUIREMENTS TO ENTER PROGRAM:

To participate in the program, a candidate must:

- be hired by a school district;

- have a bachelor's degree;

- pass Pre-Professional Skills Tests in reading, writing, and mathematics;

- have experience in a field related to the subject to be taught; and document successful experiences working with children.

PROGRAM DESCRIPTION:

Approved programs have these characteristics:

Staff development conducted by a Resident Mentorship Team made up of administrators, teachers, and postsecondary faculty members.

An instruction phase involving intensive preparation of a candidate for licensure before the candidate assumes responsibility for a classroom.

Formal instruction and peer coaching during the school year.

Assessment, supervision, and evaluation of a candidate to determine the candidate's specific needs and to ensure satisfactory completion of the program.

A research-based and results-oriented approach, focused on skills teachers need to be effective.

Assurance of integration of education theory and classroom practices.

The shared design and delivery of staff development.

NUMBER OF CREDIT HOURS TO COMPLETE:

No credit. Programs may not be driven by credit hours. Upon successful completion, a candidate will have met all of the competencies for a Minnesota initial teaching license.

WHO EVALUATES: The Resident Mentorship Team (classroom teacher, administrator, higher education faculty) must prepare for the Board of Teaching an evaluation report on the candidate's performance.

LENGTH OF TIME: Program is one year in duration (June - June).

OTHER: Since the start of the program in 1991, approximately 200 candidates have completed. The last cohort completed the program in June, 2003.

States with which the state has reciprocity of teacher licenses: None

Institutions of higher education that have *any* teacher preparation programs leading to a license to teach.

Alfred Adler Graduate School
Augsburg College
Bemidji State University
Bethel College
Bethany Lutheran College
Capella University
Carleton College
College of St. Benedict
College of St. Catherine
College of St. Scholastica
Concordia College-Moorhead
Concordia University-St. Paul
Crown College
Gustavus Adolphus College
Hamline University
Marthin Luther College

Moorhead State University
North Central College
Northwestern College
Walden University

St. Cloud State University
St. John's University
St. Mary's University
St. Olaf College
Southwest State University
University of Minnesota, Duluth Campus
University of Minnesota, Morris Campus
University of Minnesota, Twin Cities Campus
University of St. Thomas
Winona State University

TITLE: Teach Mississippi Institute

HISTORY: The Teach Mississippi Institute was mandated by the Mississippi Legislature during the 2002 legislative session, but the Institute did not begin until Jan. 1, 2003.

GRADE LEVELS AND/OR SUBJECT AREAS COVERED:

Limited to these 15 areas:

Biology	Mathematics
Business	Physics
Chemistry	Social Studies
English	Spanish
French	Special Education
German	(grades 7-12 only)
Home Economics	Speech Communication
Marketing	Technology Education

WHO OPERATES: Mississippi State Department of Education.

REQUIREMENTS TO ENTER:

The institute is available to applicants who hold a minimum of a bachelor's degree from a regionally/nationally accredited institution of higher education, but have not completed a state- or NCATE-approved teacher education program.

PROGRAM DESCRIPTION:

Teach Mississippi Institute is an eight (8) week, nine (9) semester hour summer program which shall include, but is not limited to, the following:

- Instruction in education;

- Effective teaching strategies;

- Classroom management;

- State curriculum requirement;

- Planning and instruction;

- Using tests to improve instruction; and

- A one (1) semester, three (3) semester hour, supervised internship, to be completed while the teacher is employed as a full-time teacher intern in the school district.

NUMBER OF CREDIT HOURS TO COMPLETE:

Nine (9) semester hours of course work and three (3) semester hours of internship.

WHO OPERATES: Mississippi State Department of Education.

LENGTH OF TIME: Five (5) years; renewable.

TITLE: Mississippi Alternate Path to Quality Teachers

HISTORY: The Office of Teacher Certification analyzes applicant transcripts and makes evaluations, compared to requirements in various areas of certification.

Candidates must have a bachelor's degree, meet required Praxis I scores, and pass the Praxis II Specialty Area test within a specified amount of time.

GRADE LEVELS AND/OR SUBJECT AREAS COVERED:

Limited to these 18 areas:

Art Education	Music
Biology	Physical Education
Business	Physics
Chemistry	Social Studies
English	Spanish
French	Special Education
German	(grades 7-12 only)
Home Economics	Speech Communication
Marketing	Technology Education
Mathematics	

WHO OPERATES: Mississippi State Department of Education.

REQUIREMENTS TO ENTER:

A candidate for this license must have a bachelor's degree (non-education) from a regionally/nationally accredited institution of higher learning.

Individuals who graduated from college 7 years or more ago must have a minimum 2.0 overall grade point average.

Individuals who graduated from college less than 7 years ago must have a minimum 2.5 overall grade point average or a 2.75 grade point average in their major.

PROGRAM DESCRIPTION:

Attain passing scores on the Praxis I and the Praxis II Specialty Area Test in the subject to be taught, or provide a score that is within one standard error of measurement of the passing score.

Complete the Teach Mississippi Training Institute, a two- or three-week session that introduces new teachers to the profession by providing training and hands-on field experiences.

Complete new teacher practicums, new teacher training models, and a local school district evaluation during the first year of employment. (Note: The local school district should provide an intensive induction program and provide a mentor for the new teacher.)

NUMBER OF CREDIT HOURS TO COMPLETE:

N/A

WHO OPERATES: Mississippi State Department of Education.

LENGTH OF TIME: Teachers who pass the Praxis II Specialty Area Test at the end of the third year will be issued a Standard Five-Year License.

TITLE: Master of Arts in Teaching Program

HISTORY: The Office of Teacher Certification previously
                       analyzed applicant transcripts and made
                       evaluations compared to requirements in various
                       areas of certification. However, the system was
                       changed and this responsibility was assumed by
                       Mississippi colleges with approved teacher
                       education programs after 1986.

                       Effective July 1, 1997, candidates must have a bachelor's degree, meet
                       the required Praxis I scores, and pass the Praxis II Specialty Area test.

GRADE LEVELS AND/OR SUBJECT AREAS COVERED:

                       Limited to these 18 areas:

                       Art Education   Marketing
                       Biology   Mathematics
                       Business Education   Music
                       Chemistry   Physical Education
                       Elementary Education   Physics
                           (grades 4-8 only)   Social Studies
                       English   Spanish
                       French   Speech Communication
                       German   Technology Education
                       Home Economics

WHO OPERATES: The college or university administers the MAT
                    through the graduate program.

REQUIREMENTS TO ENTER:

                       A candidate must:

                               Hold a bachelor's degree in a non-education major from a
                               regionally/nationally accredited institution of higher learning.

                               Enroll in a Master of Arts program.

PROGRAM DESCRIPTION:

The Master of Arts in Teaching Program is an alternate route program.

A candidate must pass both the Praxis I (Pre-Professional Skills Test [PPST]) and the Praxis II (Specialty Area Tests).

A candidate must complete a total of 30 to 33 semester hours of specified graduate coursework over a period of three years.

This coursework includes six (6) semester hours of pre-teaching course requirements from an approved Master of Arts in Teaching Program, including an internship prescribed by the participating college or university. And the candidate must provide program verification.

NUMBER OF CREDIT HOURS TO COMPLETE: 30 to 33 semester hours of coursework.

WHO OPERATES: The college or university administers the MAT through the graduate program.

LENGTH OF TIME: Three years; non-renewable.

Institutions of higher education that have developed alternative teacher preparation programs leading to a teaching license:

N/A

States with which the state has reciprocity of teacher licenses:

All. NASDTEC Interstate Contract.

Institutions of higher education that have *any* teacher preparation programs leading to a license to teach.

Alcorn State University
Belhaven College
Blue Mountain College
Delta State University
Jackson State University
Millsaps College
Mississippi College
Mississippi State University

Mississippi University for Women
Mississippi Valley State University
Rust College
Tougaloo College
University of Mississippi
University of Southern Mississippi
William Carey College

Contact information for persons interested in finding a teaching position in the state:

Daphne Buckley, Director
Mississippi Teacher Center
Mississippi Department of Education
P.O. Box 771
Jackson, MS 39205
Phone: (601) 359-3631

TITLE: Temporary Authorization Certificate

HISTORY: Approved November 30, 2000

                Amended September 4, 2003

MOTIVATION: The state has experienced shortages of teachers in certain content areas and in some local education agencies. This certificate was designed to allow qualifying individuals to obtain a temporary certificate of license to teach while working toward full professional certification.

SUBJECT AREAS COVERED:

All subjects and grade levels except early childhood, birth-grade 3; early childhood special education, birth-grade 3; blind or partially sighted, birth-grade 12; deaf and hearing impaired, birth-grade 12. Applicants for a temporary authorization certificate in driver's education, ESOL, gifted, and special reading must hold a certificate of license to teach or complete a certificate of license to teach in a stand-alone subject area.

WHO OPERATES: State Department of Elementary and Secondary Education

REQUIREMENTS TO ENTER:

Applicant must hold a Bachelor's degree from an accredited college or university in the content area to be taught or closely related field, or demonstrate exceptional experience in the subject area to be taught;

Applicant must have a GPA of 2.5 or higher on a 4.0 scale;

Applicant must be able to verify contracted employment with a Missouri public school district or accredited non-public school;

Applicant must complete a background check with the Missouri State Highway Patrol and/or the FBI.

PROGRAM DESCRIPTION:

The temporary authorization certificate (TAC) is valid for up to one (1) school year. It may be renewed annually by joint application from the certificate holder and the employing Missouri public school district or accredited nonpublic school upon demonstration of the following:

- Continued contracted employment with a Missouri public school district or accredited nonpublic school;

- Documentation of successful Performance Based Teacher Evaluation by the sponsoring Missouri public school district or accredited nonpublic school;

- Documentation of participation in a mentoring program by the sponsoring Missouri public school district or accredited nonpublic school;

- Taking both the Praxis II assessments, one (1) content knowledge or specialty area assessment and two (2) principles of learning and teaching for the specific grade level. An individual who currently possesses a professional certificate of license to teach will be exempted from taking the principles of learning and teaching;

- **Note:** Failure to achieve the Missouri qualifying score on either of these assessments shall be used by the certificate holder and a teacher preparation program to identify priority classes for further study; and

- Completion of nine (9) semester hours of course work toward the professional certificate of license to teach in the area of assignment.

An individual may qualify for a professional classification certificate of license to teach upon documentation of the following:

- The certificate holder has been teaching under a temporary authorization certificate of license to teach for a minimum of three (3) years;

- Achievement of the Missouri qualifying score on both the Praxis II assessments, one (1) content knowledge or specialty area assessment and two (2) principles of learning and teaching for the specific grade levels;

- Documentation of successful performance based teacher evaluation by the sponsoring Missouri public school district or accredited nonpublic school;

- Documentation of participation in a mentoring program by the sponsoring Missouri public school district or accredited nonpublic school; and

- Documentation of key course work in education as listed below:

1. Course work in education not to exceed twenty-four (24) credit hours for any temporary authorization certificate (excluding an administrator's and/or special education temporary certificate) to include competencies in:

     a. Psychology of the Exceptional Child;
     b. Behavioral Management Techniques;
     c. Measurement and Evaluation;
     d. Teaching Methods/Instructional Strategies;
     e. Methods of Teaching Reading at the appropriate level;

f. Developmental Psychology at the appropriate level; and

g. Beginning Teacher Assistance; or

2. Course work in education not to exceed twenty-nine (29) credit hours for a special education temporary authorization certificate to include competencies in the following areas:

   a. Psychology of the Exceptional Child;

   b. Behavioral Management Techniques or Supporting Challenging Behavior;

   c. Evaluation of Abilities and Achievement (to include Intelligence Testing);

   d. Introduction to Teaching Students in one of the following areas:

      (I) Cross-Categorical Disabilities; or
      (II) Severely Developmentally Disabled;

   e. Methods of Teaching Students in one (1) of the following areas:

      (I) Cross-Categorical Disabilities; or
      (II) Severely Developmentally Disabled;

   f. Methods of Teaching Reading:

      (I) Reading Methods; and
      (II) Analysis and Correction of Reading Disabilities;

   g. Methods of Teaching Mathematics:

      (I) Mathematics Methods; and
      (II) Methods of Teaching Remedial Mathematics;

   h. Counseling Techniques or Collaboration with Family, School and Community;

   i. Selection and use of assistive technology such as augmentative communication systems (only for the Severely Developmentally Disabled certificate of license to teach);

   j. Alternative formats for communication including: nonverbal communication systems (only for the Severely Developmentally Disabled certificate of license to teach); and

   k. Speech and Language Development of the Exceptional Child (only for the Severely Developmentally Disabled certificate of license to teach).

NO. OF CREDIT HOURS TO COMPLETE:

WHO EVALUATES: State Department of Elementary and Secondary Education

LENGTH OF TIME: Maximum of three years

OTHER: See http://dese.mo.gov/schoollaw/rulesregs/80800260.htm

TITLE: Missouri Alternative Certification Program Model

HISTORY: Approved October 25, 2001.

MOTIVATION: To provide an avenue for entry into the teaching profession by individuals who have not completed a traditional teacher education program.

GRADE LEVELS AND/OR SUBJECT AREAS COVERED:

WHO OPERATES: Some institutions for higher education in Missouri have been granted approval by the Missouri Department of Elementary and Secondary Education (DESE) to operate alternative programs for teacher certification. These programs are designed for non-traditional students seeking certification in critical need areas.

REQUIREMENTS TO ENTER:

The candidate must present evidence of employment by a school district in the State of Missouri contingent upon certification prior to acceptance into a Missouri Alternative Certification Program.

The candidate shall undergo a background check conducted by the Missouri Highway Patrol and the Federal Bureau of Investigation (FBI), which includes submitting to DESE two (2) full sets of fingerprints on forms provided by the board and completed by any law enforcement agency. The candidate is responsible for the payment of any fees required by the Missouri Highway Patrol and/or FBI.

The candidate shall have earned a bachelor's or higher degree in the content area or a closely allied field of the desired certificate of license to teach from a regionally accredited institution and shall have a cumulative grade point average no lower than the Missouri requirement for teacher certification (2.5 on a 4.0 scale) and a grade point average no lower than 2.5 in the major (content) area.

The candidate shall participate in a structured interview conducted by the teacher education institution to assess the candidate's beliefs regarding the nature of teaching, the nature of students and the mission and goals of education as a profession. The interview is utilized for screening, diagnostic and advising purposes.

The candidate shall enter into a four-party contract with the recommending institution, the employing school district and the Department of Elementary and Secondary Education. This contract will enable the candidate to enroll in coursework which addresses:

1. Adolescent Development.

2. The Psychology of Learning.

3. Teaching Methodology in the Content Area.

This coursework must be completed prior to provisional certification and entry into the classroom.

PROGRAM DESCRIPTION:

Upon successful completion of the coursework outlined above and upon recommendation of the higher education institution, candidates will receive a two-year provisional certificate. The candidate will:

1. Be assigned a mentor by the school district;

2. Receive additional assistance from the higher education institution;

3. Participate in the employing district's professional development program;

4. Successfully participate in the district's Performance Based Teacher Evaluation (PBTE); and

5. Continue professional growth to include thirty (30) clock-hours of in-service training as defined in criteria established by the board.

Candidates shall complete at least 8 semester hours of professional education coursework no later than the summer following the awarding of the provisional certificate.

Prior to the expiration of the provisional certificate of license to teach, the candidate must successfully complete the exit assessment designated by the State Board of Education. The exit assessment and the provisions outlined in the previous subsection must be completed prior to being granted an Initial Professional Certificate (IPC) of License to Teach.

Institutions will be responsible for the recommendation of candidates who complete innovative or alternative certification programs for professional certification in the same manner as those completing conventional programs according to the rules promulgated by the board.

NUMBER OF CREDIT HOURS TO COMPLETE:

Determined by IHE.

WHO EVALUATES: IHE

LENGTH OF TIME: Two years.

OTHER: Alternative Certification Programs (ACP) are designed for non-traditional students seeking certification in certain areas of critical need. Other information regarding program requirements may be found at http://dese.mo.gov/schoollaw/rulesregs/80805030.html

See complete list of approved programs at:
http://dese.mo.gov/divteachqual/teached/altcertprog.htm

Institutions of higher education with approved alternative teacher preparation programs leading to a teaching license:

Columbia College
Drury University
Missouri Baptist University
Missouri Southern State University
Missouri Western State College
Northwest Missouri State University
Park University
Southeast Missouri State University
Southwest Baptist University

Southwest Missouri State University
Truman State University
University of Central Missouri
University of Missouri-Columbia
University of Missouri-Kansas City
University of Missouri-St. Louis
Washington University
William Woods University
William Jewell College

States with which the state has reciprocity of teacher licenses:

NONE

Institutions of higher education that have *any* teacher preparation programs leading to a license to teach.

Avila University
Baptist Bible College
Central Methodist University
College of the Ozarks
Columbia College
Culver-Stockton College
Drury University
Evangel University
Fontbonne University
Hannibal LaGrange College
Harris-Stowe State University
Lincoln University
Lindenwood University
Maryville University
Missouri Baptist University
Missouri Southern State University
Missouri State University
Missouri Valley College
Missouri Western State University

Northwest Missouri State University
Park University
Rockhurst University
Saint Louis University
Southeast Missouri State University
Southwest Baptist University
Stephens College
Truman State University
University of Central Missouri
University of Missouri-Columbia
University of Missouri-Kansas City
University of Missouri-Rolla
University of Missouri-St. Louis
Washington University
Webster University
Westminster College
William Woods University
William Jewell College

Contact information for persons interested in finding a teaching position in the state:

Rosalyn Wieberg, Director
Educator Recruitment and Retention
Department of Elementary and Secondary Education
P.O. Box 480
Jefferson City, MO 65102-0480
Phone: (573) 751-1668 Web: http://www.moteachingjobs.com

TITLE: Class 5 (Alternative) Teaching Certificate

HISTORY: Enacted: 1975, Amended: 1976, 1978, 1980,
                      1982, 1984, 1985, 1986, 1995, 2002.

MOTIVATION: May be issued to applicants who have major
                      preparation toward regular licensure, but have
                      minor discrepancies such as lack of recent credits or
                      program deficiencies. Initiated to provide additional
                      avenue for licensure for the non-traditional
                      applicant.

SUBJECT AREAS COVERED: Elementary and Secondary Teaching Areas.

WHO OPERATES: Office of Public Instruction, Educator Licensure.

REQUIREMENTS TO ENTER:

The applicant receives and signs a plan of professional intent which
commits the applicant to a program leading to regular licensure. The
plan of professional intent initiates with the licensure office and the
applicant contacts a university to complete a professional educator
preparation program.

Elementary level: Elementary level endorsement is granted to an
applicant who submits acceptable evidence of a partially completed
elementary education program, and that the following minimum
requirements have been met:

Bachelor's degree from a regionally accredited college or university.

Minimum of 60 semester credits of academic preparation in acceptable
balance in language arts and literature, history, government and
related social science, mathematics, and any two of the following: art,
music, foreign languages, speech, dramatics, library science or health.
Professional preparation to include human growth and development,
the teaching of reading or language arts, social science and arithmetic,
and student teaching or appropriate intern experiences.

Secondary level: Secondary level endorsement is granted to an
applicant who submits acceptable evidence of a partially completed
secondary education program, and that the following minimum
requirements have been met:

Bachelor's degree from a regionally accredited college or university.

Major preparation of at least 30 semester credits in an area commonly offered in high school programs in Montana and approved by the Board of Public Education for endorsement;

6 semester credits of education coursework.

PROGRAM DESCRIPTION:

The individual must make yearly progress toward completing deficiencies for full licensure.

NUMBER OF CREDIT HOURS TO COMPLETE:

Depends on the college program the individual plans to complete.

WHO EVALUATES: The state licensure office evaluates for initial licensure; the college must verify completion of program before full licensure can be granted.

LENGTH OF TIME: Three years, not renewable and cannot be reinstated.

Institutions of higher education that have developed alternative teacher preparation programs leading to a teaching license:

Montana State University-Northern Plains Transition to Teaching Program
www.montana.edu/nptt

States with which the state has reciprocity of teacher licenses:

NASDTEC Interstate Contract.

Montana currently offers reciprocity to educators that hold a current valid out-of state license who have:

Completed an NCATE of state board approved professional educator preparation program;

Hold a bachelor's degree from a regionally accredited college or university; and

Completed student teaching or at least one year of teaching experience.

Institutions of higher education that have *any* professional educator preparation programs leading to a license to teach.

Carroll College
Montana State University - Billings
Montana State University - Bozeman
Montana State University - Northern

Rocky Mountain College
University of Great Falls
University of Montana
University of Montana - Western

Contact information for persons interested in finding a teaching position in the state:

Contact the Career Placement offices of the Montana universities. Also, access the Internet at the following address: http://jsd.dli.mt.gov.

Contact the Office of Public Instruction at the following address: http://jobsforteachers.opi.mt.gov

TITLE: Transitional Route to Regular Teacher Certification

HISTORY: Implementation begun in 2003.

MOTIVATION: 1. Shortage in some teaching areas.

                         2. Mid-life career changers and recent college
                         graduates with a BA/BS degree in an endorseable
                         area.

GRADE LEVELS AND/OR SUBJECT AREAS COVERED:

                         Secondary areas: (Elementary, Middle Grades and Special Education
                         not included.)

WHO OPERATES: SEA, IHE, LEA -- collaboratively.

REQUIREMENTS TO ENTER:

                         1. Hold a baccalaureate degree with 75% of the content required by
                         Rule 24 for the required endorsement.

                         2. Complete 3 professional education on-line modules (18 hours).

                         3. Submit transcripts and other application materials to the Nebraska
                         Statewide Assessment Center.

                         4. Develop a Transitional Plan that leads to regular certification
                         within 6 years of initial application.

                         5. Complete at least 6 hours each academic year to be eligible for
                         Transitional Certificate renewal.

PROGRAM DESCRIPTION:

                         According to the state:

                         "It provides for the person who holds a degree in specified areas to
                         begin teaching with none of the pedagogical hours of teacher education
                         having been completed. This provides access to teaching much earlier

than the older 'provisional' certificate, which required half or more of the pedagogy to be completed. The new plan, however, does not excuse the applicant from eventually completing the teacher education program in its entirety. It also requires substantial participation and up-front commitment from an employer and a teacher education institution. It is not available in elementary education, or in special education or middle grades. It attempts to address areas of critical and continuous shortage.

NUMBER OF CREDIT HOURS TO COMPLETE: Varies.

WHO EVALUATES: IHE.

LENGTH OF TIME: Six years -- one year each; renewable.

TITLE: Provisional Commitment Teaching Certificate

HISTORY: Authorized by Rule 21. Current version effective 12/03.

GRADE LEVELS AND/OR SUBJECT AREAS COVERED: All.

WHO OPERATES: IHE and SEA.

REQUIREMENTS TO ENTER:

The holder of the certificate is limited to the school requesting its issuance.

The individual must:

Submit a written request for issuance of the certificate from the superintendent or governing body of the local school district;

Have received a baccalaureate degree;

Have completed at least one-half of the pre-student teaching requirements of an approved teacher education program, including a course in teaching methods;

Have fulfilled three-quarters of the requirements for a subject or full endorsement;

Submit a statement of intent to fulfill his/her remaining program and endorsement requirements during the period in which the certificate is in effect or to make sure progress (at least six semester hours) which fulfills some or all of the remaining requirements.

The applicant must have achieved a minimum score on the Pre-Professional Skills Test unless he/she has previously held a regular (not provisional) Nebraska teaching certificate.

The applicant must complete a qualifying course in human relations training or submit a narrative describing qualifying work experience to fulfill the requirement. The narrative must be verified by a supervisor of the work experience.

The applicant must complete a qualifying three-hour course in special education or a narrative as prescribed by NDE.

The applicant must submit to a criminal history background check (fingerprints) if not a five-year or longer Nebraska resident or holder of a previous Nebraska certificate.

PROGRAM DESCRIPTION:

While teaching with a Provisional Certificate, the individual must complete 6 semester hours of credit for college coursework which fulfills some or all of his/her remaining program or endorsement requirements.

Each year, the individual must submit an application and a written request for renewal of the certificate from his/her employing school district and official transcript that documents completion of 6 hours.

NUMBER OF CREDIT HOURS TO COMPLETE:

Six (6) semester hours per year toward completing certification requirements.

WHO EVALUATES: IHE and SEA.

LENGTH OF TIME: Valid for one year. Renewable if specified progress toward completion of an IHE teacher education program is being made.

TITLE: Provisional Re-Entry Teaching Certificate

HISTORY: Effective November 12, 2000.

MOTIVATION: To provide that teachers who have been long-absent
                     from the classroom are re-tooled to be successful in
                     today's classroom.

GRADE LEVELS AND/OR SUBJECT AREAS COVERED: All.

WHO OPERATES: SEA, IHE, and LEA.

REQUIREMENTS TO ENTER:

                     Have held a lapsed regular Nebraska or other state certificate.

                     Have teaching employment in a school.

PROGRAM DESCRIPTION:

                     The individual must complete 15 semester hours of specified credit to
                     return to a regular certificate -- 6 semester hours per year -- if the
                     regular certificate is lapsed by five or more years.

                     Coursework includes school law, issues in education, curriculum
                     updating, and 100 hours of in-class practicum.

NUMBER OF CREDIT HOURS TO COMPLETE:

                     15 semester hours -- 6 hours per year. A structured program, not free
                     choice.

WHO EVALUATES: SEA and IHE.

LENGTH OF TIME: One year. Renewable if progress (6 semester hours)
                     is made.

OTHER: The human relations training course -- which is
                     mandatory for all certificate holders -- may be
                     included in the required 15 semester hours.

TITLE: Provisional Trades Teaching Certificate

HISTORY: Effective April 29, 1997.

MOTIVATION: Shortage of industrial-construction trades
                     teachers; former military teaching ROTC.

GRADE LEVELS AND/OR SUBJECT AREAS COVERED:

High school only. ROTC; industrial-construction trades, welding,
drafting, metals, graphic arts, electricity, electronics, auto.

WHO OPERATES: SEA and LEA.

REQUIREMENTS TO ENTER:

Requirements for the first issuance of the Professional Trades
Certificate, regardless of endorsement, are:

The holder of the certificate is limited to the school requesting its
issuance and may teach only in the subject, subject field, or area of
specialization and at the grade level specified.

The individual must:

1. Complete the application form.

2. Pay the application fee.

3. Submit, with the application, a written request for the
issuance of the certificate from the superintendent of the
employing school system or from the governing body of the
school system or from the personnel director of the employing
school system.

4. Pass one of the prescribed basic skills competency tests
required of teachers, and have a score report sent to the
Department of Education, Teacher Certification Office.

5. Successfully complete a qualifying human relations training
class required of all Nebraska teachers and have the official
transcript (not the grade report) sent to the Teacher Certification
Office. (A list of approved courses will be provided by the
Teacher Certification Office, upon request.) A narrative may be
submitted in lieu of the described course-work.

6. Successfully complete one or more semester hour course in a four-year college which trains teachers on special education (this must be a survey course covering all handicapping conditions). A narrative may be submitted in lieu of the described course-work.

7. If fingerprinting is required (see the application form for more information) submit fingerprints as specified in the special fingerprint memo and use the special fingerprint envelope, available from the Department of Education, and pay the additional $40 for fingerprinting.

* The renewed Provisional Trades Certificate is valid for three years and may be renewed for an unlimited number of times by meeting requirements 1, 2 and 3, and the verification of experience or the completion of three semester hours of credit. But, it never becomes a regular certificate.

** Persons who have not completed one, two, or all three requirements (4, 5 and 6) but who are employed in a Nebraska school system may be eligible to receive a one-year temporary or provisional certificate. The requirements which are not met must be completed to receive any further certification.

*** Persons who have submitted fingerprints but for whom the report of the fingerprint investigation by the Nebraska State Patrol and the Federal Bureau of Investigation is not yet completed may be eligible to receive a conditional permit, allowing teaching to be done.

PROGRAM DESCRIPTION:

● Requirements for ENDORSEMENTS on the Professional Trades Certificate:

Other trade or industrial endorsements, such as welding, auto body, construction trades, and other true 'trades areas' are based on one or more of the following qualifiers:

- Completion of a prescribed course of study in a community college or other technical trade institution.

OR

- Completion of an apprenticeship program in the trade;

OR

- Passing a proficiency examination approved by the particular trade or industry;

OR

- Demonstrated proficiency in the trade over five years of employment in the trade;

OR

- Current employment by a community college as an instructor to teach the specific trade or skill.

These endorsements generally are NOT available through traditional teacher training and do not appear on a regular teaching certificate.

- Requirements for the <u>Reserve Officers Training Corps (ROTC) endorsement</u>:

    This endorsement requires four years of full-time experience in the military, as well as a recommendation from a former military supervisor.

NUMBER OF CREDIT HOURS TO COMPLETE: N/A.

WHO EVALUATES: SEA.

LENGTH OF TIME: One year (1st certificate); three years (subsequent).

Institutions of higher education that have developed alternative teacher preparation programs leading to a teaching license:

Chadron State College – Accelerated Certification
University of Nebraska-Kearney – Online Professional Sequence
University of Nebraska-Lincoln – Project Experience

States with which the state has reciprocity of teacher licenses:

Note: Nebraska is a signatory to the MOINKAS regional exchange agreement -- with Arkansas, Illinois, Michigan, Missouri, Iowa, Kansas, Oklahoma, South Dakota and Wisconsin-- for two-year temporary certificate only.

Nebraska is a signatory of the NASDTEC Interstate teacher reciprocity agreement 2000-2005.

Institutions of higher education that have an approved teacher preparation programs leading to a license to teach.

Chadron State College
College of St. Mary
Concordia Teachers College
Creighton University
Dana College
Doane College
Grace University
Hastings College
Midland Lutheran College

Nebraska Wesleyan University
Peru State College
Union College
University of Nebraska-Kearney
University of Nebraska-Lincoln
University of Nebraska-Omaha
Wayne State College
York College

Contact information for persons interested in finding a teaching position in the state:

Teach in Nebraska Web site: http://www.nebraskaeducationjobs.com

Note: Contact the personnel office of the school system in which employment is desired.

To obtain a copy of the Nebraska Educational Directory, download it from the state's Web page at: http://www.nde.state.ne.us.

The Directory contains lists of school districts, county education officials, enrollments by grade in every school district in the state, faculty names by school building, and a wealth of similar and related data. Current year data are available after November.

Nebraska Department of Education
Teacher Education/Certification
P.O. Box 94987
301 Centennial Mall South
Lincoln, NE 68509-4987
Attn: Marge Harouff
Phone: (402) 471-4800 Fax: (402) 471-8127

TITLE: Alternative License

MOTIVATION: An alternate route to licensing for holders of a Bachelor's (or higher) degree to answer A Call To Teach.

GRADE LEVELS AND/OR SUBJECT AREAS COVERED: Early childhood, Elementary, Secondary (high need areas), and most Special Education endorsements.

WHO OPERATES: An employing school district, charter school or private school, in conjunction with an accredited college/university, and with the approval of the Nevada Department of Education.

REQUIREMENTS TO ENTER:

Bachelor's degree or higher

Passage of Praxis I (or qualified exemption).

Additional entrance requirements are specific to the grade level or type of license being sought and can include a defined number of credits in pedagogically related courses, qualifying degree majors and Praxis II subject area testing.

PROGRAM DESCRIPTION:

An Alternative license can be issued to an individual only at the request of an employing school district, charter school or private school and is restricted to use with the employing entity.

Upon completion of the approved teacher education program and three years of satisfactory teaching experience (student teaching can be waived), the holder of the Alternative license is eligible for a renewable State of Nevada License for Educational Personnel.

NUMBER OF CREDIT HOURS TO COMPLETE: 6 semester hours.

WHO EVALUATES: SEA.

LENGTH OF TIME: Three years.

OTHER: Nevada does not issue a temporary permit, emergency license, a license issued only by examination, a letter of entitlement/eligibility, or a license that does not require professional education course work completed through a regionally accredited college or university.

Institutions of higher education that have developed alternative teacher preparation programs leading to a teaching license:

Great Basin College
Nevada State College
Sierra Nevada College
University of Nevada-Las Vegas
University of Nevada-Reno
Rio Salado College (Arizona online program-Troops to Teachers)

Institutions of higher education that have *any* teacher preparation programs leading to a license to teach.

In addition to those listed above, the following have been approved to offer specific degree or licensure-only-state-approved programs in Nevada:

Nova Southeastern University (Florida)
Regis University (Colorado)
Touro University Nevada
University of Phoenix (Arizona)
Western Governor's University (Utah)

States with which the state has reciprocity of teacher licenses:

NASTEC Interstate Contract. Specific requirements governing Nevada's requirements for reciprocity can be found on our website at:

http:// **www.doe.nv.gov/licensing/license-reciprocity.html**

Contact information for persons interested in finding a teaching position in the state:

Each school district, charter school or private school must be contacted directly.

Contact information for persons interested in finding a teaching position in the state:

Note: Each school district must be contacted.

TITLE: Alternative 5: Site-Based Certification Plan

HISTORY: Effective Nov. 20, 1990.

MOTIVATION: Response to growing numbers of adults who already
                      have a bachelor's degree in a field other than
                      education and who want to become licensed to
                      teach.

GRADE LEVELS AND/OR SUBJECT AREA(S) COVERED:

                      Elementary and secondary content areas.

WHO OPERATES: State determines eligibility; LEA recommends
                      candidate for certification.

REQUIREMENTS TO ENTER:

                      The candidate shall possess a bachelor's degree from an institution
                      approved by the New Hampshire Post Secondary Education
                      Commission or a regional accrediting agency such as, but not limited
                      to, the Northeast Regional Association of Schools and Colleges; and the
                      candidate shall meet one of the following criteria:

                              a. For secondary education, candidates shall possess the
                              equivalent of a 30 credit collegiate major in the subject to be
                              taught and an overall grade point average of 2.5 or equivalent.

                              b. For elementary education, candidates shall possess a four-
                              year arts and sciences background, which includes one each of
                              an English, Mathematics, Science and Social Science and an
                              overall grade point average of 2.5 or the equivalent.

                      An individual who fails to meet the grade point average requirement
                      may still qualify for consideration providing:

                              a. All other requirements are met; and

                              b. Collegiate graduation occurred more than five (5) years prior
                              to application for the provisional plan, and

                              c. Five years of occupational experience directly related to the
                              area to be taught is documented.

Candidates who meet the requirements of part (b) of this section shall be issued a Statement of Eligibility by the Bureau of Credentialing, Division of Program Support. The Bureau of Credentialing shall maintain a list of individuals who have been issued Statement of Eligibilities.

Equivalence of credits shall be determined through analysis of such information as number of contact hours, course titles, course syllabi, required projects, and data of official transcripts. The required level of academic performance shall be equivalent to a 2.5 in a 4.0 system and shall be determined by mathematical computation or by analysis of such documents as academic recommendations.

Documentation of experience may consist of, but not be limited to, letters from previous employers, employment contracts and letters of commendation and recommendations from parties knowledgeable about the candidate's background and experience.

PROGRAM DESCRIPTION:

Superintendents or their designees may hire those individuals who possess a Statement of Eligibility, provided that the employing district agrees to the following conditions:

1. The site-based certification plan shall be developed collaboratively and agreed to by the applicant and the Superintendent of Schools.

2. The mentor shall be appointed by the superintendent of schools.

3. The mentor shall be certified in the same subject area that the applicant will be teaching and hold a valid Experienced Educator Credential with the appropriate endorsements in the same subject area in which the applicant is seeking to obtain a credential.

4. The mentor, building principal, teacher candidate, and others who may be designated by the Superintendent to be responsible for the work of the candidate shall develop the candidate's education plan.

5. The plan shall include professional education requirements, content area standards, and contain a description of how the applicant plans to meet these competencies.

6. The superintendent shall file with the Bureau of Credentialing a copy of the completed site-based plan and a description of the candidate's teaching assignment.

7. The site-based certification plan shall be completed during the period of the intern license which is valid for 1-2 years.

8. The site-based certification plan shall be developed and filed with the Bbureau. The plan may be modified by those responsible for the work of the applicant, but any modifications shall be filed with the Bureau.

9. Upon completion of the site-based certification plan, the superintendent shall submit a statement to the Bureau verifying that all portions of the plan have been implemented by the district and satisfactorily completed by the applicant. This statement shall include a recommendation for certification.

10. A positive recommendation shall not obligate a school district to continue the employment of an applicant.

11. Failure by a candidate to complete the site-based certification plan shall result in a negative certification recommendation by the superintendent.

12. Upon successful completion of the site-based certification plan and the superintendent's positive recommendation, the Bureau shall issue the credential with the endorsement sought by the applicant.

NUMBER OF CREDIT HOURS TO COMPLETE: N/A

WHO EVALUATES: State and LEA.

LENGTH OF TIME: Two years.

TITLE: Alternative 4: Individual Professional Development Plan
(Restricted)

HISTORY: New Hampshire Code of Administrative Rules,
                     effective Nov. 1, 1989.

MOTIVATION: Critical shortage.

WHO OPERATES: State.

REQUIREMENTS TO ENTER:

Employment as an educator and by completion, a bachelor's degree
from a college or university approved by an accrediting agency or state.

Minimum course/experience requirements for each endorsement area
as designated on Critical Shortage Memo.

PROGRAM DESCRIPTION:

In August, the state conducts a survey of school district
superintendents to see if they are having difficulty employing teachers
in any areas. *The state also reviews the number of graduates of in state*
teacher education institutions.

On the basis of these data, the state decides if there are critical needs
and, if so, in what areas, and prepares a list of specialties needed.

The LEA assigns a mentor certified in the content area to monitor and
develop an Individualized Professional Development Plan (IPDP) for the
teacher – The candidate has three years to complete the plan.

The teacher may be required to complete additional preparation at a
college.

NUMBER OF CREDIT HOURS TO COMPLETE: N/A

WHO EVALUATES: State.

LENGTH OF TIME: Three years from the time the Individualized
                    Professional Development Plan (IPDP) is approved.

TITLE: Conversion Programs

HISTORY: The New Hampshire Code of Administrative Rules,
                      effective Nov. 1, 1989.

MOTIVATION: "Conversion programs shall be specifically designed
                      to prepare for teacher certification persons who hold
                      baccalaureate degrees."

GRADE LEVELS AND/OR SUBJECT AREA(S) COVERED: Not specified.

WHO OPERATES: IHE.

REQUIREMENTS TO ENTER:

Programs must meet the following criteria:

Responsibility for assuring the quality of programs will be centralized
in a single specifically designated administrative unit.

Conversion programs shall be consistent with the philosophy and
objectives upon which all other education programs are based. Data
should be available to indicate that consistency exists.

One person shall be responsible for coordinating conversion programs
within each administrative unit (institution).

There will be published criteria for admission to the program.

Life experience may be accepted by the institution subject to the
following provisions:

1. No more than one-third (1/3) of the total work required for
any individual conversion program may be satisfied by life
experience.

2. A system for evaluation of life experience shall assure that:

a. experience is related to specific areas in general education,
professional education, or specialty area competency. These
are listed in Ed 609, 610, 611 and 612.

b. documentation must be provided for any life experience.

STANDARDS FOR CONVERSION PROGRAMS

The program involves individuals being given transcript evaluation by an IHE, which determines coursework and student teaching which must be completed. Conversion programs are approved by the State Department of Education.

Student Teaching. Student teaching procedures must conform to the following:

1. Any student admitted to student teaching must be competent in the basic skills of reading, writing, and mathematics according to the same criteria established for the school's undergraduate programs.

2. Student teaching or other major practicum must meet all the provisions of Ed 610.07.

Previous Collegiate Training. A process must exist to assure that any previous collegiate training is consistent with recent developments in general education, professional education, and any specialty area.

Counseling and Advising Students. Advisors must assist students in structuring individual programs designed to maximize strengths, overcome weaknesses, and reflect attention to a variety of backgrounds and potential.

NUMBER OF CREDIT HOURS TO COMPLETE:

Varies according to background and training.

WHO EVALUATES: College officials.

LENGTH OF TIME: Varies.

TITLE: Alternative 3: Demonstrated Competencies and Equivalent Experiences

HISTORY: New Hampshire Code of Administrative Rules,
                     effective 1976.

GRADE LEVELS AND/OR SUBJECT AREA(S) COVERED: Elementary and Secondary
teachers, specialists and administrators.

WHO OPERATES: State.

REQUIREMENTS TO ENTER:

> Bachelor's Degree

> Individual must successfully complete written portfolio, written test,
> and an oral board review showing the same level of competencies
> required of a beginning educator who has been through a teacher
> education program.

PROGRAM DESCRIPTION:

> The individual submits a written portfolio that is reviewed by the Board
> of Examiners prior to the oral review.

> The state agency sets up a half-day verbal interview by three board
> examiners -- a state officer and two EDUCATORS CERTIFIED in the
> subject field. These are not scheduled during the summer months.

> The examiners may recommend to the state that the individual be
> licensed if he or she has the same beginning level of competency as a
> traditionally trained educator.

NO. OF CREDIT HOURS TO COMPLETE: Not applicable.

WHO EVALUATES: State.

LENGTH OF TIME: Recommendations of having the written piece
                   completed within six (6) months of receipt of
                   materials.

Institutions of higher education that have developed alternative teacher preparation programs leading to a teaching license:

College for Lifelong Learning – Special Education Teacher Training For Special Education certification and some categorical areas.

States with which the state has reciprocity of teacher licenses:

Not limited to NASDTEC Interstate Contract and other states and jurisdictions.

Institutions of higher education that have *any* teacher preparation programs leading to a license to teach.

Antioch/New England Graduate School
Chester College
Colby Sawyer College
College for Lifelong Learning (UNH)
Dartmouth College
Franklin Pierce College
Keene State College

New England College
Plymouth State University
Rivier College
Saint Anselm College
Southern New Hampshire University
University of New Hampshire
Upper Valley Institute

Contact information for persons interested in finding a teaching position in the state:

http://www.ed.state.nh.us/education/doe/employ.htm

Bureau of Credentialing
New Hampshire Department of Education
101 Pleasant Street
Concord, NH 03301

Main Contact
Robin Warner, Administrator
Tel: 603-271-4196

Alternative 2
Jean H. Smolen, Program Specialist
Tel: 603-271-3872

Alternative 3
Arthur Brown, Education Consultant
Tel: 603-271-3874

Alternative 4
Arthur Brown, Education Consultant
Tel: 603-271-3874

Alternative 5
Jean H. Smolen, Program Specialist
Tel: 603-271-3872

TITLE: Provisional Teacher Program – Alternate Route

HISTORY: Adopted by the State Board of Education in Sept. 1984. New licensing regulations approved by the State Board of Education in January 2004 have expanded areas in which an alternate route is available to include students with disabilities (special education), bi-lingual/bi-cultural, and English as a Second Language

MOTIVATION: The Provisional Teacher Program – Alternate Route is intended to enhance both the quantity and quality of teaching candidates.

GRADE LEVELS AND/OR SUBJECT AREAS COVERED:

All.

WHO OPERATES: LEAs, supported by district consortia and colleges of education that are providing formal instruction, with coordination and authority provided by the State Department of Education.

REQUIREMENTS TO ENTER:

To be eligible for employment in the Provisional Teacher Program, applicants must present completion of the following:

1. Bachelor's degree from an accredited institution.

2. For secondary candidates: a major in the subject teaching field (e.g. English, mathematics). For elementary and pre-school through grade three candidates: a major in the liberal arts or sciences. Details about additional eligibility requirements for vocational, ESL, bi-lingual/bi-cultural, and special education certificates of eligibility are available on the New Jersey Department of Education website at: nj.gov/njded/educators/license.

3. Test requirement -- Applicants for certification in a subject teaching field must pass the appropriate Praxis II Subject Assessment/NTE Programs Specialty Area tests. Applicants for certification in elementary education must pass the Elementary Ed: Content Knowledge Test. Candidates in the following subject teaching fields available through the Alternate Route are exempt at this time from the test requirement: foreign languages other than French, German, and Spanish; health education; psychology; English as a second language, bi-lingual/bi-cultural, pre-school through

grade three, special education, military science, and vocational education.

4. Cumulative grade point average (GPA) requirement of 2.5 or higher on a 4.0 scale. Candidates graduating on or after Sept. 1, 2004, will be required to hold a GPA of 2.75 or higher.

Upon completion of the above requirements, a candidate receives a Certificate of Eligibility, which provides the opportunity to seek employment through the Provisional Teacher Program.

When offered employment, applicants are advised of documents required before a provisional license can be issued. A provisional license is required to legalize employment during the 34-week Provisional Teacher Program.

PROGRAM DESCRIPTION:

Provisional teachers attend a program of formal instruction that takes place concurrently with employment during the first year. This instruction supplements a program of on-the-job mentoring, support, and evaluation, aimed at developing and documenting the teacher's instructional competency. In 2003-2004, the Department began piloting a 20 hour pre-service experience for holders of Certificates of Eligibility. Also, several alternate route MAT programs were approved to provide formal instruction programs that lead to a graduate degree.

Mentoring is arranged by the local district and provided by an experienced mentor teacher. Other professionals, as determined by the district, may also participate.

After successful completion of the program, provisional teachers are eligible to be recommended for standard licensure in the teaching area(s) listed in the Certificate of Eligibility. Certificates are issued in subject teaching fields (N-12), elementary education (K-5), Preschool through Grade Three (P-3) and special education.

NUMBER OF CREDIT HOURS TO COMPLETE:

Formal instruction requirements vary depending on the certificate sought:

For candidates with an elementary or N-12 CE: 200 hours at a Regional Training Center or alternate route MAT program;

For candidates with a preschool through grade three CE: 13-17 credits at colleges or universities offering the specialized alternate route P-3 pedagogy;

For candidates with a special education or bi-lingual/bi-cultural CE: completion of an approved college or university program. Note that candidates teaching in these areas must also hold at minimum a CE in the subject area or grade level appropriate to the assignment.

For candidates with an ESL CE: 200 hours of formal instruction at a regional training center or alternate route MAT program <u>and</u> completion of a Department approved college or university program of 15 – 21 credits.

WHO EVALUATES: Evaluations are conducted by the school principal or administrative designee. The teacher is evaluated on at least three occasions during the initial year. The first two evaluations are used to aid the teacher's development.

The third and final evaluation is conducted after the provisional teacher has completd 34 weeks of full-time teaching. This last evaluation will contain the principal's recommendation regarding licensure. Recommendations for standard licensure are made by the principal (on forms provided by the New Jersey Department of Education), and are submitted for final action to the State Board of Examiners.

LENGTH OF TIME: 34 weeks of full-time employment. The length of the Program is extended for part-time novice teachers and for those whose formal instruction includes regional training and an approved college or university program.

CONTACT INFORMATION:

New Jersey Department of Education
Office of Licensure and Credentials
P.O. Box 500
Trenton, NJ 08625-0500
Attn: Robert R. Higgins
609-292-2045

PROVISIONAL TEACHER PROGRAM REGIONAL TRAINING CENTERS: 2006-2007

Operated by Colleges and Universities:

College or University	City
Centerary College	Clinton
College of St. Elizabeth	Dover
Monmouth University	Long Branch
Ramapo College	Pequannock
Richard Stockton College	Brick
	Linwood
	Mays Landing
	Tinton Falls
	Toms River
Rowan University	Blackwood
	Pennsauken
	Voorhees
	West Deptford
	Westampton
	Moorestown
	Pittsgrove
	Gloucester City
	Sewell
	Egg Harbor
	Millville
Rutgers University – Piscataway	Newark
	Bridgewater
	Paterson
	Hackensack
St. Peter's College	Kearny
	Jersey City
	Sayreville
Seton Hall University	Newark (TFA)
The College of New Jersey	East Brunswick
	Trenton
William Patterson University	Wayne

Operated by District Consortia:

Consortia	City
Essex County Provisional Teacher Teacher Consortium/Seton Hall University	Montclair
Morris-Union Jointure Commission Alternate Route Provisional Teacher Program/ Seton Hall University	New Providence
Elizabeth Public Schools/ Kean University	Elizabeth
Irvington Public Schools/ Fairleigh Dickinson University	Irvington
LEAP Academy/ Rutgers University – Camden	Camden
Gateway at Liberty Science Center/ Jersey City Public Schools	Jersey City

Institutions of higher education that have developed alternative teacher preparation programs leading to a teaching license:

Alternate Route MAT Programs:

New Jersey City University New Pathways to Teaching in New Jersey
Kean University Transition to Teaching
Fairleigh Dickenson University Alternate Route MAT
New Jersey Consortium for Urban Education (Montclair State et al.)
New Jersey City University World Languages Alternate Route

Pre-school through Grade Three Alternate Route Programs

Bloomfield College
Undergrad Post-baccalaureate Program – Specialized Alternate Route – 14 cr. (3.5 course units)

Caldwell College
Specialized Alternate Route – 15-18 credits

Kean University
Specialized Alternate Route Undergrad – 17 cr.

Montclair State University
Specialized Alternate Route – P-3 Undergrad level – 15 cr.

New Jersey City University
Specialized Alternate Route – 13 cr.

Rider University
Specialized Alternate Route

Rowan University
Graduate Specialized Alternate Route – 13 cr.

The College of New Jersey
Specialized Alternate Route – 15 cr.

William Paterson University
Specialized Alternate Route – 17 cr.

Bilingual/Bicultural Alternate Route Programs

Fairleigh Dickinson University
Georgian Court University
Kean University
Montclair State University
New Jersey City University
Rider University
Rowan University
Rutgers – New Brunswick
Seton Hall University
William Paterson University

ESL Alternate Route Programs

Fairleigh Dickson University
Georgian Court University
Kean University
Monmouth University
Montclair State University
NJCU
Richard Stockton College
Rider University
Rowan University
Rutgers University – Camden
Rutgers University – New Brunswick
Seton Hall University
William Paterson University

Approved Special Education Alternate Route Programs

Bloomfield College
Caldwell College
Centenary College
College of Saint Elizabeth
Fairleigh Dickinson University
Felican College – Rutherford Campus
Georgian Court University
Kean University
Monmouth University
Montclair State University
New Jersey City University
Richard Stockton College of New Jersey
Rider University
Rowan University
Rutgers University – Graduate School of Education
Seton Hall University
The College of New Jersey
William Paterson University

World Language Alternate Route Programs

New Jersey City University

States with which the state has reciprocity of teacher licenses:

NASDTEC Interstate Contract.

nstitutions of higher education that have any teacher preparation programs leading to a license to each.

Caldwell College
Centenary College
College of New Jersey
College of St. Elizabeth
Fairleigh Dickinson University
Felician College
Georgian Court College
Kean University
Montclair State University
New Jersey City University
Princeton University
Rabbinical College of America

Ramapo College of New Jersey
Rider University
Rowan University
Rutgers State University - Camden
Rutgers State University – Cook College
Rutgers State University Graduate School
Rutgers State University - Newark
Saint Peter's College
Seton Hall University
The Richard Stockton College of New Jersey
Westminister Choir College of Rider University
William Paterson University

Contact information for persons interested in finding a teaching position in the state:

NJHire.com

TITLE: Alternative Licensure

HISTORY: New Mexico Public Education Department rule effective October 31, 2007, supercedes earlier one filed July 14, 1986. Governs alternative licensure programs for persons who have earned at least a baccalaureate degree or for persons who have earned a post-baccalaureate degree and have at least five years of teaching experience at the post-secondary level but have not completed educator preparation programs and seek alternative routes to licensure in early childhood education, elementary education, middle level education, K-12 education, secondary education, or special education. Also governs alternative licensure in administration for persons who hold a post-baccalaureate degree and have administrative experience at the post-secondary level but have not completed an administrative preparation program.

MOTIVATION: Expand the pool of qualified teachers and administrators.

GRADE LEVELS AND/OR SUBJECT AREAS COVERED:

PreK-12

WHO OPERATES: Public Education Department.

REQUIREMENTS TO ENTER PROGRAM:

An applicant for alternative licensure must:

- Possess a bachelor of arts or science degree from a regionally accredited college or university including completion of a minimum of 30 semester hours of graduate or undergraduate credit in a particular field that appertains and corresponds to the subject area of instruction and level of instruction that will enable the applicant to teach in a competent manner as determined by the Public Education Department.

OR

- Possess a master of arts or science from regionally accredited college or university including completion of a minimum of 12 graduate hours in a particular field that appertains and corresponds to the subject area of instruction and level of instruction that will enable the applicant to teach in a competent manner as determined by the Public Education Department.

OR

- Possess a doctor of philosophy or doctor of education degree from a regionally accredited college or university. The degree shall correspond to the subject area of instruction and particular grade level that will enable the applicant to teach in a competent manner as determined by the Public Education Department.

PROGRAM DESCRIPTION:

Persons seeking either early childhood birth-grade 3, elementary K-8, or special education pre K-12 licensure, must complete various semester hours of credit earned through a regionally accredited college or university that has a Public Education Department-approved alternative licensure program containing no less than twelve (12) nor more than twenty-one (21) semester hours of credit and meeting the following criteria:

- the credits must include six (6) semester hours of coursework in the teaching of reading; and
- the credits must include the PED competencies for entry level teachers that correspond to the license being sought; and
- the credits must be in a program approved by the PED; and
- the program must include a student teaching or field-based component.

Persons seeking either middle level 5-9, secondary 7-12 or specialty area pre K-12 licensure, must complete various semester hours of credit earned through a regionally accredited college or university that has a PED-approved alternative licensure program containing no less than twelve (12) nor more than eighteen (18) semester hours of credit and meeting the following criteria:

- the credits must include three (3) semester hours of coursework in the teaching of reading; and
- the credits must include the PED's competencies for entry level teachers that correspond to the license being sought; and
- the credits must be in a program approved by the PED; and
- the program must include a student teaching or field-based component.

OR

Successfully demonstrate the PED's approved competencies for entry level teachers that correspond to the license being sought by presenting for assessment by trained reviewers an internet web-based Online Portfolio for Alternative Certification (OPAL). Such applicants shall:
- Complete the reading coursework required for the type of license sought and
- serve as the teacher of record for a full school year (minimum of 160 days) prior to being granted a portfolio review.

A candidate for alternative licensure may be permitted to assume the functions of a teacher prior to completion of licensure requirements and be issued a three-year non-renewable internship license

All applicants for alternative licensure must pass all of the New Mexico Teacher Assessments (www.nmta.nesinc.com).

Completion of the program will lead to a Level 1A, 5-year alternative license or if 5

OR

Alternative licensure for these individuals with 5 or more years of experience at the post-secondary level may receive a level 2 or level 3A license after completing the above requirements, not including portfolio or program.

OR

An applicant for alternative administrator licensure who has earned a post-baccalaureate degree and has at least six years administrator experience at the post-secondary level but has never completed an administrator preparation program must

- complete an internship of at least one full school year while holding an administrator internship license working as an administrator in a school district, charter school, private school or state agency education program.
- Meet PED-approved administrator competencies as verified to the PED by the candidate's employer.
- Pass the New Mexico Administrator Test

Completion of this program will lead to a Level 3B, 9-year administrative license.

NUMBER OF CREDIT HOURS TO COMPLETE:

Determined by each Program.

WHO EVALUATES: Public Education Department.

LENGTH OF TIME: One to three years.

Institutions of higher education that have developed alternative teacher preparation programs leading to a teaching license:

Central New Mexico College
Clovis Community College
College of Santa Fe
Eastern New Mexico University
New Mexico Institute of Mining and Tech.
New Mexico State University
Northern New Mexico Community College

San Juan Community College
Santa Fe Community College
University of New Mexico
Western New Mexico University

States with which the state has reciprocity of teacher licenses:

NASDTEC Interstate Contract. New Mexico has signed the NASDTEC Interstate Contract in the areas of teaching and school administration.

In addition, any applicant who has a valid out-of-state license, has completed a teacher preparation program and has taken a licensure exam or has teaching experience may receive a comparable license in New Mexico.

Institutions of higher education that have teacher preparation programs leading to a license to teach.

Central New Mexico College
Clovis Community College
College of Santa Fe
College of Southwest
Diné College
Eastern New Mexico University
New Mexico Highlands University
New Mexico Institute of Mining and Tech.

New Mexico State University
Northern New Mexico Community College
San Juan Community College
Santa Fe Community College
University of New Mexico
University of Phoenix
Wayland Baptist University
Western New Mexico University

Contact information for persons interested in finding a teaching position in the state:

New Mexico Regional Education
Applicant Program (NM REAP)
4216 Balloon Park Road, NE
Albuquerque, NM 87109-5801
Phone: (505) 344-5470

TITLE: Alternative Teacher Certification - Transitional B

HISTORY:　　　　　Instituted through action of the Board of Regents in July 2000.

GRADE LEVELS AND/OR SUBJECT AREAS COVERED:

All.

WHO OPERATES:　IHE and LEA

REQUIREMENTS TO ENTER PROGRAM:

Secondary teaching: Baccalaureate degree with major in subject appropriate to the certificate.

Elementary teaching: Baccalaureate degree with a liberal arts and sciences major.

At least 30 semester hours in the certification area that may include up to 12 semester hours in cognates (related subjects).

A 3.0 cumulative grade-point average or written recommendation of officer of the college program.

PROGRAM DESCRIPTION:

Regulations require an introductory component of 200 clock hours of pedagogical study, including 40 hours of field experiences, prior to beginning mentored teaching with a Transitional B certificate. All programs currently being offered exceed the 40 hour field experience requirement.

Prior to beginning mentored teaching with a Transitional B certificate, the candidate must pass the New York State Liberal Arts and Sciences Test (LAST) and the Content Specialty Test (CST) in the area in which s/he plans to teach. If a CST is not available in the subject, the candidate may take and pass the CST in any area.

As part of the introductory component, candidates must complete an approved two clock-hour course in the identification and reporting of suspected child abuse or maltreatment and an approved two clock-hour workshop on school violence prevention and intervention.

After successfully completing the 200-hour introductory pedagogical component and passing the required certification exams, the candidate continues part-time collegiate study in pedagogy, while teaching, to qualify for the initial certificate. Upon successful completion of the program, the candidate is eligible to apply for initial certification.

NUMBER OF CREDIT HOURS TO COMPLETE:

Determined by the individual colleges that offer the programs, and approved by the state. Programs are sufficient in length to meet all requirements for an initial certificate.

WHO EVALUATES: Programs are reviewed, approved and registered by the State Education Department. The IHE and the LEA collaborate to offer the programs; the IHE awards the degree and recommends the candidate to the New York State Education Department for initial certification. Oversight of programs is by the State Education Department.

LENGTH OF TIME: The Internship (Transitional B) certificate is valid for three years.

OTHER: A similar alternative teacher certification program is available for candidates who hold graduate degrees in subjects appropriate to the certificate. These candidates may begin at least two years of mentored teaching with a Transitional C certificate upon passing the NYS Liberal Arts and Sciences Test and the Content Specialty Test. The program includes pedagogical core study required for the initial certificate in the area of the candidate's transitional certificate, integrated into an intensive, streamlined course of study, except that field experience, student teaching ,or practica requirement shall not be applicable. A portion of the pedagogical core may be met through an assessment of previous knowledge and skills.

TITLE: Internship Certificate

HISTORY: In effect for over 30 years.

MOTIVATION: To enable talented persons to teach during the last
                      half of their teacher education graduate program
                      leading to teacher certification.

GRADE LEVELS AND/OR SUBJECT AREAS COVERED: All.

WHO OPERATES: IHE and LEA.

REQUIREMENTS TO ENTER PROGRAM:

A baccalaureate degree in an appropriate field.

The individual applies for admission to a registered master's degree
program that includes an internship and leads to certification.

The college applies to the state for issuance of the internship certificate
for the individual's specific school assignment.

PROGRAM DESCRIPTION:

Following completion of at least one half of the degree program, the
institution of higher education may recommend candidates judged to
be ready to be placed in a teaching position in a local school district
under appropriate supervision.

The length of classroom teaching is determined by the participating
institution of higher education.

The internship is the culminating graduate program activity.

The certificate enables qualified individuals to receive remuneration for
the services provided, as well as to legalize the individual's
employment.

The individual must complete an approved two clock-hour course in the identification and reporting of suspected child abuse or maltreatment and an approved two-hour workshop on school violence prevention and intervention prior to teaching.

NUMBER OF CREDIT HOURS TO COMPLETE:

Determined by the college, but at least 30 semester hours for the award of a master's degree.

WHO EVALUATES: IHE and LEA, with oversight by the State Education Department

LENGTH OF TIME: The internship certificate is valid for two years.

TITLE: Individual Evaluation (Transcript Evaluation)

HISTORY: More than 60 years.

MOTIVATION: To address the teacher shortage by enabling candidates who have not completed a state-approved teacher education program to establish eligibility for an initial teaching certificate.

GRADE LEVELS AND/OR SUBJECT AREAS COVERED: Effective February 2, 2007, this pathway is no longer as a means to obtain a first teaching certificate in childhood (grades 1-6) education. The pathway remains in effect for all other certificates.

WHO OPERATES: State Education Department.

REQUIREMENTS TO ENTER PROGRAM:

Baccalaureate degree.

Applicants submit an application, fee, and official transcripts of collegiate-level study for evaluation.

PROGRAM DESCRIPTION:

The applicant must fulfill academic, pedagogical, and examination requirements for an initial certificate. These requirements are comparable to those completed by graduates of registered teacher preparation programs.

If there are deficiencies in the transcript, the applicant is informed and must complete those requirements before a certificate is issued.

Evaluation is conducted and certificates issued by the Office of Teaching Initiatives in the New York State Education Department. For specific requirements, see www.highered.nysed.gov/tcert.

The individual must complete an approved two clock-hour course on the identification and reporting of suspected child abuse or maltreatment and an approved two clock-hour workshop on school violence prevention and intervention.

NUMBER OF CREDIT HOURS TO COMPLETE: Varies by certificate title.

WHO EVALUATES: Staff in the Office of Teaching Initiatives or Regional Certification Offices.

LENGTH OF TIME: N/A.

TITLE: Visiting Lecturer

HISTORY: Available since the early 1960s.

MOTIVATION: To supplement a local school district's regular
                        program of instruction.

GRADE LEVELS AND/OR SUBJECT AREAS COVERED: All.

WHO OPERATES: LEA.

REQUIREMENTS TO ENTER PROGRAM:

> Applicant must have unusual qualifications and expertise in a specific
> subject area.
>
> Examples of persons who have received Visiting Lecturer credentials
> include higher education faculty, persons from the arts, the judiciary,
> legal profession, bank officers, etc.

PROGRAM DESCRIPTION:

> The individual works under the general supervision of a certified
> teacher.
>
> The individual does not replace a regular, certified, full-time teacher.

NUMBER OF CREDIT HOURS TO COMPLETE: Not applicable.

WHO EVALUATES: LEA.

LENGTH OF TIME: Valid for one year, but renewable.

Institutions of higher education that have developed alternative teacher preparation programs leading to a teaching license:

Transitional B Certificate Programs:

Bank Street College
City Univesity of New York (CUNY)
   Brooklyn College
   City College
   College of Staten Island
   Herbert H. Lehman College
   Hunter College
   Queens College
College of New Rochelle
Fordham University
Utica College

Iona College
Long Island University-Brooklyn
Mercy College-Bronx, Manhattan
Mount Saint Mary College
Pace University
Roberts Wesleyan College
State University of New York
   College at Buffalo
   Empire State College
St. John's University

States with which the state has reciprocity of teacher licenses:

New York has interstate contracts with over 40 other states and jurisdictions. As outlined in the NASDTEC's Interstate Agreement of Qualification of Education Personnel, a person who is prepared in one of the contract states and meets the conditions of the contract is eligible for certification in other member states. For a list of states, please see
http://www.highered.nysed.gov/tcert/certificate/teachrecother.htm

Institutions of higher education that have *any* teacher preparation programs leading to a license to teach.

Adelphi University
Alfred University
Bank Street College of Education
Bard College
Barnard College
Boricua College
Canisius College
Cazenovia College
Colgate University
College of Mount St. Vincent
College of New Rochelle-Main Campus
College of St. Rose
Concordia College
CUNY-Brooklyn College
CUNY-City College
CUNY-College of Staten Island
CUNY-Herbert H. Lehman College
CUNY-Hunter College
CUNY-Medgar Evers College

Manhattan College
Manhattanville College
Marist College
Marymount Manhattan College

Medaille College
Mercy College*
Metropolitan College of New York
Molloy College
Mount St. Mary's College
Nazareth College
New York Institute of Technology*
New York University-Main Campus
Niagara University
Nyack College
NYS College of Agriculture and Life
    Sciences at Cornell
Pace University*
Pratt Institute
Roberts Wesleyan College
Rochester Institute of Technology
Sarah Lawrence College
School of Visual Arts
Siena College
Skidmore College
St. Bonaventure University
St. Francis College
St. John Fisher College
St. John's University*
St. Joseph's College*

CUNY-New York City Technical College
CUNY-Queens College
CUNY-York College
Daemen College
Dominican College of Blauvelt
Dowling College
D'Youville College
Elmira College
Five Towns College
Fordham University*
Hartwick College
Hobart & William Smith Colleges
Hofstra University
Houghton College
Iona College*
Ithaca College
Keuka College
Le Moyne College
Long Island University*
St. Lawrence University
St. Thomas Aquinas College
State University of New York (SUNY)
    College-Brockport

SUNY College-Buffalo
SUNY College-Cortland
SUNY College-Fredonia
SUNY College-Genesco
SUNY College-New Paltz
SUNY College-Old Westbury
SUNY College-Oneonta
SUNY College-Oswego
SUNY College-Plattsburgh
SUNY College-Potsdam
SUNY Empire State College
SUNY-Albany
SUNY-Binghamton
SUNY-Buffalo
SUNY Stony Brook
Syracuse University
Teachers College
The Sage Colleges*
Touro College*
Union Graduate College
University of Rochester
Utica College
Vassar College
Wagner College
Wells College
Yeshiva University

TITLE: Lateral Entry License

HISTORY: Effective January 1, 1985.

MOTIVATION: The 1984 session of the North Carolina General
                          Assembly approved an amendment, stating that: "It
                          is the policy of the State of North Carolina to
                          encourage lateral entry into the profession of
                          teaching by skilled professionals from the private
                          sector."

GRADE LEVELS AND/OR SUBJECT AREA(S) COVERED:

Major teaching areas for which the state has established licensure.

WHO OPERATES: The Local Education Agency (LEA).

REQUIREMENTS TO ENTER:

An individual who has not completed an approved teacher education program may be licensed under the following lateral entry provisions:

(1)   Be selected for employment by a North Carolina school system;

(2)   Hold at least a bachelor's degree from a regionally accredited college or university in the subject area in which they are employed to teach or hold at least a bachelor's degree from a regionally accredited college or university and have satisfied Praxis II testing requirements for the license area and meet the requirements to be designated "highly qualified" as prescribed by No Child Left Behind. To be designated "highly qualified," elementary and exceptional children's teachers must pass a rigorous state assessment (currently Praxis II exams). To be designated "highly qualified," middle school, high school, and special subject area teachers (e.g., art, music, second languages) must hold a bachelor's or master's degree in the specific area, or have 24 semester hours in the area, or pass a rigorous state assessment (currently Praxis II exams) in the area.

(3)   Have a minimum cumulative grade point average (GPA) of 2.5 or have five years of experience considered relevant by the LEA, or have passed the Praxis I exams and have attained one of the following:

(a)   a GPA of at least 3.0 on all work completed in the senior year;

(b)   a GPA of at least 3.0 in the major; or

(c)   a GPA of at least 3.0 in a minimum of 15 semester hours of course work completed within the last 5 years.

PROGRAM DESCRIPTION:

A. A person who holds a lateral entry license shall complete a program that includes the following components:

(1) completion of an approved teacher education program in the area of licensure at a college or university or completion of a program of study outlined by the Regional Alternative Licensing Centers;

Prescribed academic *content* coursework that is available through community colleges may be used to satisfy licensure requirements. General pedagogy competencies can be satisfied as follows.

General Pedagogy Competencies	Completed Through
Educational/Instructional Technology	Approved Teacher Education Program or Community College or Local Education Agency (if employed)
Understanding the Learner: Human Growth and Development	Approved Teacher Education Program or Community College
Learning Theory; Learning Styles; Motivation; How Children/Adolescents Learn	Approved Teacher Education Program or Community College
Meeting Special Learning Needs; Exceptionalities; Diversity	Approved Teacher Education Program
Literacy/Reading Methods	Approved Teacher Education Program
Instructional Methods	Approved Teacher Education Program

General Pedagogy Competencies	Completed Through
School Policies/Procedures	Approved Teacher Education Program or Community College or Local Education Agency (if employed)
Home/School/Community Collaborations	Approved Teacher Education Program or Community College or Local Education Agency (if employed)
Classroom Management/Organizing the Classroom to Maximize Learning	Approved Teacher Education Program or Community College or Local Education Agency (if employed)

(2) attaining passing score on appropriate PRAXIS subject exam(s) during the first three school years of holding the lateral entry license if the exam(s) was/were not the basis of qualifying for the license;

(3) completion of a staff development program that includes a two-week training course prior to beginning the work assignment;

(4) completion of a cumulative of six semester hours of course work in the approved program each school year;

(5) successful completion of at least a three-year initial licensure program in the lateral entry license area;

(6) completion of all above requirements within 3 years of becoming eligible for a lateral entry license and recommendation of the IHE or RALC for clear licensure.

B. **Individuals who possess five or more years of experience considered relevant by the LEA and satisfy testing requirements (currently Praxis II) for the licensure area within the first year of teaching shall be issued a Standard Professional 1 License upon:**

a. Completion of the NC TEACH modules or the equivalent through an approved teacher education program:

1) The Teacher, The Learner, and The School;

2) Diversity;

3) Content Area Pedagogy. (Note: The NC TEACH modules are offered and administered through NC colleges and universities with approved teacher education programs.

and

b. Completion of the NC TEACH module on Instructional Technology or the equivalent through an approved teacher education program, community college, or through professional development offered by the LEA;

and

c. Completion of one year of successful teaching as verified by the employing LEA.

The employing school system shall formally commit to supporting the lateral entry teacher by:

(1)   providing a two-week orientation that includes:

a. lesson planning,

b. classroom organization,

c. classroom management, including positive management of student behavior, effective communication for defusing and deescalating disruptive or dangerous behavior, and safe and appropriate use of seclusion and restraint,

d. an overview of the ABCs Program including the standard course of study and end-of-grade and end-of-course testing, and

e. the identification and education of children with disabilities.

(2)   assignment of a mentor on or before the first day on the job;

(3)   providing working conditions that are appropriate for all novice teachers;

(4)   giving regular focused feedback to the teacher for improving instruction; and

(5)   assisting the individual in accessing prescribed course work and professional development opportunities.

TITLE: Alternative Entry License

HISTORY: Effective January 1, 1985. Adapted 2006. LEAs shall report semi-annually to the SBE the number of individuals employed as teachers under each eligibility criteria. This policy expires September 1, 2006 but remains in effect for any teacher employed by it prior to September 1, 2006.

MOTIVATION: Alternative entry licenses shall be issued to individuals if requested by an employing LEA that has determined there is or anticipates there will be a shortage of qualified teachers available for specified subjects or grade levels.

GRADE LEVELS AND/OR SUBJECT AREA(S) COVERED:

Specified shortage teaching areas.

WHO OPERATES: The Local Education Agency (LEA) and the Department of Public Instruction Teacher Licensure Section.

REQUIREMENTS TO ENTER:

To qualify for an alternative entry license, the individual must:

1) hold at least a bachelor's degree from a regionally accredited college or university;
2) be eligible for re-employment by his or her prior employer; and must:
3)
   (a) hold a valid (current) out-of-state certificate with a minimum of one year of classroom teaching experience considered relevant by the local board to the grade of subject to be taught; or
   (b) have at least one year of full-time classroom teaching experience considered relevant by the local board to the grade or subject to be taught, as a professor, associate professor, assistant professor, instructor, or visiting lecturer at a regionally accredited college or university; or
   (c) have three years of other experience provided the local board determines that both the individual's experience and postsecondary education are relevant to the grade or subject to be taught.

PROGRAM COMPONENTS

1) During the period of employment with an alternative entry license, the individual shall receive an annual evaluation and multiple observations.

2) The individual's competence as a teacher, including review of the performance of students taught by the individual, shall be assessed according to the plan developed by the local board.

3) If the individual does not have one year of classroom teaching experience, a mentor teacher shall be provided by the local board.

4) If the individual qualifying for the alternative license under eligibility criteria 3a is deemed competent based on the plan adopted by the local board and recommended for re-employment, she/he is then eligible for a Standard Professional 1 or Standard Professional 2 NC teacher license and is not required to take and pass a standard examination. It shall be the responsibility of the local board to submit the required forms to the Licensure Section for the license to be processed. An individual who receives a Standard Professional 1 or Standard Professional 2 NC teacher license under this option shall be subject to the same requirements for continuing licensure and license renewal as other teachers who hold initial or continuing NC teacher licenses.

5) If the individual qualifying for this license under eligibility criteria 3b or 3c is deemed competent based on the plan adopted by the local board and recommended for re-employment by the local board and the individual has passed the Praxis examinations applicable for the area of licensure, the individual is then eligible for a Standard Professional 1 or Standard Professional 2 NC teacher license. It shall be the responsibility of the local board to submit the required forms to the Licensure Section for the license to be processed. An individual who receives a Standard Professional 1 or Standard Professional 2 NC teacher license under this option shall be subject to the same requirements for continuing licensure and license renewal as other teachers who hold initial or continuing NC teacher licenses.

If the individual qualifying for this license under eligibility criteria 3b or 3c does not pass the required Praxis examinations within the first year of alternative entry licensure, she/he may be employed under the provisions of lateral entry.

Institutions of higher education that have developed alternative teacher preparation programs leading to a teaching license:

N/A

States with which the state has reciprocity of teacher licenses:

ILA; NASDTEC Interstate Contract; NCATE.

Out-of-state applicants from non-reciprocal states are eligible for provisional licensure upon employment in North Carolina, if they have completed an education program approved by their states, although not accredited by NCATE or based on NASDTEC standards.

Institutions of higher education that have *any* teacher preparation programs leading to a license to teach.

Appalachian State University
Barton College
Barber-Scotia College
Belmont Abbey College
Bennett College
Campbell University
Catawba College
Southeastern College at WF
Duke University
East Carolina University
Elizabeth City State University
Elon College
Fayetteville State University
Gardner-Webb University
Greensboro College
Guilford College
High Point University
Johnson C. Smith University
Lees-McRae College
Lenoir-Rhyne College
Livingstone College
Mars Hill College
Meredith College

Methodist College
Montreat-Anderson College
North Carolina A&T State University
North Carolina Central University
North Carolina State University
North Carolina Wesleyan College
Pembroke State University
Pfeiffer College
Queens College
Salem College
Shaw University
St. Andrews College
St. Augustine's College
University of North Carolina-Asheville
University of North Carolina-Chapel Hill
University of North Carolina-Charlotte
University of North Carolina-Greensboro
University of North Carolina-Wilmington
Wake Forest University
Warren Wilson College
Western Carolina University
Wingate College
Winston-Salem State University

Contact information for persons interested in finding a teaching position in the state:

Center for Recruitment and Retention
6330 Mail Service Center
Raleigh, NC 27699-6330
Phone: (919) 807-3375

Institutions of higher education that have developed alternative teacher preparation programs leading to a teaching license:

None

States with which the state has reciprocity of teacher licenses:

All

Institutions of higher education that have *any* teacher preparation programs leading to a license to teach.

Dickinson State College	Sitting Bull College/Sinte Gleske University
Jamestown College	Trinity Bible Institute
Mayville State College	University of Mary
Minot State College	University of North Dakota
North Dakota State University	Valley City State College

Contact information for persons interested in finding a teaching position in the state:

Note: Contact any college placement office.

TITLE: Alternative Educator License

HISTORY: Rule for Alternative Educator, effective January 1, 2000.

GRADE LEVELS AND/OR SUBJECT AREAS COVERED: Secondary school (7-12) subjects. Intervention Specialist areas (K-12).

WHO OPERATES: Ohio Department of Education, Office of Certification Licensure.

REQUIREMENTS TO ENTER:

The candidate:

1. Holds a bachelor's degree from an accredited institution;

2. Has completed a major (30 S.H.) in the subject area to be taught, OR evidence of extensive work experience directly related to the area to be taught;

3. Has completed six semester hours of professional education coursework in the past five years with a GPA of 2.5, and from a college or university approved to prepare teachers, including:

   A. Three semester hours in the developmental characteristics of the adolescent through young adult students, and

   B. Three semester hours in teaching methods (this course must include field experience).;

4. Successful completion of the PRAXIS II examination for teacher licensure that measures content knowledge in the teaching subject.

PROGRAM DESCRIPTION:

Employing school district agrees to provide a structured mentoring program.

The individual enters the classroom to teach full-time in the teaching subject for two years under the alternative educator license.

Must complete 12 additional semester hours of professional education coursework, with a GPA of 2.5 or above, prior to expiration of the alternative educator license, from a college or university approved to prepare teachers, in the principles and practices of teaching, student development and learning; pupil assessment procedures; curriculum development; classroom management; and teaching methodology.

Must successfully complete the Praxis II examination required for teacher licensure that measures professional knowledge.

The school district can then recommend licensure and the individual can be licensed as a two-year provisional teachers -- the initial teaching license issued to all beginning teachers.

After receiving the two-year provisional license, the educator must then meet the teacher licensure standards to transfer from a provisional to a professional license, and then to renew that license.

NUMBER OF CREDIT HOURS TO COMPLETE:

If major is held in the subject area: Up to two years to complete a total of 18 hours of professional education coursework, including six semester hours of pre-service and 12 semester hours of in-service course work.

LENGTH OF TIME: Two years, nonrenewable.

TITLE: **Conditional Teaching Permit for Intervention Specialist (K-12)**

HISTORY: Authorized in House Bill 196, enacted November 2001.

GRADE LEVELS AND/OR SUBJECT AREAS COVERED: Intervention Specialist areas.

WHO OPERATES: Ohio Department of Education, Office of Certification
Licensure and employing school/district.

REQUIREMENTS TO ENTER:

Prospective employing school district agrees to provide a structured mentoring program.

The candidate:

Holds a bachelor's degree from an accredited institution.

Must pass the basic skills test prescribed by the State Board of Education.

Has completed 15 semester hours (or equivalent) in the principles and practices of teaching exceptional children, including such topics as child and adolescent development, diagnosis and assessment of children with disabilities, curriculum design and instruction, applied behavioral analysis, and methods of teaching students from culturally diverse backgrounds with the different learning styles.

PROGRAM DESCRIPTION:

The individual enters the classroom to teach full-time in the intervention specialist area for one year under the Conditional Teaching Permit.

Must complete an additional three semester hours in the content and methods of teaching reading during the year for which the Conditional Teaching Permit is issued.

Must complete the requirements for the Alternative Educator License for Intervention Specialist at the end of the year for which the Conditional Teaching Permit is issued.

NUMBER OF CREDIT HOURS TO COMPLETE:

One year to complete a total of 18 hours of professional education coursework, including 15 semester hours of pre-service and three semester hours of in-service coursework.

LENGTH OF TIME: One year, nonrenewable.

TITLE: Conditional Teaching Permit for Adolescence to Young Adult (7-12)

HISTORY: Authorized in House Bill 196, enacted November 2001.

GRADE LEVELS AND/OR SUBJECT AREAS COVERED: Secondary (7-12) subject areas.

WHO OPERATES: Ohio Department of Education, Office of Certification/Licensure and employing school/district.

REQUIREMENTS TO ENTER:

Prospective employing school district agrees to provide a structured mentoring program.

The candidate:

1. Holds a bachelor's degree from an accredited institution.

2. Must pass the basic skills test prescribed by the State Board of Education.

3. Has completed 15 semester hours (or equivalent) in the teaching subject area or subject area for which license is sought.

4. Has completed, within the previous five years, an additional six semester hours (or equivalent) of coursework, with a minimum GPA of 2.5, in one or more of the following areas: teaching content area, characteristics of student learning, diversity of learners, planning instruction, instructional strategies, learning environments, communication, assessment, and/or student support.

PROGRAM DESCRIPTION:

The individual enters the classroom to teach full-time for one year under the Conditional Teaching Permit.

Must complete an additional three semester hours in the teaching or subject area during the year for which the Conditional Teaching Permit is issued.

Must complete the requirements for the Alternative Educator License at the end of the year for which the Conditional Teaching Permit is issued.

NUMBER OF CREDIT HOURS TO COMPLETE:

One year to evidence a total of 30 semester hours of coursework in the teaching or subject area, six semester hours of specified professional education coursework, and three semester hours of in-service coursework., to advance to the alternative educator license.

LENGTH OF TIME: One year, nonrenewable.

Institutions of higher education that have developed alternative teacher preparation programs leading to a teaching license:

States with which the state has reciprocity of teacher licenses:

NASDTEC Interstate Contract.

Institutions of higher education that have *any* teacher preparation programs leading to a license to teach.

Antioch College	Mt. Vernon Nazarene College
Ashland University	Muskingum College
Baldwin-Wallace College	Notre Dame College
Bluffton College	Oberlin College
Bowling Green State University	Ohio Dominican College
Capital University	Ohio Northern University
Case Western Reserve University	Ohio State University
Cedarville College	Ohio University
Central State University	Ohio Wesleyan University
Cleveland State University	Otterbein College
College of Mount St. Joseph	Shawnee State University
College of Wooster	University of Akron
Defiance College	University of Cincinnati
Denison University	University of Dayton
Franciscan University of Steubenville	University of Findlay
Heidelberg College	University of Rio Grande
Hiram College	University of Toledo
John Carroll University	Urbana University
Kent State University	Ursuline College
Lake Erie College	Walsh University
Lourdes College	Wilmington College
Malone College	Wittenberg University
Marietta College	Wright State University
Miami University	Xavier University
Mount Union College	Youngstown State University

Contact information for persons interested in finding a teaching position in the state:

For employment, contact: each school or school district.

For licensure, contact:

Jennifer Kangas, Administrator
Office of Certification/Licensure
25 S. Front St. Mail Stop 105
Columbus, OH 43215
Phone: (614) 466-3593

Teacher Competency Review Panel

Beginning July 1, 1997, Oklahoma law created the Teacher Competency review Panel to make recommendations to the State Board of Education for the licensure and certification of people who have not graduated from an approved teacher education program in the state, or who have never held a standard teaching certificate in the state, or who are not currently certified to teach in another state.

According to the state regulation, "No person shall be certified to teach pursuant to the provisions of this section unless the person holds at least a baccalaureate degree from an accredited institution of higher education, has successfully completed the required competency tests, and has been assessed by and received a favorable recommendation from the Teacher Competency Review Panel. . . . The State Board of Education shall assess candidates seeking certification to teach through the recommendation of the Teacher Competency Review Panel fees for this service in an amount sufficient to fully fund the duties of the Teacher Competency Review Panel."

Applicants who do not receive a favorable recommendation from the panel may appeal to the State Board of Education.

NOTE: Attorney General Opinion Number 99-63, Sept. 23, 1999, determined that the requirement to be assessed by and receive a favorable recommendation from the Teacher Competency Review Panel includes applicants to the Alternative Certification program.

TITLE: Alternative Placement Program

HISTORY: Passed by the state legislature in 1991, this program replaced the Alternative Certification Program enacted in 1990.

MOTIVATION: To meet teacher shortages and expand the areas in which degreed, but non-certified, individuals possessing exceptional expertise can become certified.

GRADE LEVELS AND/OR SUBJECT AREAS COVERED:

Elementary-Secondary (grades PK-12); Secondary (grades 6-12); Career-Technology (6-12). Does not include early childhood education (PK-3) and elementary education (1-8).

WHO OPERATES: Operated under guidance from the State Board of Education through the Professional Standards Section of the State Department of Education. The Teacher Competency Review Panel was created by the state legislature in 1997.

REQUIREMENTS TO ENTER PROGRAM:

Pre-requisites: Prior to beginning work, an individual must meet the following conditions:

1. Hold a baccalaureate degree from an institution whose accreditation is recognized by the Oklahoma State Regents for Higher Education;

2. Have completed a major in a field that corresponds to an area of specialization for an elementary-secondary, secondary, or career-technology certificate;

3. Have passed the competency test in the subject area of specialization for which certification is sought and passed the general education test;

(Note: The professional education competency test may be taken after receiving a license, but would be required for a standard, five-year certificate).

4. Have provided documentation of at least two years of work experience which is related to the subject area of specialization if the person has only a baccalaureate degree

with no postbaccalaureate work in a related area. The State Board of Education may grant an exception to the requirements for licensure and certification and, upon demonstration by the individual of competency in the area of specialization, may grant a license or certificate to the individual.

5. The applicant must declare the intent to earn a Standard Certificate in not more than three years;

6. Have on file a plan for meeting standard certification requirements within three years; and

7. File appropriate application and fee with the Professional Standards Section of the State Department of Education.

PROGRAM DESCRIPTION:

In addition to meeting the prerequisites, the applicant must never have been denied admittance to a teacher education program approved by the Oklahoma State Regents for Higher Education, the North Central Association of Colleges and Schools, or the Oklahoma State Board of Education, nor have enrolled in and subsequently failed courses necessary to successfully meet the minimum requirements of such a program.

Qualified applicants must declare the intention to seek employment as a teacher at an accredited public school district in the state and have on file a plan for meeting certification requirements of the Alternative Placement Program.

Applicants who have no previous teaching experience must participate in the Resident Teacher Program with the same duties and responsibilities as other Resident Teacher program participants.

Participants will have three years in which to complete a block of up to 18 semester hours or 270 clock hours of professional education. The required hours may be reduced proportionately by advanced degrees, work experience, or a combination of both. In no instance, however, will the required number of hours be reduced to less than 6 semester hours or 90 clock hours.

Participants will have three years to pass the professional educational competency test.

The license is valid for one year, but can be renewed.

The program waives requirements of pre-student teaching field experiences, as well as student teaching.

NUMBER OF CREDIT HOURS TO COMPLETE:

A maximum of 18 semester hours or 270 clock hours of professional education courses are required for completion.

WHO EVALUATES: Evaluations of credentials presented in this program are conducted by the Professional Services Section of the State Department of Education.

LENGTH OF TIME: Participants have a maximum of three years to complete the requirements for standard certification.

Institutions of higher education that have developed alternative teacher preparation programs leading to a teaching license:

By legislative mandate, all 20 of Oklahoma's teacher preparation institutions must participate in the Oklahoma Alternative Placement Program.

States with which the state has reciprocity of teacher licenses:

NASDTEC Interstate Contract.

Out-of-State Applicant Certification ---

Applicants holding out-of-state certificates may either:

- Meet current Oklahoma certification requirements for standard certification; or

- Receive a Two-year certificate and have two years to fulfill the following requirements:

    Assessment and one year of successful employment in an Oklahoma school district.

States That Have Signed Certification Agreements for Oklahoma Teachers Going Out-of-State ---

Alabama	Illinois	New York
Alaska	Indiana	North Carolina
Arizona	Kentucky	Ohio
Arkansas	Louisiana	Oregon
California	Maine	Pennsylvania
Colorado	Maryland	Rhode Island
Connecticut	Massachusetts	South Carolina
Delaware	Michigan	Tennessee
District of Columbia	Mississippi	Texas
Florida	Montana	Utah
Georgia	Nebraska	Vermont
Guam	Nevada	Virginia
Hawaii	New Hampshire	Washington
Idaho	New Mexico	West Virginia

Institutions of higher education that have *any* teacher preparation programs leading to a license to teach.

Bacone College
Cameron University
East Central University
Langston University
Mid-American Christian University
Northeastern State University
Northwestern Oklahoma State University
Oklahoma Baptist University
Oklahoma Christian University
   of Science/Arts
Oklahoma City University
Oklahoma Panhandle State University

Oklahoma State University
Oklahoma Wesleyan University
Oral Roberts University
Rogers State University
St. Gregory's University
Southeastern Oklahoma State University
Southern Nazarene University
Southwestern Oklahoma State University
University of Central Oklahoma
University of Oklahoma
University of Science and Arts of Oklahoma
University of Tulsa

Contact information for persons interested in finding a teaching position in the state:

Note: Applicants should contact individual school districts.

Institutions of higher education that have developed alternative teacher preparation programs leading to a teaching license:

None

States with which the state has reciprocity of teacher licenses:

NASDTEC Interstate Contract.

Alabama	Illinois	New York
Alaska	Indiana	North Carolina
Arizona	Kentucky	Ohio
Arkansas	Louisiana	Oregon
California	Maine	Pennsylvania
Colorado	Maryland	Rhode Island
Connecticut	Massachusetts	South Carolina
Delaware	Michigan	Tennessee
District of Columbia	Mississippi	Texas
Florida	Montana	Utah
Georgia	Nebraska	Vermont
Guam	Nevada	Virginia
Hawaii	New Hampshire	Washington
Idaho	New Mexico	West Virginia

Institutions of higher education that have *any* teacher preparation programs leading to a license to teach.

Cascade College
Concordia College
Corban College
Eastern Oregon University
George Fox College
Lesley University
Lewis and Clark College
Linfield College
Northwest Christian College
Multnomah Bible College
Western Oregon University
Oregon State University

Pacific University
Portland State University
Southern Oregon University
University of Oregon
University of Phoenix
University of Portland
Warner Pacific College
Willamette University

Contact information for persons interested in finding a teaching position in the state:

Confederation of Oregon School Administrators (COSA)
707 13th St. SE, Suite 100
Salem, OR 97301-4035
Phone: (503) 581-3141

http://www.cosa.k12.or.us/

Oregon Education Association (OEA)
1 Plaza SW, 6900 SW Haines Rd.
Tigard, OR 97223
Phone: (503) 684-3300
http://www.oregoned.org/site/pp.asp?c=9dKKKYMDH&b=123024

TITLE: ABCTE and the Pennsylvania Department of Education

HISTORY: Initial resolution of the State Board of Education to collaborate with the American Board for the Certification of Teacher Excellence and the issuance of a Pennsylvania teaching certificate: September 2003. Current agreement reached between ABCTE and the PA Department of Education in August 2004.

REQUIREMENTS TO ENTER:

Individuals holding the Passport to Teaching are eligible for a Temporary Teaching Permit, valid for one calendar year.

PROGRAM DESCRIPTION:

During that year, the teacher must complete the following:

- One-on-one mentoring under a supervising mentor from a college/university that has Department approval to offer teacher preparation programs. The two universities selected for this component are St. Joseph's University in Philadelphia and Point Park University in Pittsburgh. This component also includes the school or district teacher/coach as part of the induction program to provide direct support to the new teacher. The teaching experience may be in a public, private or nonpublic religious school.

- Attendance at two one-day retreats provided by ABCTE for all American Board teachers and supervising mentors. One retreat will be scheduled in September/October and the second retreat will be held in January/February. These will be opportunities for professional development and program evaluation.

- Complete two graduate level courses offered by St. Joseph's University Learning Institute from an approved list of topics aimed at strengthening a teacher's pedagogical skills. The courses are offered in a four-day format. ABCTE is helping to underwrite the cost of the courses for the current group of candidates.

WHO EVALUATES:

When all of the requirements of the mentoring component have been met, the university can recommend the individual for the Instructional I certificate, the same certificate issued to completers of a Pennsylvania teacher education program. There is no additional testing required.

LENGTH OF TIME: One Year

OTHER: Number of PA individuals holding the Passport to Teaching certificate: 14

Number of PA individuals currently completing the mentoring component: 7

Institutions of higher education that have developed American Board for Certification of Teacher Excellence (ABCTE) Programs:

Point Park University   St. Joseph's University

Institutions of higher education that have developed Intern Programs:

Intern Programs

Alvernia College
Arcadia University
Bloomsburg University of PA
Cabrini College
Carnegie Mellon University
Cedar Crest College
Chestnut Hill College
Cheyney University of Pennsylvania
De Sales University
Delaware Valley College
Drexel University
Duquesne University
East Stroudsburg Univ. of PA.
Eastern College
Gwynedd-Mercy College
Holy Family University
Immaculata College
Indiana University of Pennsylvania (English & Elementary only)

Kutztown University of PA
LaRoche College
Lehigh University
Lincoln University
Lycoming College
Mansfield University of Pennsylvania
Marywood University
Millersville University of Pennsylvania
Moore College of Art and Design
Pennsylvania State University/Main
Saint Joseph's University
Susquehanna University
Temple University
University of Pennsylvania
University of Pittsburgh/Main
West Chester University of Pennsylvania
Widener University
Wilkes University
Wilson College

States with which the state has reciprocity of teacher licenses:

NASDTEC Interstate Contract.

Institutions of higher education that have *any* teacher preparation programs leading to a license to teach. **Contact individual school districts if interested in finding a teaching position in the state.**

Albright College
Alvernia College
Arcadia University
Baptist Bible College
Bloomsburg University of Penn.
Bryn Mawr College
Bucknell University
Cabrini College
California University of Penn
Carlow College
Carnegie-Mellon University
Cedar Crest College
Chatham College
Chestnut Hill College
Cheyney University of Pennsylvania
Clarion University of Pennsylvania
College Misericordia
Delaware Valley College
DeSales University
Dickinson College
Drexel University
Duquesne University
East Stroudsburg University of Penn.
Eastern College
Edinboro University of Pennsylvania
Elizabethtown College
Gannon University
Geneva College
Gettysburg College
Grove City College
Gwynedd-Mercy College
Holy Family College
    Johnstown Campus-Pittsburgh
Immaculata College
Indiana University of Penn.
Juniata College
Keystone College
King's College
Kutztown University of Penn.
LaRoche College
Lebanon Valley College
Lancaster Bible College
LaSalle College
Keystone College
Lehigh University
Lincoln University
Lock Haven State University
Lycoming College
Mansfield University of Pennsylvania

Marywood University
Mercyhurst College
Messiah College
Millersville University of Pennsylvania
Moravian College
Moore College of Art and Design
Mount Aloysius College
Muhlenberg College
Neumann College
Pennsylvania College of Optometry
Pennsylvania State University   /Main
Pennsylvania State University/Harrisburg
Philadelphia Biblical University
Philadelphia College of Osteopathic Medicine
Philadelphia University
Point Park College
Robert Morris University
Rosemont College
St. Bonaventure University (located in New York
Saint Francis University
Saint Joseph's University
Saint Vincent College
Seton Hill College
Shippensburg University of Pennsylvania
Slippery Rock University of Pennsylvania
Susquehanna University
Swarthmore College
Temple University
Thiel College
University of Pennsylvania
University of Pittsburgh/Main
University of Pittsburgh/Bradford
University of Pittsburgh/Johnstown
University of Scranton
University of the Arts
University of the Sciences in Philadelphia
Ursinus College
Valley Forge Christian College
Villanova University
Washington & Jefferson College
Waynesburg College
West Chester University of Pennsylvania
Westminster College
Wilkes College
Wilson College
Widener University
York College

TITLE: Project RITER – Aspiring Teachers Program

HISTORY: Implemented during Summer 2006 under federal
                         grant funds.

MOTIVATION: To eliminate issuance of emergency permits for
                         shortage areas.

GRADE LEVELS AND/OR SUBJECT AREA (S) COVERED: Secondary chemistry,
physics, mathematics and special education; middle-school special education.

WHO OPERATES: Collaboration between a higher education
                   institutions and school districts

REQUIREMENTS TO ENTER:

Minimum of a bachelor's degree from and accredited institution with a
major in, or closely related to, the intended teaching field.

Minimum grade point average of B (3.00 on a 4.00 scale) in
undergraduate studies, or the same average in at least 24 semester
horus of graduate study.

At least three years of career experience in an area related to the
desired certification area.

Passing score on Praxis I PPST (or comparable skills test).

Documented experience with children and/or young adults.

Completed application which includes reflective essay, resume, official
transcripts of all college study, and three letters of recommendation.

Successful interview by the admitting program.

PROGRAM DESCRIPTION:

Intensive summer program that assess candidate performance to the
"readiness to teach" standards of the
RIBTS with a minimum of 200 contact hours to include experience in
instruction in teaching methods, growth and development,
microteaching, classroom teaching, law and regulations and reflective
practice in teaching. (This component has been modified, see note
below)

At least one year of teaching experience that is heavily mentored and verified by the approved school district and the approved institution of higher education.

Completion of the individualized plan that is verified by staff at the RI Department of Education. (This component has also been modified)

Successful completion of the State Licensure Exam.

Note: The program outlined above is still operating for four (4) individuals who are in their second year. No new candidates will be admitted under that design. Currently, the RITER- Aspiring Teacher Program is functioning as a clearinghouse. Potential candidates must meet the eligibility requirements outlined above. Then, the indviiual is directed to an exisiting post-baccalaureate program at one of the four (4) participating institutions. No new candidates are serving as teachers of record while completing one of the approved programs.

NUMBER OF CREDIT HOURS TO COMPLETE:

Varies by candidate.

WHO EVALUATES: Members of the collaborative support team who will review the RIBTS portfolio and individualized plan to ensure that candidate meets the Rhode Island Beginning Teachers Standards (RIBTS). This is in place for the first cohort. Any new candidates are evaluated according to the requirements of the program at the institution.

LENGTH OF TIME: 2 years.

Institutions of higher education that have developed alternative teacher preparation programs leading to a teaching license:

Johnson & Wales University

Providence College

Rhode Island College

University of Rhode Island

States with which the state has reciprocity of teacher licenses:

NASDTEC Interstate Contract. Rhode Island has signed reciprocity contracts with 45 states under this contract through 2010.

Institutions of higher education that have *any* teacher preparation programs leading to a license to teach.

Brown University
Johnson & Wales University
Providence College
Rhode Island College

Rhode Island School of Design
Roger Williams University
Salve Regina University
University of Rhode Island

Contact information for persons interested in finding a teaching position in the state:

Note: Contact individual school districts. All employment decisions are made at the school district level. There is no central employment service in Rhode Island for teachers.

TITLE: Program of Alternative Certification for Educators

HISTORY: Established in 1984 by state law.

MOTIVATION: Shortage.

GRADE LEVELS AND/OR SUBJECT AREA(S) COVERED:

> Areas of teacher shortage deemed critical by the State Board of
> Education. Areas are evaluated annually.

WHO OPERATES: State.

REQUIREMENTS TO ENTER PROGRAM:

> A bachelor's degree in an initial certification subject.
>
> A passing score on the appropriate PRAXIS Specialty Area
> Examination(s).
>
> Two years full time work experience.
>
> Employment by a public school district.
>
> Successful completion of a pre-service institute to prepare the
> prospective teacher for the opening of school.

PROGRAM DESCRIPTION:

> The individual completes:
>
> A pre-service institute to prepare the prospective teacher for the
> opening of school (or in January). Training sessions throughout the
> first school year. Together, these should total 14 days.

An institute during the second summer of employment. Training sessions throughout the second school year. Together, these should total 12 days.

Over a three-year period, completion of three graduate-level professional education courses as prescribed in the teacher's professional development plan.

The individual must successfully complete no fewer than three years of full-time employment in an instructional role in a public school after issuance of the initial alternative certificate.

Participant must pass the Principals of Learning and Teaching exam prior to completion of the PACE program and issuance of the professional certificate.

All program expenses must be paid by the applicant.

NUMBER OF CREDIT HOURS TO COMPLETE:

Over a period of three years, completion of three graduate-level professional education courses as prescribed in the teacher's professional development plan.

WHO EVALUATES: State.

LENGTH OF TIME: The individual must complete the requirements within three years.

Institutions of higher education that have developed alternative teacher preparation programs leading to a teaching license:

N/A

States with which the state has reciprocity of teacher licenses:

NASDTEC Interstate Contract.

Institutions of higher education that have *any* teacher preparation programs leading to a license to teach.

Allen University
Anderson College
Benedict College
Bob Jones University
Charleston Southern University
Citadel Military College
Claflin College
Clemson University
Coastal Carolina University
Coker College
College of Charleston
Columbia College
Columbia International University
Converse College
Erskine College
Francis Marion University

Furman University
Lander College
Limestone College
Morris College
Newberry College
North Greenville College
Presbyterian College
South Carolina State College
Southern Wesleyan University
University of South Carolina-Aiken
University of South Carolina-Columbia
University of South Carolina-Spartanburg
Winthrop University
Wofford College

Contact information for persons interested in finding a teaching position in the state:

South Carolina Center for Recruitment,
Retention, and Advancement
Winthrop University
Rock Hill, SC 29733
Phone: 1-800-323-4032

TITLE: Department of Education Alternative Route to Certification

HISTORY: Has existed as a pilot since 1985. It was formally
enacted as a rule by the State Board of Education,
effective July 1, 1991.

MOTIVATION: It is intended for a school district which is unable to
fill a position with a properly certified teacher.

GRADE LEVELS AND/OR SUBJECT AREA(S) COVERED: Secondary only.

WHO OPERATES: State.

REQUIREMENTS TO ENTER PROGRAM:

To be eligible for the alternative certification program, a person must
meet the following requirements.

1) Holds a bachelor's degree or higher, with the bachelor's degree
obtained at least two-years prior to admittance into the alternative
certification program;

2) Has maintained an overall grade point average of 2.5 grade point on
a 4.0 scale or higher on the undergraduate degree transcript;

3) Holds a college major in the subject area to be taught or has five
years experience in a related field, as determined by the department;

4) Has an offer of employment from a South Dakota accredited system
that operates a mentoring program approved by the department;

5) Submits to a criminal background investigation pursuant to a
SDCL chapter 13-10;

6) Adheres to the Code of Professional Ethics pursuant to chapter
24:08:03. as adopted by the Professional Teachers Practices and
Standards Commission;

7) Completes a screening interview with school personnel and the
department's program coordinator prior to being hired by a school
system; and

8) Effective July 2005, submits to the department an official copy of all test scores on the state certification exams for each subject or area authorization and for the pedagogy exam for each age or grade span in which the alternative certification applicant will be certified.

ADMISSION REQUIREMENTS:

Contact Roxie Thielen, Accreditation & Teacher Quality, 700 Governors Drive, Pierre SD 57501-2291, (605) 773-4669, Fax (605) 773-6139, roxie.thielen@state.sd.us

1) Eligibility for the Alternative Certification Program is determined by review of a candidate's completed application. The candidate must be employed by a South Dakota accredited school. Candidate must forward a copy of the "employment contract" to the address listed above;

2) Candidate must submit the following items to the address listed above:

   a) Application for Alternative Route to Certification;

   b) Applicant Conduct Review Statement;

   c) A $20 processing fee for two-year instructor certificate;

   d) Official transcripts of all undergraduate and graduate course work; and,

   e) A copy of the signed teaching contract.

3) Each candidate participates in an "approved teacher mentoring program" or receives intensive supervision that consists of structured guidance and regular ongoing support;

4) Complete all coursework, with a minimum grade of "C" necessary to complete the current alternative certification program (Chapter 24:15:04); and

5) Submit passing scores or the appropriate Praxis II content test(s) and for a pedagogy exam for the appropriate grade span.

PROGRAM DESCRIPTION:

The three (3) year alternative route to certification program shall consist of on-the-job classroom training during 2 semesters, mentorship during the on-the-job training, an orientation program provided by the employer, and six semester hours of education coursework in pedagogy and related fields. Also, Alternative Route to Certification candidates must complete a three (3) semester hour course in both Human Relations and South Dakota Indian Studies. The coursework shall be delivered by an accredited college or university with an approved program or endorsement program in the discipline and coordinated with the Department of Education and the employing school system.

NUMBER OF CREDIT HOURS TO COMPLETE:

Pedagogy & Other Educational Coursework

a) Human Relations..........................3 semester hours

b) South Dakota Indian Studies........3 semester hours

Six (6) credits of pedagogy coursework will be assigned based on a review of candidate's transcripts and collaboration with the Department of Education.

State Licensure Exam

The South Dakota state licensure exam, Praxis II (http://doe.sd.gov/oatq/praxis/index.asp), must be completed with passing scores in order to be considered for full state certification. A copy of the candidate's Praxis score(s) must be received by the South Dakota Department of Education

WHO EVALUATES:

Mentorships and school administration will provide assistance to the alternative certification instructor regarding purpose, expectations, and procedures involved in the evaluation process and whatever guidance may be needed. A minimum of two evaluations will be completed by administrative staff annually and a copy of each evaluation forwarded to the Office of Accreditation and Teacher Quality for review and inclusion in the instructor's official file.

OTHER:

Salary and benefits are established by the local schools. All costs related to the college and university credits required and state licensure exam will be the responsibility of the alternative certification candidate.

STATE CERTIFICATION:

Upon successful completion of all aspects of this program, including coursework, licensure examinations (Praxis II), and a positive recommendation from the on-the-job mentor, the candidate must apply for a Department of Education teaching certificate from the Office of Accreditation and Teacher Quality.

TITLE: Northern Plains Transition to Teaching

HISTORY: Created through a grant awarded by the U.S Department of Education.

MOTIVATION: The Northern Plains Transition to Teaching (NPTT) program at Montana State University-Bozeman (MSU) has developed an implemented a sustainable program to provide highly qualified and competent educators to meet the hiring needs of secondary rural schools in South Dakota, Montana, and Wyoming.

GRADE LEVELS AND/OR SUBJECT AREA(S) COVERED: Secondary

WHO OPERATES: Montana State University-Bozeman

REQUIREMENTS TO ENTER: A baccalaureate degree in a teachable subject area, must have a documented history of productive engagement in the workforce, and must have a demonstrated capacity and the willingness to engage in serious, concentrated study and preparation in order to move rapidly through the demanding, highly concentrated course of study.

PROGRAM DESCRIPTION:

Candidate enrolled in this program will:

1. Complete nine credits of coursework delivered at a distance with web-based technology, six credits prior to entry into the classroom as a teacher;

2. Complete an internship, which entails teaching for one school year; and

3. Complete the final nine credits delivered at a distance with web-based technology, after the first year of teaching.

Candidates completing this program have the option to earn a Master of Education degree by completing an additional six credits.

NUMBER OF CREDIT HOURS TO COMPLETE: 24 credits

WHO EVALUATES: Montana State University-Bozeman

LENGTH OF TIME: One year.

TITLE: Teach For America

HISTORY: South Dakota's participation in this program began
                    in 2004. Teachers have been recruited to teach in
                    schools on South Dakota Indian Reservations.

MOTIVATION: Recognition of the high quality of individuals
                    recruited into this program.

GRADE LEVELS AND/OR SUBJECT AREA(S) COVERED: All content areas.

WHO OPERATES: Teach For America – local education agencies.

REQUIREMENTS TO ENTER PROGRAM:

Recruitment is done through the Teach for America program under
their guidelines. The following are South Dakota's requirements:

Teach For America, in coordination with the South Dakota Department
of Education, shall administer a program that provides an alternative
route to certification. The Teach For America alternative certification
program is inclusive of K-8, 7-12, and K-12 age/grade span
authorizations issued at the approved education program level.

To be eligible for the program, a person must meet the following
requirements:

1) Hold a bachelor's degree or higher;

2) Have maintained an overall grade point average of 2.5 or higher on
an undergraduate transcript;

3) Submit to a criminal background investigation pursuant to SDCL
chapter 13-10;

4) Adhere to the Code of Professional Ethics pursuant to chapter
24:08:03, as adopted by the Professional Teachers Practices and
Standards Commission;

5) Complete a screening interview with Teach For America and an
interview with the school district;

6) Complete the intensive Teach For America application process and is accepted into the Teach For America program; and,

7) Meet the requirements for "highly qualified teacher" status by taking and earning a qualifying score on state certification exams for each subject or area authorization in which the corps member may be certified in order to prove the corps member's competency if the corps member is placed in a core content area outside of the corps member's undergraduate preparation.

PROGRAM DESCRIPTION:

24:15:05:03. Program description. The Teach For America two-year alternative certification program requires corps members to:

(1) Participate in the comprehensive, classroom-focused pre-service summer training institute provided by Teach For America;

(2) Participate in a local regional orientation at the assigned school district;

(3) Complete six semester hours of education coursework in pedagogy and related fields of the education school curriculum based on the core standards developed by the Interstate New Teacher Assessment and Support Consortium (INTASC). The program shall be delivered by an accredited college or university with an approved program or endorsement program in the discipline and coordinated with the department and the employing school system;

(4) Complete three semester hours of South Dakota Indian Studies and three semester hours of Human Relations;

(5) Participate in an on-the-job classroom mentorship in collaboration with other Teach For America corps members under the guidance of Teach For America and the employing school district for the duration of the two years; and,

(6) Earn a qualifying score on The Praxis II content test and pedagogy exam for the age or grade span in which the alternative certification corps member will be certified. All test scores, including any subtest corps provided by the testing company for both the content and pedagogy test must be submitted to the department.

NUMBER OF CREDIT HOURS TO COMPLETE:

12 hours to include Human Relations and South Dakota Indian Studies

WHO EVALUATES:

Department of Education

LENGTH OF TIME:

2 years

TITLE: Certification Only Program

HISTORY: Formally enacted in administrative rule by the South Dakota Board of Education effective July 5, 2004.

MOTIVATION: Provides individuals with a bachelor's degree an option to complete a teacher education program to obtain certification only.

GRADE LEVELS AND/OR SUBJECT AREAS(S) COVERED: Secondary only.

REQUIREMENTS FOR CERTIFICATION-ONLY PROGRAMS.

An accredited institution with approved education programs may request approval for K-12 and 7-12 certification-only programs for teacher education candidates who have completed at least a baccalaureate degree from an accredited institution. Certification-only programs are modifications of the study and experience requirements of any education program of article 24: 16.

Certification-only programs incorporate the applicable general education, professional education and program standards and requirements for admission, matriculation, and exit from such programs, but allow an institution to accept previous demonstrations of knowledge, skill, and attitudes judged to meet satisfactorily those preparation standards or program requirements.

Before admission to the program, institutions shall require candidates in certification-only programs to pass the state certification content exam. Institutions shall recommend candidates for certification and successful completion of the certification-only program.

TITLE: Western Governors University

HISTORY: Established its teacher college in 2003, Western Governors University(WGU) is a nonprofit, degree-granting, competency-based online university designed initially to represent the strategic educational interests of the governors of its 19 founding states.

MOTIVATION: Western Governors University is a non-profit online university offering a convenient, flexible online education.

GRADE LEVELS AND/OR SUBJECT AREA(S) COVERED: All areas

WHO OPERATES: Western Governors University

REQUIREMENTS TO ENTER PROGRAM: Available on the WGU Web site at http://www.wgu.edu/admissions/requirements.asp

PROGRAM DESCRIPTION: Learn about the various programs from the Western Governors University Web site at: http://www.wgu.edu/index.asp

NUMBER OF CREDIT HOURS TO COMPLETE: Varies

WHO EVALUATES: Western Governors University

LENGTH OF TIME: Varies

States with which the state has reciprocity of teacher licenses:

ALL. NSADTEC Interstate Contract.

Institutions of higher education that have *any* teacher preparation programs leading to a license to teach.

Augustana College
Black Hills State University
Dakota State University
Dakota Wesleyan University
Mount Marty College
Northern State University

Oglala Lakota College
Sinte Gleska College
South Dakota State University
University of Sioux Falls
University of South Dakota

Contact information for persons interested in finding a teaching position in the state:

South Dakota Teacher Placement
P.O.Box 1059
Pierre, SD 57501-1059
Telephone: 605.773.2508
Fax: 605.773.2501
Website: www.asbsd.org

Teach Tennessee

Teach Tennessee is a special project of the the Office of the Comissioner of Education. It is focusing on math and science teachers who are second career with a major in one of these areas and a minimum of five years of career experience that had a focus on the area to be taught. For licensure purposes, these people have been working on an Alternative "C" License. When Tenessee switches to the new Alternative Licenses next year, there is a proposed "Teach Tennessee" License that will be used for these people only.

For more information, contact:

Becky Kent, Executive Assistant for Research & Development

(615) 532-2815

Becky.Kent@state.tn.us

The website describing Teach Tennessee is located at the following address:

http://www.tennessee.gov/education/teachtn

**TITLE: Alternative License Type C --
          Alternative Preparation for Licensure**

HISTORY: Approved by the State Board in Nov. 1990. The University of
                      Tennessee - Knoxville, the University of Tennessee - Chattanooga
                      and the University of Memphis offer this program. Beginning Fall
                      of 2003, all Tennessee Board of Regents IHEs offer Alt C Licenses
                      through the Regents Online Degree Program (RODP).

MOTIVATION: Desire to attract extremely capable persons with
                      maturity and a variety of work experiences to the
                      teaching profession.

GRADE LEVELS AND/OR SUBJECT AREA(S) COVERED:

                      All licensure areas.

WHO OPERATES: IHE, in collaboration with LEA.

REQUIREMENTS TO ENTER:

                      An Alternative Type C Teacher License may be issued to an individual
                      who holds a Bachelor's degree from a regionally accredited
                      college/university.

                      The candidate must be accepted into an approved Alternative C
                      Licensure program at one of the participating Tennessee higher
                      education institutions.

                      The candidate must complete an intensive summer program at the
                      university prior to becoming employed on an Alternative C License.

PROGRAM DESCRIPTION:

                      The Alternative Type C licensure program requires very close
                      coordination between the university and the employing Tennessee
                      school district. Once employed, the candidate should be assigned a
                      mentor by the employing school district. The mentor shall provide
                      support to the candidate during the first year of teaching and
                      participate with the candidate in a university seminar at the end of the
                      year.

                      The Alternative C License is available in all endorsement areas for
                      which the institutions offer approved programs.

NUMBER OF CREDIT HOURS TO COMPLETE: Variable.

WHO EVALUATES: IHE, LEA.

LENGTH OF TIME: One year. May be reissued one time if requirements
not completed within one year.

TITLE: Alternative License Type E --
Alternative Licensure for persons not completing college programs

HISTORY: Approved by the State Board in May 2000.

MOTIVATION: To attract qualified individuals into the teaching field
by offering a more flexible licensure route.

GRADE LEVELS AND/OR SUBJECT AREA(S) COVERED:

Elementary and Middle Grades.

WHO OPERATES: State Department of Education.

REQUIREMENTS TO ENTER:

Option 1

Completion of an appropriate degree with an academic major in the desired
area of endorsement; OR

Option 2

Obtaining written verification from the college certification officer at a
university with an approved program in the desired area of endorsement
stating that admission requirements to the program have been satisfied and
that the applicant does not lack content courses in the desired area of
endorsement; OR

Option 3

Successful completion of the Praxis Exams Specialty Test(s) required for the
desired area of endorsement.

PROGRAM DESCRIPTION:

An individual with a Bachelor's degree from a regionally accredited
college/university may be employed on an Alternative E License for up to three
years while completing 24 semester hours of professional education
coursework to advance to a full Tennessee license.

An applicant is eligible for the Alternative E License if it can be documented
that he or she has met the required knowledge and skills in the specific
endorsement area.

Certain areas such as School Administrator, School Counselor, School Psychologist, Library Information Specialist and Speech/Language Pathologist require a prerequisite of an acceptable Master's degree in order to be placed on an Alternative E License.

Alternative E Licenses may be issued for all initial licensure endorsement areas <u>except</u> for Elementary Education and Middle Grades Education.

Applicants already holding a full Tennessee license are not eligible for the Alternative E License, as it is designed to assist with initial licensure, not with additional endorsements.

An Alternative Type E License is issued for the duration of one school year at a time and always expires on the August 31 following the academic school year of its issuance. An individual may not be issued an Alternative Type E License more than three times. This includes initial issuance plus two renewals.

NUMBER OF CREDIT HOURS TO COMPLETE: 24 semester hours of professional education coursework.

WHO EVALUATES: IHE, State Department of Education.

LENGTH OF TIME: One year. Renewal for two additional years if renewal requirements are met each year.

OTHER: The candidate must have met admission requirements to a teacher education program before the first renewal and obtain a program of study signed by a college certification officer outlining the professional education requirements lacking for full licensure <u>not to exceed 24 semester hours</u>. The candidate must complete at least six semester hours of coursework toward the program of study to renew the Alternative E License each year.

TITLE: Alternative License Type A

HISTORY: Legislation enacted in 1984.

GRADE LEVELS AND/OR SUBJECT AREA(S) COVERED:

Available in all endorsement areas.

WHO OPERATES: Office of Teacher Licensing in the Tennessee State
Department of Education and IHEs.

REQUIREMENTS TO ENTER:

An Alternative Type A Teacher License is issued to an individual who
holds a Bachelor's degree from a regionally accredited institution of
higher education with an academic major in the endorsement area
sought.

A superintendent/director of schools in Tennessee must sign a
statement of intent to employ the applicant and must provide a mentor
for the applicant during the first two years of teaching.

If the applicant's transcripts do not reflect an academic major in the
area of endorsement sought, he/she must be admitted to an approved
teacher preparation program and obtain a written statement signed by
the certification officer at the university verifying that the applicant
has satisfied all coursework in the subject area component of the
approved program.

PROGRAM DESCRIPTION:

Alternative Type A Licenses are available in all initial licensure
endorsement areas.

All persons seeking an Alternative Type A License in the areas of early
childhood education, elementary education, and middle grades
education must be admitted to an approved teacher preparation
program and must have made adequate academic progress as
prescribed by the college/university **prior** to the issuance of the
Alternative A License .

An individual may not be issued an Alternative Type A License more than three times. This includes initial issuance plus a limit of two renewals.

NUMBER OF CREDIT HOURS TO COMPLETE:

Variable. To renew this license, one must be officially admitted to an approved teacher preparation program. His/her areas of deficiency must be identified on a program of studies signed by the certification officer at the college/university, and the applicant must earn six semester/nine quarter hours of credit in these areas of deficiency each year for renewal. Once a person has met all the deficiencies as outlined by the college/university, that institution can recommend the individual for a full Tennessee teacher license.

The individual may not be issued a Type A license more than three times.

Upon completion of program and test requirements, a candidate may be issued a full teaching license.

WHO EVALUATES: LEA and IHE.

LENGTH OF TIME: Valid for one calendar year -- until the following August 31. May be renewed twice for a total of not more than three years.

OTHER: Thirty-nine Tennessee institutions of higher education (IHEs) offer approved post-baccalaureate programs which lead to initial licensure and a graduate degree in some instances. These programs range from twelve to fifteen months and include either a semester of student teaching or a year-long internship.

Institutions of higher education that have developed alternative teacher preparation programs leading to a teaching license:

These Institutions offer Alternative C License programs (as of now):

Austin Peay State University
East Tennessee State University
Middle Tennessee State University
Tennessee State University

Tennessee Technological University
University of Memphis
University of Tennessee – Knoxville
University of Tennessee – Chattanooga

States with which the state has reciprocity of teacher licenses:

NASDTEC Interstate Contract.

Institutions of higher education that have *any* teacher preparation programs leading to a license to teach.

Aquinas College
Austin Peay State University
Belmont University
Bethel College
Bryan College
Carson-Newman College
Christian Brothers College
Crichton College
Cumberland University
David Lipscomb University
East Tennessee State University
Fisk University
Free Will Baptist Bible College
Freed-Hardeman University
Johnson Bible College
King College
Lambuth College
Lane College
LeMoyne-Owen College
Lee College
Lincoln Memorial University

Maryville College
Martin Methodist College
Middle Tennessee State University
Milligan College
Peabody College of Vanderbilt University
Rhodes College
South College
Southern Adventist University
Tennessee State University
Tennessee Technological University
Tennessee Wesleyan College
Trevecca Nazarene College
Tusculum College
Union University
University of Memphis
University of the South
University of Tennessee-Chattanooga
University of Tennessee-Knoxville
University of Tennessee-Martin

Contact information for persons interested in finding a teaching position in the state:

Teach Tennessee web site: http://www.tennessee.gov/education/mtjobs.htm
Note: No central placement service in Tennessee.

TITLE: Alternative Teacher Certification

HISTORY: First implemented in 1985 with single program in
the Houston school district. The state currently
has 67 programs, including 21 programs in
community colleges and 8 programs conducted by
private entities.

MOTIVATION: Originally to alleviate shortages, but state legislation
passed in 1989 eliminated that requirement.

GRADE LEVELS AND/OR SUBJECT AREAS COVERED:

The alternative preparation programs are approved to offer teacher
preparation in all grade levels and content areas offered by the State of
Texas. In addition, alternative preparation programs are currently
available for administrators to include principal, superintendent,
educational diagnostician, master teacher, school counselor and school
librarian.

WHO OPERATES: Typically, each program involves a combination of
three entities ---LEA, IHE, and regional education
service center. Development of each certification
area includes practitioners from the field. Recently,
community colleges and private for-profit companies
have created programs in partnership with LEAs.

REQUIREMENTS TO ENTER:

The individual must:

Hold a bachelor's degree.

Demonstrate acceptable college level skills in reading, oral and
written communication, critical thinking, and mathematics as
determined by the program.

Complete screening activities to determine appropriateness for
the certification sought.

If seeking a Bilingual Education/English as a second language
(ESL) certificate, must give evidence of oral and written language
proficiency before being assigned to a bilingual education
classroom.

PROGRAM DESCRIPTION:

All programs may be jointly created through a collaborative process involving the local school districts, colleges, and education service center. Participants from these entities develop the curricula, based on the State's standards that are necessary to prepare teachers for the target certificate. The curricula cover the same State standards that would be included in traditional undergraduate programs, as well as any unique local needs. Instruction is delivered by the partners most suited to the task, either in coursework or in contact hours, and includes a one-year paid internship or a one semester non-paid clinical teaching experience..

During the one-year internship, the intern holds a one-year probationary certificate and receives close support and assistance on a regular basis from a certified mentor teacher who is teaching either in the same or in a related subject area.

Since the intern is on a probationary certificate, he or she receives the full financial benefits of a classroom teacher (i.e., salary and benefits.)

Provisions are made for the intern to observe the teaching of the mentor teacher, and for the mentor teacher to observe the intern.

The intern must complete any training in teaching methods and classroom management prescribed by the state, either during the pre-assignment training or during the internship year.

The internship leads to a standard teaching certificate, identical to that received by a graduate of a traditional undergraduate teacher preparation program.

NUMBER OF CREDIT HOURS TO COMPLETE:

Individual certificate programs require varying amounts of additional coursework to meet unique competency requirements of each certificate.

WHO EVALUATES: The school principal, ACP program supervisor or ACP director.

LENGTH OF TIME: Probationary certificate is valid for one year. It may be renewed annually for up to two additional years.

Institutions of higher education that have developed <u>post-baccalaureate</u> teacher preparation programs leading to a teaching license:

Abilene Christian University
Amerton University
Angelo State University
Arlington Baptist College
Austin College
Baylor University
Concordia University
Dallas Baptist University
East Texas Baptist University
Hardin-Simmons University
Houston Baptist University
Howard Payne University
Huston-Tillotson University
Jarvis Christian College
Lamar University
LeTourneau University
Lubbock Christian University
McMurry University
Midwestern State University
Our Lady of the Lake University
Paul Quin College
Prairie View A&M University
Rice University
Sam Houston State University
Schreiner University
Southern Methodist University
Southwestern Adventist University
Southwestern Assemblies of God University
Southwestern University
St. Edward's University
Stephen F. Austin State University
St. Mary's University
Sul Ross Univeristy- Alpine
Sul Ross University- Uvalde
Tarleton State University
Texas A & M University-College Station
Texas A & M University- Corpus Christi

Texas A & M University - Texarkana
Texas A & M University-Commerce
Texas A & M University-Kingsville
Texas A & M International University
Texas College
Texas Christian University
Texas Lutheran University
Texas Southern University
Texas State University- San Marcos
Texas Tech University
Texas Wesleyan University
Texas Woman's University
Trinity Univeristy
University of Dallas
University of Houston
University of Houston- Clear Lake
University of Houston- Downtown
University of Houston- Victoria
University of Mary Hardin-Baylor
University of North Texas
University of St. Thomas
University of Texas at Arlington
University of Texas at Austin
University of Texas at Brownsville
University of Texas at Dallas
University of Texas at El Paso
University of Texas at San Antonio
University of Texas at Tyler
University of Texas of the Permian Basin
University of Texas Pan American
University of the Incarnate Word
Western Governors University
Wayland Baptist University
West Texas A&M University
Wiley College

Community Colleges that have developed alternative teacher preparation programs leading to a teaching license:

Alamo Community College District
Austin Community College
Blinn College
Brookhaven College
Collin County Community College
Cy-Fair College
Del Mar College- DMC-ACP
Galveston County Alternative Teacher
Certification Program
Houston Community College System
Kingwood College
Lamar State College-Orange
Laredo Community College

Lamar State College-Port Arthur
McLennan Community College
Mountain View College
Montgomery College
North Harris College
Richland College
San Antonio College Center for Educator
Preperation
San Jacinto College North
Tyler Junior College
Tomball College
Weatherford College

Private entities that have developed alternative teacher preparation programs leading to a teaching license:

21st Century Leadership
A Career in Teaching
ACT- San Antonio (Alt Cert for Teachers)
Alternative Cert for Teachers NOW!
Alternative Certification for Teachers-Houston (ACT-Houston)
Alternative Certification for Teachers-Rio Grande Valley (ACT-RGV)
Alternative-South Texas Educator Program (A-STEP)
Education Career Alternatives Program (ECAP)
IteAChtexas.com
Phonoscope Education Network
Qualit ACT: Alternative Certified Tchrs
South Texas Transition to Teaching Alternative Certification Program
Steps to Teaching-ACP
TeacherBuilder.com
Teachers for the 21st Century
Texas Alternative Center for Teachers
Texas Alternative Certification Program
Texas Teachers of Tomorrow

Texas Teaching Fellows
Training vie E-Learning: An Alternative
Certification Hybrid (T.E.A.C.H)
Web-Centric Alternative Certification
Program

States with which the state has reciprocity of teacher licenses:

Note: Texas has no formal reciprocity agreements with any other state. Texas recognizes all states' certified teachers in areas in which Texas recognizes teachers' certificates. Texas is a member of the NASDTEC Interstate Contract, through which about 35 states now recognize Texas certification

Institutions of higher education that have *any* teacher preparation programs leading to a license to teach.

Abilene Christian University
Amberton University
Angelo State University
Argosy University
Arlington Baptist College
Austin College
Baylor University
Concordia University
Dallas Baptist University
Dallas Christian College
East Texas Baptist University
Hardin-Simmons University
Houston Baptist University
Howard Payne University
Huston-Tillotson University
Jarvis Christian College
Lamar University
Letourneau University
Lubbock Christian University
McMurry University
Midwestern State University
Our Lady of the Lake University
Paul Quinn College
Prairie View A&M University
Rice University
St. Edwards University
St. Mary's University
Sam Houston State University
Schreiner University
Southern Methodist University
Southwestern Adventist University
Southwestern Assemblies of God University
Southwestern University
Stephen F. Austin State University
Sul Ross State University-Alpine
Sul Ross State University-Uvalde
Tarleton State University

Texas A&M International University
Texas A&M University-College Station
Texas A&M University-Commerce
Texas A&M University-Corpus Christi
Texas A&M University-Kingsville
Texas A&M University-Texarkana
Texas Christian University
Texas College
Texas Southern University
Texas Lutheran University
Texas State University- San Marcos
Texas Tech University
Texas Wesleyan University
Texas Woman's University
Trinity University
University of Dallas
University of Houston
University of Houston-Clear Lake
University of Houston-Downtown
University of Houston-Victoria
University of Mary Hardin-Baylor
University of North Texas
University of St. Thomas
University of Texas at Arlington
University of Texas at Austin
University of Texas at Brownsville
University of Texas at Dallas
University of Texas-Pan American
University of Texas of the Permian Basin
University of Texas at San Antonio
University of Texas at Tyler
University of Incarnate Word
Wayland Baptist University
West Texas A&M University
Wiley College
University of Texas at El Paso

Contact information for persons interested in finding a teaching position in the state:

Program Approval and Assessment Branch
Maryland State Department of Education
200 West. Baltimore St.
Baltimore, MD 21202
Phone: (410) 767-0390

Independent School Districts (ISDs) that have teacher preparation programs leading to a certificate to teach:

Alief ISD
Dallas ISD
Frenship ISD
Houston ISD
Pasadena ISD

Regional Education Service Centers (ESCs) that have teacher/administrator preparation programs leading to a certificate to teach/administrate:

ESC Region I
ESC Region II
ESC Region III
ESC Region IV
ESC Region VI
ESC Region VII
ESC Region VIII
ESC Region X
ESC Region XI
ESC Region XII
ESC Region XIII
ESC Region XIV
ESC Region XVIII
ESC Region XIX
ESC Region XX

Additional information about ACP programs in Texas is available on the SBEC Web site at: www.sbec.state.tx.us or by contacting:

Karen L Loonam, Ed.D.
Director of Educator Standards
1701 N. Congress Avenue, 5th Floor
Austin, TX 78748
Phone: (512) 936-8304

Or

SBEC Information and Support Center

1-888-863-5880

TITLE: Alternative Routes to Licensure (ARL)

HISTORY: In April 2002, the Utah State Board of Education
                        adopted Administrative Rule 277-503, which
                        governs alternative routes to licensure and
                        endorsements.

MOTIVATION: To increase the number of eligible, qualified, and
                        prepared teachers through non-traditional paths to
                        licensure.

GRADE LEVELS AND/OR SUBJECT AREA(S) COVERED:

                        Early childhood, elementary, and secondary teaching.

WHO OPERATES: Utah State Office of Education (USOE).

REQUIREMENTS TO ENTER:

                        There are two eligibility requirements for the program:

                        1. To hold a minimum of a bachelor's degree in a subject area taught
                        in Utah schools; and

                        2. To be employed by a Utah school district or an accredited Utah
                        school.

PROGRAM DESCRIPTION:

                        The program is a cooperative effort between USOE and Utah school
                        districts. USOE is responsible for: administration of the program;
                        evaluation of the candidates' course requirements; developing
                        curriculum; tracking candidates' progress toward licensure; and
                        recommending the candidates for licensure. Districts are responsible
                        for assigning trained mentors and conducting observations of
                        classroom performance skills and dispositions.

                        Program participants are required to show competency in four areas:
                        content knowledge, pedagogical knowledge, classroom performance
                        skills and dispositions. Content knowledge is required coursework
                        established by USOE curriculum specialists, A streamlined
                        curriculum of pedagogical knowledge was established by USOE, in

partnership with Weber State University College of Education. University courses, district professional development classes, or achieving a passing score on state-approved content tests can fill program requirements.

Participants' transcripts are evaluated by the ARL Advisor, and a Professional Growth Plan is developed. ARL allows participants to teach under a temporary license while fulfilling licensure requirements. Participants have three years to complete the program, and they must make yearly progress. Participants must document progress toward licensure in their first years, successfully pass two observations of their classroom teaching skills, work with a trained mentor, and achieve passing scores on required tests. Participants who meet the above requirements will be issued an ARL license prior to June 30 of each year, which will allow them to be reported as highly qualified. The ARL license may be renewed for two additional years, as long as the particiapant continues to make progress each year. ARL participants must be assigned to teach in the area of their university major in order to be reported as highly qualified. ARL participants who are teaching subjects for which they do not have a major or a major equivalency cannot be reported as highly qualified. Once requirements are completed, the participant is recommended for a three year, Level 1, Utah Professional Educator License.

NUMBER OF CREDIT HOURS TO COMPLETE:

The number varies with each candidate, but the core curriculum is 15 semester hours of pedagogical course work. The remaining 15 semester hours are earned through a strong mentor/professional support program.

WHO EVALUATES: The ARL Advisor and the principal.

LENGTH OF TIME: Three years.

TITLE: Troops To Teachers

HISTORY: Ronald M. Stanfield, (LTC, Retired) Coordinator
                    Utah Transition to Teaching Alternative Program,
                    is the Utah representative.

MOTIVATION: To relieve overall teacher shortages and to improve
                    teacher quality by attracting mature, highly-
                    experienced personnel to the classroom.

GRADE LEVELS AND/OR SUBJECT AREA(S) COVERED: All subjects.

WHO OPERATES: Utah State Office of Education (USOE).

REQUIREMENTS TO ENTER:

                    Candidates must be:

                    Active Duty

                    1.   Retired from active duty

                    2.   Active duty members with approved date of retirement

                    Reserve Component

                    1.   Retired from drilling reserves

                    2.   Currently serving in drilling reserves with over 10 years
                    service and a commitment to serve an additional 3 years.

                    AND

                    Hold a bachelor's degree

                    AND

                    Successfully complete a background clearance check.

PROGRAM DESCRIPTION:

                    The program has a referral and placement assistance program for
                    candidates.

NUMBER OF CREDIT HOURS TO COMPLETE:

                    Varies with each candidate; core program is 15 semester hours.

WHO EVALUATES: The Alternative Routes to Licensure Advisor and the
                    principal.

LENGTH OF TIME: 1-2 years.

Institutions of higher education that have developed alternative teacher preparation programs leading to a teaching license:

None.

States with which the state has reciprocity of teacher licenses:

ICA.

Institutions of higher education that have *any* teacher preparation programs leading to a license to teach.

Brigham Young University
Dixie State College
Southern Utah University
University of Phoenix
University of Utah

Utah State University
Utah Valley State College
Weber State University
Westminster College

Contact information for persons interested in finding a teaching position in the state:

Visit the Web site at: http://www.usoe.k12.ut.us/cert
Click on job vacancies

TITLE: License by Evaluation

HISTORY: Regulations issued in 1971.

GRADE LEVELS AND/OR SUBJECT AREA(S) COVERED: Not specified.

WHO OPERATES: State.

REQUIREMENTS TO ENTER:

>   A bachelor's degree.
>
>   Competence, preparation, and experience in the subject to be taught.

PROGRAM DESCRIPTION:

>   The individual may be licensed by the Office of Educator Licensing and
>   Professional Standards through an evaluation process.
>
>   The evaluation is conducted by a peer review panel consisting of
>   educators who are licensed and practicing in the appropriate
>   endorsement area. For example, to evaluate a person seeking a
>   science endorsement, the panel members would be licensed science
>   teachers.
>
>   The peer review panel shall recommend individuals for licensure based
>   on evidence of competence, preparation, and experience in the field for
>   which a license is being sought.
>
>   The panel may recommend that the individual be licensed without
>   reservation or that he/she be licensed only after documentation of
>   evidence addressing the competencies identified as "not met" has been
>   received and deemed satisfactory.

NUMBER OF CREDIT HOURS TO COMPLETE: Coursework may be required.

WHO EVALUATES: Panel of licensed and practicing educators in the
endorsement area and chosen by the Office of
Educator Licensing and Professional Standards.

LENGTH OF TIME: Applicant must submit portfolio for evaluation
within one year of letter of eligibility to the Peer
Review Process.

TITLE: Transcript Analysis

HISTORY: In operation since about 1964.

GRADE LEVELS AND/OR SUBJECT AREA(S) COVERED: Not specified.

WHO OPERATES: State.

REQUIREMENTS TO ENTER:

Must hold a valid Vermont license.

PROGRAM DESCRIPTION:

For Initial License: Transcript Review is performed only for endorsements for which Vermont does NOT have a state approved educator preparation program. **For additional endorsements:** All endorsements can be evaluated by transcript review for additional endorsements.

The state will specify competencies the individual must complete in order to qualify for certification.

NUMBER OF CREDIT HOURS TO COMPLETE: Varies for applicants.

WHO EVALUATES: Office of Educator Licensing and Professional Standards.

LENGTH OF TIME: New requirements can be added at any time if competencies are revised.

OTHER: Transcript analysis is used only for additional endorsement purposes OR for areas of licensure in which there are no Vermont preparation programs.

Institutions of higher education that have developed alternative teacher preparation programs leading to a teaching license:

None.

States with which the state has reciprocity of teacher licenses:

NASDTEC Interstate Contract. A graduate of a state-approved teacher preparation program, whether or not a Vermont resident, is entitled to an initial Vermont license. This license may used to obtain an initial license/certificate in states that are participants, along with Vermont, in the NASDTEC Interstate Contract.

Contact the Vermont Department of Education, Office of Educator Licensing, 120 State Street, Montpelier, VT 05620 for more information.

Institutions of higher education that have *any* teacher preparation programs leading to a license to teach.

Bennington College
Castleton State College
Champlain College
College of St. Joseph
Goddard College
Green Mountain College
Johnson State College
Lyndon State College

Middlebury College
Norwich University
St. Michael's College
School for International Training
University of Vermont
Vermont College of Union Institute & University
Vermont Technical College

Contact information for persons interested in finding a teaching position in the state:

linda.hendrickson@state.vt.us

TITLE: Alternate Routes to Licensure

HISTORY: The implementation of the current licensure regulations for Virginia school divisions became effective September 21, 2007. Career Switcher Program was created in response to Senate Joint Resolution 384 and the 1999 Appropriation Act (Item 127D and 129Q). A pilot for military personnel was conducted in summer 2000. Four pilots were conducted in summer 2001 to prepare individuals in other professions to become teachers. In March 2002, six program providers were established. Virginia currently has nine Career Switcher Programs statewide.

MOTIVATION: Alternate route programs are available to individuals employed by an education agency in Virginia who seek teaching endorsements in grades PreK-12. The Career Switcher program was designed for individuals who have not completed a teacher preparation program but had considerable life experiences, career achievements, and an academic background relevant for teaching in PreK through grade 12.

GRADE LEVELS AND/OR SUBJECT AREA(S) COVERED:
PreK-12. All teaching areas can be pursued through an alternate route program. Special education endorsement is not available through the Career Switcher Program, but is available through another alternate route as described below.

WHO OPERATES: IHE, LEA, and State.

REQUIREMENTS TO ENTER AND PROGRAM DESCRIPTIONS:

8VAC20-22-90. Alternate routes to licensure.

A. Career switcher alternate route to licensure for career professions. An alternate route is available to career switchers who seek teaching endorsements preK through grade 12 with the exception of special education.

1. An individual seeking a Provisional License through the career switcher program must meet the following prerequisite requirements:

a. An application process;

b. A baccalaureate degree from a regionally accredited college or university;

c. The completion of requirements for an endorsement in a teaching area or the equivalent through verifiable experience or academic study;

d. At least five years of full-time work experience or its equivalent; and

e. Virginia qualifying scores on the professional teacher's assessments as prescribed by the Board of Education.

2. The Provisional License is awarded at the end of Level I preparation. All components of the career switcher alternate route for career professions must be completed by the candidate.

3. The Level I requirements must be completed during the course of a single year and may be offered through a variety of delivery systems, including distance learning programs. If an employing agency recommends extending the Provisional License for a second year, the candidate will enter Level III of the program. Career switcher programs must be certified by the Virginia Department of Education.

a. Level I preparation. Intensive Level I preparation includes a minimum of 180 clock hours of instruction, including field experience. This phase includes, but is not limited to, curriculum and instruction, including technology, reading, and other specific course content relating to the Standards of Learning, differentiation of instruction, classroom/behavior management, instructional design based on assessment data, and human growth and development.

b. Level II preparation during first year of employment.

(1) Candidate seeks employment in Virginia with the one-year Provisional License.

(2) Continued Level II preparation during the first year of employment with a minimum of five seminars that expand the intensive preparation requirements listed in subdivision 3 a of this subsection. The five seminars will include a minimum of 20 cumulative instructional hours. A variety of instructional delivery techniques will be utilized to implement the seminars.

(3) One year of successful, full-time teaching experience in a Virginia public or accredited nonpublic school under a one-year Provisional License. A trained mentor must be assigned to assist the candidate during the first year of employment. Responsibilities of the mentor include, but are not limited to, the following:

(a) Collaborate with the beginning teacher in the development and implementation of an individualized professional development plan;

(b) Observe, assess, coach, and provide opportunities for constructive feedback, including strategies for self-reflection;

(c) Share resources and materials;

(d) Share best instructional, assessment, and organizational practices; classroom and behavior management strategies; and techniques for promoting effective communication; and

(e) Provide general support and direction regarding school policies and procedures.

(4) Upon completion of Levels I and II of the career switcher alternate route to licensure program and submission of a recommendation from the Virginia educational employing agency,

the candidate will be eligible to apply for a five-year, renewable license. Renewal requirements for the regular license will be subject to current regulations of the Board of Education.

c. Level III preparation, if required.

(1) Post preparation, if required, will be conducted by the Virginia employing educational agency to address the areas where improvement is needed as identified in the candidate's professional improvement plan; and

(2) Upon completion of Levels I, II, and III of the career switcher alternate route to licensure program and submission of a recommendation from the Virginia educational employing agency, the candidate will be eligible to receive a five-year renewable license.

4. Verification of program completion will be documented by the certified program provider and the division superintendent or designee.

5. Certified providers implementing a career switcher program may charge a fee for participation in the program.

B. An alternate route is available to individuals employed by an educational agency who seek teaching endorsements preK through grade 12.   Individuals must complete the requirements for the regular, five-year license within the validity period of the provisional license.

1. An individual seeking a license through this alternate route must have met the following requirements:

a. Are entering the teaching field through the alternate route to licensure upon the recommendation of the Virginia employing educational agency;

b. Hold a baccalaureate degree from a regionally accredited college or university with the exception of individuals seeking the Technical Professional License;

c. Have met requirements for the endorsement area; and

d. Need to complete an allowable portion of professional studies and licensure requirements.

2. The professional studies requirements for the appropriate level of endorsement sought must be completed. A Virginia educational agency may submit to the Superintendent of Public Instruction for approval an alternate program to meet the professional studies requirements. The alternate program must include training (seminar, internship, coursework, etc.) in human growth and development, curriculum and instructional procedures (including technology), instructional design based on assessment data, classroom and behavior management, foundations of education and reading.

3. One year of successful, full-time teaching experience in the appropriate teaching area in a Virginia public or accredited nonpublic school must be completed. A fully licensed experienced teacher must be available in the school building to assist the beginning teacher employed through the alternate route.

C. Alternate route in special education. The Provisional License is a three-year nonrenewable teaching license issued to an individual employed as a special education teacher in a public school or a nonpublic special education school in Virginia who does not hold the appropriate special education endorsement. This alternate route to special education is not applicable to individuals employed as speech pathologists. To be issued the Provisional License through this alternate route, an individual must:

1. Be employed by a Virginia public or nonpublic school as a special educator and have the recommendation of the employing educational agency;

2. Hold a baccalaureate degree from a regionally accredited college or university;

3. Have an assigned mentor endorsed in special education; and

4. Have a planned program of study in the assigned endorsement area, make progress toward meeting the endorsement requirements each of the three years of the license, and have completed coursework in the competencies of foundations for educating students with disabilities and an understanding and application of the legal aspects and regulatory requirements associated with identification, education, and evaluation of students with disabilities. A survey course integrating these competencies would satisfy this requirement. The Provisional License through this alternate route shall not be issued without the completion of these prerequisites.

D. Alternate programs at institutions of higher education or Virginia school divisions. Alternate programs developed by institutions of higher education (i) recognize the unique strengths of prospective teachers from nontraditional backgrounds and (ii) prepare these individuals to meet the same standards that are established for others who are granted a license through an alternate route.

E. Experiential learning. Individuals applying for an initial license through the alternate route as prescribed by the Board of Education must meet the following criteria to be eligible to request experiential learning credits in lieu of the coursework for the endorsement (teaching) content area:

1. Hold a baccalaureate degree from a regionally accredited college or university;

2. Have at least five years of documented full-time work experience that may include specialized training related to the endorsement sought; and

3. Have met the qualifying score on the content knowledge assessment prescribed by the Board of Education.

The criteria do not apply to teachers of special education and elementary education (preK-3 and preK-6).

NUMBER OF CREDIT HOURS TO COMPLETE:
A minimum of a bachelor's degree; 15 to 18 semester hours of professional studies coursework; specific endorsement area course requirements.
Those enrolled in Career Switcher programs must meet the requirements of their specific program.

WHO EVALUATES: State

LENGTH OF TIME: Provisional licenses are issued for a period not to exceed three years. Provisional (Career Switcher) licenses are issued for one year. Renewable licenses are issued for five years.

INSTITUTIONS OF HIGHER EDUCATION THAT HAVE DEVELOPED TEACHER PREPARATION PROGRAMS LEADING TO A TEACHING LICENSE:

Career Switcher Program Providers:
- George Mason University
- Old Dominion University
- Regent University
- Shenandoah University
- Spotsylvania County Schools
- University of Virginia Richmond Center
- Virginia Beach City Public Schools
- Virginia Community College System
- Western Virginia Public Education Consortium (WVPEC)

Virginia College and University with approved programs:

Averett University
Bluefield College
Bridgewater College
Christopher Newport University
College of William and Mary
Council of Higher Education
Eastern Mennonite University
Emory and Henry College
Ferrum College
George Mason University
Hampton University
Hollins University
James Madison University
Liberty University
Longwood University
Lynchburg College
Mary Baldwin College
Marymount University
Norfolk State University

Old Dominion University
Radford University
Randolph College
Randolph-Macon College
Regent University
Roanoke College
Saint Paul's College
Shenandoah University
Sweet Briar College
University of Mary Washington
University of Richmond
University of Virginia
University of Virginia's College at Wise
Virginia Commonwealth University
Virginia Intermont College
Virginia State University
Virginia Tech
Virginia Union University
Virginia Wesleyan College

STATES WITH WHICH THE STATE HAS RECIPROCITY OF TEACHER LICENSES: Virginia recognizes all states who participate in the NASDTEC Interstate Agreement.

CONTACT INFORMATION FOR PERSONS INTERESTED IN FINDING A TEACHING POSITION IN THE STATE: Individuals must contact each school division for vacancy information.

TITLE: Regional Consortia Alternative Route Program

HISTORY: Create consortia programs including multiple higher education institutions, educational service districts, and local school districts.

MOTIVATION: Increase access to alternative route programs in eastern Washington and solve local shortages locally.

GRADE LEVELS AND/OR SUBJECT AREA(S) COVERED: Secondary shortage areas, special education, bilingual education, ESL.

WHO OPERATES: Professional Educator Standards Board.

REQUIREMENTS TO ENTER:

Route 2: Currently employed classified staff with baccalaureate degrees in subject matter or "subject matter related" (i.e. engineering for math or science) shortage areas (special education, mathematics, chemistry, physics, biology, instrumental music, early childhood special education, choral music, English as a Second Language, bilingual, and Japanese) and/or working in an area of shortage due to geographic location as documented by partnerships and districts, AND

a. District validation of qualifications, including three years of successful student interaction and leadership as a classified staff;
b. A baccalaureate degree from a regionally accredited institution of higher education);
c. Meet the age, good moral character, and personal fitness requirements for all teachers (all candidates must have fingerprint clearance prior to assignment to classroom); and
d. Successful passage of the statewide basic skills exam (WEST-B) and PRAXIS II subject area test.

Route 3: Mid-career professionals with baccalaureate degrees or higher who are not employed in a school district. Priority shall be given to individuals with degrees that qualify them for endorsements in the subject matter shortage areas noted above or identified by partnership districts within the consortia programs. In addition, candidates via this route must have:

a. Five years career work experience;
b. A baccalaureate degree from a regionally accredited institution of higher education;
c. External validation of qualifications, including demonstrated successful experience with students or children, such as reference letters and letters of support from previous employers;

d. Meet the age, good moral character, and personal fitness requirements for teachers (all candidates must have fingerprint clearance prior to assignment to a classroom); and

e. Successful passage of the statewide basic skills exam (WEST-B) and PRAXIS II subject area test.

Route 4: Individuals teaching with conditional or emergency substitute certificates. The eligibility criteria for mid-career professionals apply to these individuals. Priority will be given to individuals teaching in shortage areas and/or "core academic subjects" as defined by federal legislation (No Child Left Behind).

PROGRAM DESCRIPTION:

- A Summer Academy during which prior learning and experience are assessed in order to create a Teacher Development Plan that identifies program requirements for each candidate. Candidates must be prepared to attend a full day orientation, six two day seminar sessions and participate in school-based experiences with students during June and July.

- A performance-based mentored internship of one school year or less. Interns are assigned to work full-time with a mentor teacher in his/her classroom beginning with the first day of school in the district and concluding with the last day. Early exit is an option for interns who complete a minimum of half of the year, provide evidence that verifies that the learner outcomes for the program have been met, and for whom the mentor teacher and consortium program supervisor concur that all program requirements have been met.

- Formalized learning opportunities offered by the colleges/universities on or near school/ESD sites, on-line, or via K-20. Interns register for modules with up to four institutions during the course of the summer and first semester/fall-winter quarters of the internship. The modules focus on specific learner outcomes and performance indicators. The delivery of the modules is a combination of face-to-face meetings, on-line opportunities, and interaction via K-20. Interns will create a portfolio that contains evidence related to the program learner outcomes and performance indicators.

NUMBER OF CREDIT HOURS TO COMPLETE:

12.5 – 16.0 semester credits

LENGTH OF TIME::   One year or less

WHO EVALUATES: Higher education institution and district.

TITLE: Alternative Route under Partnership Grants Program

HISTORY: Legislation creating this program was signed into
                     law on May 3, 2001. Access www.pesb.wa.gov for
                     more information.

MOTIVATION: The program permits creation of four different
                     alternative routes, "aimed at recruiting candidates to
                     teaching in subject matter shortage areas and areas
                     with shortages due to geographic location." Stipends
                     for both interns and mentors are available
                     contingent upon legislative funding.

GRADE LEVELS AND/OR SUBJECT AREA(S) COVERED:

                     Secondary subject shortage areas, special education, bilingual, and
                     ESL.

WHO OPERATES: Washington Professional Educator Standards Board.

REQUIREMENTS TO ENTER:

                     Route 1: Currently employed classified instructional employees with
                     transferable associate degrees seeking residency certification with
                     endorsements in special education, bilingual education, or ESL, AND

                     a. District validation of qualifications, including three years of
                         successful student interaction and leadership as a classified
                         instructional employee;
                     b. Successful passage of the statewide basic skills exam (WEST-B);
                     c. Meeting the age, good moral character, and personal fitness
                         requirements for all teachers

                     Route 2: Currently employed classified staff with baccalaureate
                     degrees in subject matter or "subject matter related" (i.e. engineering
                     for math or science) shortage areas (special education, mathematics,
                     chemistry, physics, biology, instrumental music, early childhood
                     special education, choral music, English as a Second Language,
                     bilingual, and Japanese) and/or working in an area of shortage due to
                     geographic location as documented by partnerships and districts, AND

                     a. District validation of qualifications, including three years of
                         successful student interaction and leadership as a classified staff;
                     b. A baccalaureate degree from a regionally accredited institution of
                         higher education);

c. Meet the age, good moral character, and personal fitness requirements for all teachers (all candidates must have fingerprint clearance prior to assignment to classroom); and

d. Successful passage of the statewide basic skills exam (WEST-B) and PRAXIS II for subject area

Route 3: Mid-career professionals with baccalaureate degrees or higher who are not employed in a school district. Priority shall be given to individuals with degrees that qualify them for endorsements in the subject matter shortage areas noted above or identified by partnership districts within the consortia programs. In addition, candidates via this route must have:
a. Five years career work experience;
b. A baccalaureate degree from a regionally accredited institution of higher education;
c. External validation of qualifications, including demonstrated successful experience with students or children, such as reference letters and letters of support from previous employers;
d. Meet the age, good moral character, and personal fitness requirements for teachers (all candidates must have fingerprint clearance prior to assignment to a classroom); and
e. Successful passage of the statewide basic skills exam (WEST-B) and PRAXIS II subject area test.

Route 4: Individuals teaching with conditional or emergency substitute certificates. The eligibility criteria for mid-career professionals apply to these individuals. Priority will be given to individuals teaching in shortage areas and/or "core academic subjects" as defined by federal legislation (No Child Left Behind).

PROGRAM DESCRIPTION:

- A Summer Academy during which prior learning and experience are assessed in order to create at Teacher Development Plan that identifies program requirements for each candidate. Candidates must be prepared to attend a full day orientation, seminar sessions and participate in school-based experiences with students during June and July.

- A performance-based mentored internship of one school year or less. Interns are assigned to work full-time with a mentor teacher in his/her classroom beginning with the first day of school in the district and concluding with the last day. Early exit is an option for interns who complete a minimum of half of the year, provide evidence that verifies that the learner outcomes for the program have been met, and for whom the mentor teacher and consortium program supervisor concur that all program requirements have been met.

- Formalized learning opportunities are offered by the colleges/universities on or near school/ESD sites, on-line, or via K-20 during the internship.

NUMBER OF CREDIT HOURS:

Varies, depending on prior credits applicable and the subject area in which candidate is being certified.

LENGTH OF TIME: Varies, depending on the program and the IHE.

WHO EVALUATES: IHE and LEA.

TITLE: Conditional Certificate

HISTORY: Instituted in 1989; changed in 1990 and 1998.

MOTIVATION: Shortage. No person with regular certification in the
field is available as verified by the local school
district or educational service district
superintendent or the applicant has unusual
distinction.

GRADE LEVELS AND/OR SUBJECT AREA(S) COVERED:

Persons highly qualified and experienced in fields of knowledge to be
taught in the common or non-public schools.

WHO OPERATES: State; employing school district or educational service district
superintendent.

REQUIREMENTS TO ENTER:

Conditional certificates are issued to individuals who are screened by
the local school district or educational service district superintendents,
who verify that these conditions have been met:

1. The applicant is highly qualified and experienced in the
subject matter to be taught and has unusual distinction or
exceptional talent;

2. No person with regular teacher certification in the
endorsement area is available or that circumstances warrant
consideration of issuance of a conditional certificate;

3. Conditional certificates are issued only if no person with
regular certification is available.

PROGRAM DESCRIPTION:

The educational service district or local district superintendent or
administrator of an approved private school will verify that the
following criteria have been met when requesting the conditional
certificate:

The individual is competent for the assignment and is being
certified for that specific assignment only;

The individual will be delegated primary responsibility for planning, conducting, and evaluating instructional activities with the assistance of the district and will not be serving in a paraprofessional role which would not require certification;

The individual will complete a minimum of 60 clock hours of pedagogy and child/adolescent development within the first 60 working days.

LENGTH OF TIME: Valid for two years, and only for the activity specified. The certificate may be reissued upon completion of 60 clock hours (6 quarter hours) of coursework.

OTHER: The State of Washington also issues EMERGENCY CERTIFICATES. Emergency certification for specific positions may be issued upon the recommendation of local school district and educational service district superintendents to persons who hold the appropriate degree and have substantially completed a program of preparation in accordance with Washington requirements for certification: Provided, that a qualified person who holds regular certification is not available or that the position is essential and circumstances warrant consideration of issuance of an emergency certificate.

TITLE: Troops To Teachers Program

HISTORY: The Department of Defense Troops to Teachers (TTT)
                    Program was officially established on Jan. 19, 1994,
                    and is managed by the federal Defense Activity for Non-
                    Traditional Education Support (DANTES).

MOTIVATION: This program was established to help relieve teacher
                    shortages, provide positive role models in the
                    nation's public schools, and to assist military and
                    civilian personnel impacted by military reductions to
                    enter a new career in public education.

GRADE LEVELS AND/OR SUBJECT AREA(S) COVERED: K-12 all areas

WHO OPERATES: The Office of Superintendent of Public Instruction,
                    IHE, LEA, and DANTES cooperatively work together
                    to provide resources and a plan for the TTT
                    applicant.
                    Washington state contact person for this program:
                    Dr. George Willett
                    Phone: (800) 743-2357

REQUIREMENTS TO ENTER:

                    Bachelor's degree with 45 quarter hours in an endorsement area or an
                    associate degree to be accepted into the TTT program which leads to
                    certification.

PROGRAM DESCRIPTION:

                    DANTES and the local TTT office assist interested individuals in
                    locating a certification program, and/or securing a position as a
                    teacher (or teacher's aide if there is only an associate's degree).

NUMBER OF CREDIT HOURS:

                    Varies, depending on prior credits applicable and the subject area in
                    which candidate is being certified.

LENGTH OF TIME: Varies, depending on the program and the IHE.

WHO EVALUATES: DANTES, IHE, and LEA.

TITLE: Paraprofessional Pipeline

HISTORY: In April 2007 the Washington State Legislature expanded Alternative Route programs by allocating funds to support paraprofessionals who hold no college degree to earn an AA in Math Education followed by a BA in Education with an endorsement in Secondary Math through Alternative Route Programs.

MOTIVATION: Math Shortage

SUBJECT AREAS COVERED:
Secondary Math

GRADES: 9-12

WHO OPERATES: Professional Educator Standards Board

REQUIREMENTS TO ENTER:
Currently employed classified instructional employees with no transferable degrees seeking residency certification with an endorsement in secondary math AND

a.   District validation of qualifications, including three years of successful student interaction and leadership as a classified instructional employee;
b.   Successful passage of the statewide basic skills exam (WEST-B);
c.   Meeting the age, good moral character, and personal fitness requirements for all teachers

PROGRAM DESCRIPTION:

Candidates enter a two year community college program designed to earn a Math Education Associate of Arts Degree. Upon completion of this program and successful passing of the Praxis II in Secondary Math, candidates enter an Alternative Route program to complete an additional year of coursework in education in year three and complete a yearlong mentored internship in year four.

NUMBER OF CREDIT HOURS TO COMPLETE: 180

WHO EVALUATES: LEA's and IHE's

LENGTH OF TIME:
Four Years

Institutions of higher education that have developed alternative teacher preparation programs leading to a teaching license:

City University- Seattle
Saint Martin's University
Pacific Lutheran University
ESD 105 Regional Consortia Program: Central Washington University, Western Washington University, Heritage University, Pacific Lutheran University

States with which the state has reciprocity of teacher licenses:

NASDTEC Interstate Agreement.

Institutions of higher education that have *any* teacher preparation programs leading to a license to teach.

Antioch University-Seattle
Argosy University
Central Washington University
City University
Eastern Washington University
Evergreen State College
Gonzaga University
Heritage University
Lesley University
Northwest University
Pacific Lutheran University

St. Martin's University
Seattle Pacific University
Seattle University
University of Puget Sound
University of Washington – Bothell
University of Washington – Seattle
University of Washington – Tacoma
Walla Walla College
Washington State University
Western Washington University
Whitworth College

Contact information for persons interested in finding a teaching position in the state:

Note: Interested persons should contact individual school district personnel officers or access www.wateach.com

Saint Martin's University - Ann Gentle: 360-438-4566
http://www.stmartin.edu/education/transitions.htm

Pacific Lutheran University - Tony Aho: 253-535-7276
http://www.plu.edu/~educ/CO.htm

ESD 105 Regional Consortia Programs - Jim Seamons: 509-961-7779
ESD 105 Route 1- Mickie Clise: 509-865-8653

City University- Seattle – Corll Morrissey: 800-426-5596 ext. 5332

TITLE: : Alternative for General Education Certification

MOTIVATION: Assist individuals to obtain a specialization in a general education field.

SUBJECT AREAS COVERED: All general education areas

WHO OPERATES: Institutions of higher education & RESAs.

REQUIREMENTS TO ENTER:

- Minimum of a bachelor's degree from a regionally accredited institution of higher education with a minimum 2.5 GPA;

- Meet the WVBE – required proficiency scores on the Praxis I or qualify for an exemption;

- Meet the WVBE – required proficiency score(s) on the Praxis II content or qualify for an exemption;

- Be offered employment in a shortage area in a West Virginia school district: and

- Complete a West Virginia State Police and Federal Bureau of Investigation background check.

PROGRAM DESCRIPTION:

Individuals complete a minimum of 18 semester hours of instruction in the areas of student assessment, development and learning, curriculum, classroom management, the use of educational computers and other technology, and special education and diversity.

All programs must contain a minimum of three semester hours of instruction in special education and diversity.

Individuals also complete three phases of training which include supervision by a professional support team as well as formal observations and evaluations.

Please visit the following website for more information:

http://wvde.state.wv.us/certification/educator/alternative/general.html

NUMBER OF CREDIT HOURS TO COMPLETE: 18 semester hours

WHO EVALUATES:

Institutions of Higher Education and RESAs

LENGTH OF TIME:

Maximum of 3 years

TITLE: Alternative for Special Education Certification

MOTIVATION: To assist individuals to obtain a specialization in multi-categorical (BD, MI, SLD) special education.

SUBJECT AREAS COVERED: Multi-categorical (BD, MI, SLD)

WHO OPERATES: Institutions of higher education and RESAs

REQUIREMENTS TO ENTER:

- Minimum of a bachelor's degree from a regionally accredited institution of a higher education with a minimum 2.5 GPA;

- Meet the WVBE- required proficiency scores on the Praxis I or qualify for an exemption; and

- Complete a West Virginia State Police and Federal Bureau of Investigation background check.

PROGRAM DESCRIPTION:

Individuals complete a minimum of 21 semester hours in special education including:

- Research-based reading strategies (six semester hours);
- Research-based mathematics strategies (three semester hours);
- Introduction to special education and legal foundations (three-six semester hours);
- Diagnostic evaluation and early intervention strategies (three semester hours).

The West Virginia Content Standards & Objectives, differentiated instruction, consultation, and Positive Behavioral Intervention & Supports must be woven throughout the program as well as other research-based strategies.

Individuals completing this alternative route who DO NOT HOLD a valid, West Virginia professional teaching certificate or ARE NOT EMPLOYED and HOLD a valid, West Virginia alternative teaching certificate MUST ALSO COMPLETE a clinical experience. Please visit the following website for more information:**http://wvde.state.wv.us/certification/educator/alternative/special/html**

NUMBER OF CREDIT HOURS TO COMPLETE: 21 semester hours

**WHO
EVALUATES:**　　Institutions of higher education and RESAs

**LENGTH OF
TIME:**　　Maximum of 3 years

TITLE: Alternative for Special Educators to Obtain a Content Endorsement(s)

MOTIVATION: To assist special educators (delivering direct instruction in a departmentalized setting) to meet the NCLB and IDEA definitions of highly qualified special educator.

SUBJECT AREAS COVERED:

Biology, English, General Science, Mathematics and Social Studies.

WHO OPERATES: West Virginia Department of Education.

REQUIREMENTS TO ENTER:

- Minimum of a bachelor's degree from a regionally accredited institution of higher education with a minimum 2.5 GPA and

- Meet the WVBE – required proficiency scores on the Praxis I or qualify for an exemption.

PROGRAM DESCRIPTION:

Individuals wishing to obtain a content endorsement(s) must complete 21 semester hours of content appropriate to the specific endorsement(s). For more information, please visit: **http://wvde.state.wv.us/certification/educator/alternative/special.html**

NUMBER OF CREDIT HOURS TO COMPLETE: 21 semester hours

WHO EVALUATES: West Virginia Department of Education

LENGTH OF TIME: Maximum of 3 years

Institutions of higher education that have developed alternative teacher preparation programs leading to a teaching license:

Concord University, Fairmont State University, Marshall University and West Virginia State University

States with which the state has reciprocity of teacher licenses:

NASDTEC Interstate Contract.

Institutions of higher education that have _any_ teacher preparation programs leading to a license to teach.

Alderson-Broaddus College
Appalachian Bible College
Bethany College
Bluefield State College
Concord University
Davis & Elkins College
Fairmont State University
Glenville State College
Marshall University Graduate College **
Ohio Valley _University_
Salem International University
Shepherd University

University of Charleston
West Liberty State College
West Virginia University
   Institute of Technology *
West Virginia State University
West Virginia University
West Virginia University-Parkersburg
West Virginia Wesleyan College
Wheeling Jesuit College
* Vocational/technical program only
_** West Virginia Graduate College and
   Marshall University merged in July 1997_

State Contact information :

Serena Starcher
Coordinator, Teacher Education

West Virginia Department of Education
Officer of Professional Preparation
1900 Kanawha Blvd., East
Building 6, Room 252
Charleston, WV 25305

Phone: 304.558.2703
Fax: 304.558.7843
Email: slstarch@access.k12.wv.us

TITLE: Alternative Programs Leading to Initial Educator Licensing

HISTORY: Under new rules promulgated in 2000, the state superintendent could approve alternative programs that lead to initial educator licensing, beginning in 2004. Some pilot programs are underway.

MOTIVATION: In order to address shortages and provide accelerated, performance-based programs to non-traditional students, new rules were promulgated, which allow colleges and universities, agencies, school districts, and others to develop alternative programs.

These programs are required to have students demonstrate proficiency in Wisconsin's teaching standards, in order to be recommended for the Initial Educator License.

GRADE LEVELS AND/OR SUBJECT AREA(S) COVERED:

Depends on the individual program.

WHO OPERATES: Not limited.

REQUIREMENTS TO ENTER:

Defined by the individual program through a standard application process.

PROGRAM DESCRIPTION:

Varies from program to program.

Programs submitted for approval must include the following:

Components to assure program completers are proficient in the Wisconsin standards:

1. Need, Mission, Philosophy of Program

2. Goals and Objectives

3. Resources Statement

4. Instructional Design

5. Student Admission Criteria

6. Student Assessment and Program Completion Requirements

7. Program Evaluation Plan

NUMBER OF CREDIT HOURS TO COMPLETE:

Dependent on a candidate's background and the individual program.

WHO EVALUATES: Program provider **evaluates candidate performance; the Departmetn of Public Instruction evaluates program for continued approval.**

LENGTH OF TIME: Dependent on individual program.

OTHER: A list of the programs is available online on the Web site at: http://www.dpi.state.wi.us/dlsis/tel/altern.html.

TITLE: Experimental and Innovative Teacher Education Programs

HISTORY: Began as a pilot in 1991.

Continues as an option for colleges and universities under: Rules, effective July 1, 2004.

MOTIVATION: To provide colleges and universities with approved teacher education programs opportunities to apply for approval of pilot programs. Programs submitted must be substantially different from existing traditional programs to qualify for approval as an experimental or innovative program.

GRADE LEVELS AND/OR SUBJECT AREA(S) COVERED: Not specified.

WHO OPERATES: IHEs which have approved teacher education programs.

REQUIREMENTS TO ENTER:

IHEs may apply to the state for approval to pilot models of experimental or innovative preparation programs, containing a heavy evaluation component.

An IHE must provide evidence of a screening process for admitting candidates to the program, a plan for formative evaluation during the period the candidate is in the program, and a summative evaluation prior to exiting the program -- the institutional endorsement for a teaching license. There must also be a plan for an evaluation of the pilot program itself.

IHE proposals must contain program goals and specific objectives which define the intent and expectations of the program's outcomes, as well as specific objectives to be obtained by individuals enrolled in the experimental or innovative program.

Proposals must also: verify how the program will meet state standards for minimum competencies in teacher preparation; include a listing of standards for which waivers are being sought and a rationale for each exception; provide documentation of admission criteria, faculty qualifications, and institutional support, including budget data, syllabi or detailed descriptions of any courses expressly developed for the program; provide documentation of recruitment processes; and show evidence of a direct relationship between the program's structure and its goals and objectives.

PROGRAM DESCRIPTION:

> May vary with each program.

NUMBER OF CREDIT HOURS TO COMPLETE: May vary with each program.

WHO EVALUATES: IHE responsible for evaluation of candidates and evaluation of its pilot program.

LENGTH OF TIME: May vary with each program.

OTHER: A state official said this program should allow IHEs to develop a variety of models -- with evaluations of each. Then, the state can weigh the results in deciding whether to adopt any of the models.

Institutions of higher education that have developed alternative or innovative/experimental teacher preparation programs leading to a teaching license:

Alverno College
Cardinal Stritch University
Carthage College
Concordia University
Lakeland College

Mt. Mary College
University of Wisconsin-Milwaukee
University of Wisconsin-Oshkosh

University of Wisconsin- Platteville

Contact information for persons interested in finding a teaching position in the state:

Laurie Derse
Department of Public Instruction
125 S. Webster, P.O. Box 7841
Madison, WI 53707
Phone: (608) 266-1028

States with which the state has reciprocity of teacher licenses:

None.

Institutions of higher education that have *any* teacher preparation programs leading to a license to teach.

Alverno College
Beloit College
Cardinal Stritch University
Carroll College
Carthage College
Concordia University
Edgewood College
Lakeland College
Lawrence University
Maranatha Baptist Bible College
Marian College of Fond du Lac
Marquette University
Mount Mary College
Northland College
Ripon College
St. Norbert College

Silver Lake College
Viterbo University
University of Wisconsin-Eau Claire
University of Wisconsin-Green Bay
University of Wisconsin-LaCrosse
University of Wisconsin-Madison
University of Wisconsin-Milwaukee
University of Wisconsin-Oshkosh
University of Wisconsin-Parkside
University of Wisconsin-Platteville
University of Wisconsin-River Falls
University of Wisconsin-Stevens Point
University of Wisconsin-Stout
University of Wisconsin-Superior
University of Wisconsin-Whitewater
Viterbo College
Wisconsin Lutheran College

Contact information for persons interested in finding a teaching position in the state:

Note: "The Wisconsin Department of Education doesn't serve as a clearinghouse. Contacts should be made directly to the districts where the individual is interested in teaching."

Jobs: www.wisconsin.gov

TITLE: Northern Plains Transition to Teaching

HISTORY: Created by Wyoming, in conjunction with
                                Montana and South Dakota, under a grant from
                                the Transition to Teaching Program, awarded by
                                the U.S. Department of Education.

MOTIVATION: Wyoming needed a program that could be
                                delivered online for individuals who already have a
                                bachelor's degree and want to become teachers.

GRADE LEVELS AND/OR SUBJECT AREA (S) COVERED: Secondary.

WHO OPERATES: Montana State University – Bozeman.

REQUIREMENTS TO ENTER:

                                A bachelor's degree, preferably in a content area.

PROGRAM DESCRIPTION:

                    Candidates:

                                Enroll in the program and complete 9 semester hours of
                                coursework, prior to entry into the classroom as teachers;

                                Complete an internship, which entails teaching for one school
                                year;

                                Complete the final 9 semester hours of coursework after the
                                first year of teaching.

                    They may also enroll in a master's degree program.

NUMBER OF CREDIT HOURS TO COMPLETE:

                    24 semester hours.

WHO EVALUATES: Montana State University – Bozeman.

LENGTH OF TIME: 1 year.

TITLE: Portfolio Certification

MOTIVATION: Recognition of an individual's knowledge and
competencies gained through a variety of life
experiences.

GRADE LEVELS AND/OR SUBJECT AREA (S) COVERED:

The portfolio can be used either to receive a standard teaching
certificate or to add an endorsement area to a current Wyoming
teaching certificate. All areas of endorsement are accepted.

WHO OPERATES: Professional Teaching Standards Board.

REQUIREMENTS TO ENTER:

A bachelor's degree from an NCATE or regionally accredited college or
university.

PROGRAM DESCRIPTION:

The portfolio certification method allows the Professional Teaching
Standards Board to certify teachers based upon professional,
educational and life experiences. A portfolio is a collection of
documented evidence that shows the applicant's lifetime of activities
and verifies how these activities meet Wyoming certification standards.
The portfolio certification process is an alternative way to obtain a
standard teaching certificate or to add an endorsement area to a
current Wyoming teaching certificate.

NUMBER OF CREDIT HOURS TO COMPLETE: N/A.

WHO EVALUATES: A two-four member team evaluates portfolios and
makes a recommendation to the Professional
Teaching Standards Board., who votes on the
approval.

LENGTH OF TIME: After an *intent letter* is filed with the Professional
Teaching Standards Board, the individual has one
year to complete the portfolio.

Institutions of higher education that have developed alternative teacher preparation programs leading to a teaching license:

States with which the state has reciprocity of teacher licenses:

All states.

Institutions of higher education that have *any* teacher preparation programs leading to a license to teach.

University of Wyoming and Regis University

Contact information for persons interested in finding a teaching position in the state:

University of Wyoming
Career Services
College of Education
P.O. Box 3374
Laramie, WY 82071
(307) 766-2019

Also, visit the Professional Teaching Standards Board Web site at: http://ptsb.state.wy.us